Untold Truths

Exposing Slavery and Its Legacies at
Loyola University Maryland

Edited by
Alexis Faison, Israel White,
Lisa Zimmerelli, and David Carey Jr.

Apprentice
House Press
Loyola University Maryland

"Slavery is dead, but the spirit which animated it still lives."
—*Frances Harper, 1892*

First Edition

Hardcover ISBN: 978-1-62720-543-6
Paperback ISBN: 978-1-62720-544-3

Printed in the United States of America

Design by Katie McDonnell
Edited by Alexis Faison, Israel White, Lisa Zimmerelli, and David Carey Jr.

Cover Credits:
    Top Left: Photograph of Louisa Mahoney Mason (seated on left), one of the 272 Black men, women, and children enslaved by the Jesuits and sold in 1838. Photograph title: "St. Inigoes -- Bob Mason and family, our workman" circa 1900, photograph by John Brosnan, S.J., Brosnan Photo Collection, Woodstock Theological Library. http://hdl.handle.net/10822/1067977. Courtesy of the Archives of the Maryland Province of the Society of Jesus, on deposit at the Booth Family Center for Special Collections, Georgetown University Library, Washington, D.C.
    Top Right: Photograph of Madison Fenwick, who worked at Loyola for some forty years. Photograph title: "Maddie and his 'pets'," circa 1897. Courtesy of Archives of St. Ignatius Church, Baltimore, MD.
    Bottom: Loyola College campus, circa 1920s (looking east at the intersection of Charles Street and Cold Spring Lane). Courtesy of Loyola Notre Dame Library Archives and Special Collections, Loyola University Maryland Photograph Collection.

Published by Apprentice House Press

Apprentice
House Press
Loyola University Maryland

Apprentice House Press
Loyola University Maryland
4501 N. Charles Street
Baltimore, MD 21210
410.617.5265
www.ApprenticeHouse.com
info@ApprenticeHouse.com

This work is for the descendants of the 272.

Table of Contents

Foreword..xi
    Cheryl Moore-Thomas, Provost, Loyola University Maryland

Acknowledgements...xiii

Introduction: Slavery and Its Legacies at Loyola 1
    David Carey Jr. and Lisa Zimmerelli

Undergraduate Research: Truth and Insights....................................16
    (A note to the reader: Some student-authors deployed empirical evidence from their primary source research to analyze the past. In short, they deployed historical analysis. Other student-authors used student research to inspire a range of creative writing, which includes rhetorical analysis, creative nonfiction and fiction, and argument. A parenthetical after each student's name indicates which methodology they used.)

Era One: Foundations of Loyola (1852 - 1921) 17

Historical Documents 18
Portraits 18
Structures.. 22
Letters, Censuses, and Land Deeds.. 25
Historical Student Publications 30

Student Essays..36
'Strong Truths, Well Lived': The Truth Behind Loyola University
    Maryland's Ties to Slavery.. 37
    Alysa Krause (historical analysis)
After Contrition 45
    Evelyn Ryan (creative writing)
Loyola, the Civil War, and the Long Shadow of the Lost Cause.................. 56
    Brandon Jay Lyda (historical analysis)
Spotlighting Loyola College's Foundation of Black Labor.......................... 68
    Anna Young (historical analysis)

Loyola Yesterday: A Look at the Unrevealed Culture of Early Loyola
    University Maryland 81
    Deidra Jackson (historical analysis)
Ludeema 93
    Justine Amedson (creative writing)
Era Two: Building Architecture, Developing Culture (1921 – 1970)..**106**
Historical Documents **107**
Portraits 107
Structures... 110
Faculty on Race Relations... 112
Historical Student Publications 116
Night School & World War II.. 125
Student Essays..**131**
Building White Success & Preventing Black Prosperity 132
    Alexis Faison (historical analysis)
Columbia's Rising.. 144
    Israel White (creative writing)
Evergreen Pastures: Upholding Jesuit White Supremacy on Loyola's Stages.....163
    Lucy Marous (historical analysis)
The Desegregation of Loyola College.. 171
    Ikia Robinson (historical analysis)
Facing the Archives.. 181
    Brandon Nefferdorf (creative writing)
Era Three: Contemporary Challenges (1971 – 2023) **191**
Loyola Student Researchers 192
Student Essays..**197**
Stuck in the Grey 198
    Noah Hileman (historical analysis)
Black Notes in a Bottle.. 204
    Jacolby Lacy (creative writing)
The Half of Loyola Buried in 1971 211
    Natasha Saar (creative writing)
Two Different Campuses, Two Different Experiences 221
    Maya du Plessis (historical analysis)
Scio Nihil.. 235
    Camille Barrón (creative writing)
Reflections & Recollections..**240**
Finding Answers in the Archives.. 241
    Jenny Kinniff

Archaeology and Jesuit-enslaved Ancestors 248
    Laura E. Masur

Epilogue 260
    Terrence M. Sawyer, President of Loyola University Maryland

Afterword(s): Descendant Voices 263

Here I Am 264
    Mélisande Short-Colomb

The Mahoney Mason Line: A Journey of Redemption 288
    Dr. Lynn Locklear Nehemiah

Freedom on Trial 301
    Kevin Porter

Bibliography 316

Index 324

Foreword

Cheryl Moore-Thomas

Most forewords are written by individuals who have a connection to the content of the book at hand and some sort of tie to the author. The writer hopes to lend credibility to the book and stir interest in the topic in such a way that potential readers are drawn to the text. A foreword typically attempts to stamp a book as a good and worthwhile read. The task of a foreword is lofty. The writer must hit a mighty aim. In this case, however, the task is an easy one.

It is my honor and privilege to write this foreword for *Untold Truths*. As interim provost and vice president of academic affairs for Loyola University Maryland, I could not be prouder of the dedication, initiative, creativity, and openness that went into developing this book. The book contains historical analyses, presentations of maps and historical documents, artwork, creative writings, essays, and literary arguments written, created, and presented by outstanding Loyola students under the guidance of the esteemed Loyola faculty, Dr. Lisa Zimmerelli, Associate Professor of Writing, and Dr. David Carey Jr., Doehler Chair and Professor of History.

At Loyola, we push ourselves to wrestle with the tough questions and issues of our own time and those of the past. The Loyola student authors of the many writings and creative works that make up this text have done just that. Their research and creative expressions have applied the theories, approaches, and frameworks of their fields of study in well-disciplined and rigorous manners. They have unfolded and shared the voices and stories of history in profound, yet sensitive ways. In exploring the uncomfortable and painful realities of the legacy of slavery, the inextricable involvement of the Catholic Church and the Jesuits, and the beginnings of Loyola University Maryland, the works presented here serve as a sieve for us to sift the aspects and notions of our own lives, so that by seeing more fully we can more fully align with our values, purpose, and calling. In the noble tradition of liberal arts education, *Untold Truths* offers readers a chance to wrestle with the deeply disturbing reality of slavery, the complex involvement of the Catholic Church, and the legacies of this human atrocity in the context of Loyola and higher education more broadly.

I am a longstanding member of the Loyola community. I attended Loyola as an undergraduate and am now honored to serve as its first Black provost; one who is a descendant of enslaved people known to have lived, toiled, cried, and died on plantation fields not far from the land on which Loyola's Evergreen campus sits, on land purchased through the sale of slaves' bodies. As a long-term Loyola community member, a descendant of enslaved persons, and one who now has the tremendous responsibility for the education of college students who will one day lead the world, I know the work of this book tells an important story that must be read and felt. This book must be read and felt because it tells painful yet important truths about the origin and establishment of our beloved institution and many institutions across the nation. It tells a story that is marked by the courageous lives and valued voices of a proud people who previously had been hidden from us. Until now they have not been appropriately acknowledged nor respected for all that they gave, for all that was stolen from them, for all they never had an opportunity to experience or imagine, for all the evil and pain and injustice they endured in service . . . to us. In this compelling volume, the authors use their scholarship, creative expressions, and challenging, thought-provoking work as an invitation to join their powerful call to action, their call to know and confront the legacy of slavery in higher education, and work toward true equity and justice in our world today.

Provost and Vice President,
Loyola University Maryland, January 2023

Acknowledgements

This book was born of collaboration. We have been enriched by the process and want to acknowledge the many debts we incurred along the way. A generous Aperio grant, awarded by the Loyola University Maryland Center for the Humanities, made the research, writing, and publication of this volume possible. For the insights, expertise, and experience that they so generously and copiously shared with us, we extend our heartfelt appreciation to Meli Short-Colomb and Dr. Lynn Locklear Nehemiah, descendants of Louisa Mahoney, who was born in 1813 and enslaved by Jesuits her entire life.

The head of Archives and Special Collections at the Loyola Notre Dame Library, Jenny Kinniff, guided our research there and at other archives. We also are indebted to the archivists and librarians who facilitated our research at Georgetown University (especially Mary Beth Corrigan), the Maryland Center for History and Culture, Enoch Pratt Free Library, and Loyola Blakefield.

A number of scholars and colleagues, including Matt Mulcahy, Tom Pegram, Allen Wells, Martha Jones, Jenny Kinniff, Martin Camper, Marian Crotty, and Lucas Southworth, offered critical feedback that greatly improved the volume. In addition to creating the index, Michael Lettieri adeptly copyedited and proofread the volume. Katie McDonnell expertly shepherded the manuscript through the editorial process at our partner, Apprentice House Press.

Members of the Presidential Task Force Studying Slavery (2022-2023) expressed their enthusiasm for this project at every turn. We also appreciate the working group that met during the summer of 2022 to consider Loyola's connections to slavery. President Terry Sawyer unwaveringly supported this project from its nascent stages. He visited students as they were conducting research in the archives, introduced their panel when they presented their findings to the community, and consulted with the editors as the volume entered its final stages. Through his actions and words, he continues to advance Loyola's efforts to reckon with its history of slavery and its legacies.

Slavery and Its Legacies at Loyola[1]

David Carey Jr. and Lisa Zimmerelli

Few educational institutions in the United States can claim no connection to, or association with, slavery or Jim Crow. Indeed, this reality has become painfully evident in the last decade or so as many universities and colleges have confronted direct evidence of the powerful linkages that existed between slavery and almost all aspects of British American and U.S. life during the eighteenth and nineteenth centuries when many universities were founded. The most striking example was the revelation that the Society of Jesus sold 272 African women, men, and children, many of whose families had lived in the Maryland colony and then state for more than a century, to keep Georgetown University open in 1838 and establish other colleges thereafter, including Loyola. It has become clear that without a deep understanding and reckoning of past injustices, universities cannot forge campuses and climates that move beyond desegregation to embrace integration with all the nuances, opportunities, and resources needed to allow Black and other marginalized minorities to thrive.

Loyola University Maryland is no exception to this narrative. Since at least 1717 and likely since the late seventeenth century, Jesuits purchased enslaved men, women, boys, and girls to work on their tobacco, corn, and wheat forced labor camps in Maryland.[2] When the 1838 sale of enslaved people to fund Georgetown University was first reported in 2016, Loyola was quick to claim that since the college was founded in 1852, it was not linked to that sale or its profits.[3] Indeed, a university spokesperson asserted: "From examination of our archives…we have no reason to believe that slavery or the slave trade has ties to Loyola."[4] Six years later, Loyola has made significant efforts to face its past, notably by institutionalized support of a 2022 Loyola Center for the Humanities research grant that explored those links and by the Loyola Apprentice House Press publication of this volume. The research and writing contained herein presents a kaleidoscope of histories and an intellectual posture of transparency and integrity that compels readers to reflect deeply. Even before the publication of this volume, Loyola had begun the process of recognition and reckoning: on November 30, 2022, student contributors presented their findings to an audience comprised of Loyola students, staff, alumni, and faculty, the Baltimore community, and descendants of the men, women, and children Jesuits had enslaved and sold. The following spring still more Loyola students publicly presented their findings from oral history interviews they had conducted with descendants. Yet much work remains to be done. As an institution and community, Loyola can build on this work by creating spaces for compassionate, empathetic, and difficult conversations that invite informed diverse perspectives about the past, present, and future of the institution and the people so intimately connected to it.

This volume reveals historical threads of slavery, racism, and white power. Woven from Loyola's foundation from the sale and exploitation of enslaved Africans, those threads were tightened with Lost Cause discourse and during the Jim Crow era. Today those tattered threads bind the institution to that past and continue to haunt the university. We live in the shadow of this lingering legacy because of the vestiges of discrimination. The Loyola University Maryland undergraduate students who conducted the research and wrote the essays contained in this volume together with descendants of those the Jesuits enslaved have set a brave and firm path toward truth and justice. The students have embarked on this intellectual journey with diligence, intellectual curiosity, and a keen eye for detail often associated with graduate students. The integrity, transparency, and humility with which they approached this material has made their findings all the more compelling.

In addition to crafting narratives—both historical and fictional—about Loyola's relationship to slavery and its legacies, this volume decenters the 1838 sale from Georgetown University and highlights how all institutions connected to the Maryland Province of the Society of Jesus—from parishes and high schools to colleges and universities—are linked to that sale and the larger slave economy. Our hope is that a deep examination of Loyola University Maryland's history of slavery and racism will elucidate the varied and complex ways the effects of the 1838 sale and Jesuit slaveholding and profits from slavery more generally reverberate throughout Jesuit institutions all along the eastern part of the United States. In doing so, we aim to redirect media and popular attention away from a narrow focus on Georgetown University to Jesuit institutions more broadly.

***

Five years before the 1838 sale, "The jolly old president" [of Georgetown University], Reverend Thomas F. Mulledy, proudly showed "a piece of a *Negro's* hide tanned—[that] was as thick as calves skin," to Henry Barnard.[5] Highlighting what Mulledy apparently considered one of the Maryland Province of the Society of Jesus' treasures in 1833, he reflected the racist and colonialist ideologies at the heart of Catholic and educational institutions—including Loyola—that were founded and/or funded in part with proceeds from the 1838 sale.[6] As is now well-known, that sale helped secure the future for Georgetown University and stabilized the finances of the Jesuit province in Maryland. What is less well known is that the impact of the funds from that sale stretched well beyond 1838. Most of the enslaved people were purchased on credit and payment was spread over decades during which the Jesuits used their newfound wealth to expand their operations and institutions. Since the Louisiana buyers could not afford to purchase the enslaved people outright, the Jesuits effectively offered them a mortgage payable over more than twenty years. After Mr. J. R. Thompson had purchased many of the enslaved from the original buyers and thus incurred their outstanding debt, he asked the Jesuits to extend their loan on the sale. On January 27, 1859, the Jesuits responded, "I am sorry to inform you that it is quite out of our power to accede to your first proposition viz: to lend you $30,000. As we yet owe a very large amt [sic] for a college built in Baltimore a few years ago" (see figures on pp. 26-27).[7] In short, funds from the 1838 sale provided the cornerstones for what is now Loyola University Maryland, as Alysa Krause explores in this volume.

The impact of slavery in Loyola's early years extended beyond financing the institution. When the Jesuits opened Loyola College in 1852, both enslaved and free Blacks lived in the city. Although free Blacks far outnumbered enslaved Blacks in Baltimore—in 1860, Baltimore's population of 212,418 people was comprised of 25,680 free and 2,218 enslaved Blacks— Loyola Jesuits depended on slave labor. Like their counterparts at Georgetown, they preferred to rent rather than to own the enslaved people who maintained the campus, residence, and college.[8] From July 1855 through December 1860, Loyola Jesuits including its first president Father John Early (figure on p. 19) rented "servants" from Mrs. Henry S. Manning, whose family were slaveholders according to the 1850 and 1860 censuses.[9] Historically, such arrangements for servants involved enslaved men and women, as Anna Young explains in her essay. Particularly in southern cities, the practice of hiring enslaved laborers was common.[10] The 1860 U.S. census for Baltimore City also records a 60-year-old enslaved Black woman held by the "Order of the Jesuits." (see figure on p. 28).[11] Like Dominic Butler, Madison Fenwick (see cover top right image), and other free Black men and women who labored at Loyola after the Civil War, those servants and the enslaved woman in the 1860 census contributed to the college's development. There were many other Black workers in the late nineteenth and early twentieth centuries, but their stories remain frustratingly opaque in historical records even as their impact on Loyola resonates into the twenty-first century.

During the Civil War, Loyola students fought for both the Union and the Confederacy, though far more joined the latter, as Brandon Lyda documents in his essay. At least one faculty member, James A. Noonan, a

4

southern-sympathizing Jesuit, was drafted into and (begrudgingly) served in the Union army. A faculty member from 1862-1867 (and later President of Loyola from 1891-1900), Father John Abell Morgan detailed his strong support for the Confederacy in a diary he kept from 1862 to 1867.[12] Morgan's family had owned slaves in southern Maryland, although he was not blind to efforts to serve Black Baltimoreans, as is evident in his positive assessment of Reverend Peter Miller's ministry for Black Catholics in Baltimore. Still, Morgan and other Loyola Jesuits and leaders had sympathy for the South and supported white slaveholders, white power, and the exploitation of enslaved Black people. In short, those of us at Loyola today are members of an institution whose founders financed its development through slavery, and whose subsequent stakeholders embraced discriminatory practices often intentionally crafted to advance white power.

Slavery died out in Maryland with the passage of a new state constitution in 1864 (followed by the 13th amendment in 1865) less than two decades after Loyola's founding, but the racism at the root of slavery lingered for decades, and those attitudes continued to influence Loyola, as it did U.S. law and culture more broadly. The college remained wedded to racist notions including supporting the emergence of the ideology of the Lost Cause of the Confederacy. The Lost Cause was a racist mythology that emerged in the post war years until it became a fixed belief among white southerners (and even nationally) by the turn of the century. Lost Cause tropes were promoted by former Confederate General Jubal Early (in the 1870s-1880s), the United Daughters of the Confederacy (in the 1890s), and popularized in a wave of public sculpture and art that filled municipal spaces in the early twentieth century, including several in Baltimore.[13] In an attempt to dissociate the Civil War from slavery, Lost Cause proponents asserted a romanticized notion of the Confederacy and the Old South as idyllic and uniquely American, the Civil War as just and a defense of states' rights, and Confederate soldiers—particularly General Robert E. Lee—as saintly and heroic. Lingering to this day in some places is the rhetoric of the happy, devoted slave, loyal to their enslavers and uninterested and unprepared for independent living.

Such beliefs found a home on Loyola's campus. In December 1880, Loyola Jesuits hosted the "Poet Priest of the Lost Cause" Father Abram J. Ryan (see figure on p. 20) in their home as he lectured and wrote poetry in Baltimore for the month. Appreciative of their hospitality, Ryan donated proceeds from his public reading to establish a prize for poetry at Loyola.[14] Ryan was not the only such visitor. In his essay, Lyda details how Loyola Jesuits also welcomed to campus Richard Malcolm Johnston (see figure on p. 21), another Lost Cause literary giant. Indeed, Johnston developed an intimate friendship with Loyola College faculty member and later president Reverend Morgan.[15]

Loyola's embrace of racist poetry, literature, and entertainment continued into the twentieth century. For example, Loyola's Drama Department and theatre regularly put on blackface (and yellowface) minstrel shows (see figures on pp. 31-33, 122, 184), thus participating in a popular form of entertainment in the late nineteenth and early twentieth-century United States, as Lucy Marous and Brandon Nefferdorf examine in their essays. Another student at Loyola, Leo A. Codd penned an ode to the Ku Klux Klan entitled "Clansmen" in 1913 (see figure on p. 34).[16] He lauded the Reconstruction Klan that was valorized in Lost Cause mythology rather than the revived movement founded in 1915. The latter grew influential across the United States during the 1920s, but was noted for its anti-Catholicism. So beloved was Codd as an alumnus that Loyola invited him to speak at the Parent's Day Celebration on May 9, 1943.[17]

When the college moved from downtown to northern Baltimore in 1922, its new location was connected to racial discrimination and redlining. Informed by the Roland Park Company, which had developed the area around the campus with restrictive covenants in place that barred Black people from owning property, the 1921 land deed that the college signed abided by those covenants and restricted education on its campus to "white persons" (see figure on p. 29). The deed further stipulated that "any negro or person of negro extraction" was barred from living on the property unless they were employed by the college. Even after Loyola admitted its first Black undergraduate student, Charles Dorsey, in 1949, the restriction remained on record and occasional blackface performances persisted.[18]

When Dorsey first applied to Loyola in 1947, he was rejected because he had taken courses at a Josephite seminary that had not been accredited by the Middle States Association. To facilitate Dorsey's enrollment in 1949, Loyola President Father Francis X. Talbot (1947-1950) consulted the Josephites about Dorsey's intellectual acumen and other attributes. When Talbot announced Dorsey's matriculation to alumni in April 1950, the reaction was mixed. Some parents asked their students if they wanted to transfer out of the newly desegregated college. Four years later in the 1954 *Brown v the Board of Education of Topeka* case, the Supreme Court ruled that racially segregating children in public schools was unconstitutional. Baltimore City desegregated public schools shortly thereafter.[19] After leaving Loyola to serve in the Air Force during the Korean War, Dorsey returned and graduated in 1957. He subsequently earned a law degree and ultimately became the executive director of the Maryland Legal Aid Bureau, where he worked assiduously to alleviate the plight of Baltimore's marginalized populations, as Ikia Robinson documents in her essay.

Dorsey pioneered a path for other Black students, among them his future brother-in-law Paul Smith. Nonetheless, the presence of increasing numbers of Black students did not significantly alter the campus climate, but rather sometimes fueled the fears of racists. In an *Evergreen Quarterly* article about the Supreme Court's decision to desegregate public schools, Smith warned his peers about the "southern sentiment" of virulent racism.[20] He knew discrimination at Loyola firsthand. For example, since the 1940s, Loyola's junior prom had been celebrated off campus in white-only establishments. One year, to accommodate Black students such as Dorsey and Smith, Loyola junior-class officers rented out the Friendship Airport terminal because it was one of the few desegregated event spaces in the Baltimore region. That unequivocal welcoming of Black students at the prom was short lived, however. The following year, Loyola students backslid, renting a country club in neighboring Anne Arundel County that allowed Black people on the grounds but not in the pool.[21] Thereafter the college continued—and the university continues—to fall short of full integration, at times making strides toward inclusivity but at other times failing to embody its core values of diversity and justice, as Maya du Plessis' interviews in this volume demonstrate.[22]

In 1983, without a hint of irony, Loyola awarded Dorsey the Andrew White Medal. Viewed through an historical lens, the college bestowing an award named after an individual who exploited and denigrated Native Americans, on an alumnus who faced similarly hostile conditions because of his race is particularly poignant. When the Sidney Hollander Foundation bestowed its award for contributions "toward the achievement of equal rights and opportunities for Negroes in Maryland" on Loyola in 1951, the award jury lauded Loyola "for fully integrating minority students into both its curricular and extracurricular activities."[23] That assertion rang particularly hollow when set against the blackface and Confederate flags that marked the campus during Dorsey's tenure at Loyola. Racist structures and thought continued to influence Loyola through the second half of the twentieth century.

This painful history notwithstanding, enslaved and free Black people's achievements and contributions to Loyola and the United States more broadly are noteworthy. The first Black students at Loyola, including Dorsey who became a lawyer, Smith who became a Catholic priest, and Mary Frazier who in 1952 became the first Black student to earn a graduate degree from Loyola and was a high school teacher in Baltimore, forged opportunities for future Black students at Loyola.[24] It is particularly fitting that some of the descendants of those sold by the Jesuits including Dr. Lynn Locklear Nehemiah and Mélisande (Meli) Short-Colomb, both of whom have contributions in this volume, have been instrumental in guiding the President's Task Force Examining Loyola's Connections to Slavery and other efforts (including the student research and scholarship that appears in this volume) to trace Loyola's and the Maryland Province of the Society of Jesus' historical ties to slavery and its legacies.[25]

***

This volume also provides a potential model for how Loyola University Maryland might tell the history of its engagement with indigenous peoples, Latin American immigrants, and other marginalized groups and address the lingering vestiges of outdated attitudes that remain visible on campus. For example, the university has crafted a land acknowledgement, but has yet to reckon with the stained-glass window in the chapel that depicts a Native American (presumably Mohawk) killing Jesuit saint Isaac Jogues or the student center named after Andrew White, the first Jesuit to arrive in Maryland (1634) who advanced colonialism by disparaging and subjugating Native Americans ostensibly under the auspices of education and conversion.[26] These histories, which Alexis Faison analyzes in her essay, and those of Black Americans need not be approached discretely. Some descendants of those sold by the Society of Jesus traced rich indigenous histories and lineages. Such is the case with Dr. Nehemiah who is also a member of the Nanticoke tribe. In 1946, her maternal great aunt, Ruth Harmon Walker, wrote to President Harry S. Truman to advocate for Nanticoke peoples' rights and to explain that "268 years have taught us to lay away the gunpowder, bows and arrows" for more peaceful and productive relations that could only result from honest accountings of the past and shared goals for the future.[27]

Our own honest accounting of the past through the student research and writing in this volume provides Loyola's contemporary community of students, staff, and faculty a keen sense of the white men who created, crafted, and curated Loyola College as an institution grounded in racism and misogyny, as Deidra Jackson demonstrates in her essay. Paradoxically, that history offers hope: If we accept the premise that such unjust foundations, infrastructure, and social relations were socially constructed, then we can accept the possibility that a more diverse group of people—like us—can deconstruct those vestiges of colonialism, racism, and sexism. We can reshape and mold a more just institution where Black American, Latin American, Native American, Asian American, and other students of color are not singled out to speak for their communities in the classroom, where women are paid the same as men, and where our campus benefits from more authentic integration that intentionally dismantles white power.

Racist policies always have been embedded in U.S. higher education, even for colleges and universities with no direct historical ties to slavery. As *Atlantic* staff writer Adam Harris argues, we cannot understand current inequities without understanding that history.[28] Exploring our past raises difficult questions we must confront. Making links between histories of slavery, injustice, and racism helps to identify direct pathways to address contemporary inequalities, injustices, and racism. The question, however, is how do we integrate histories of marginalization to craft transparent and honest historical narratives about Loyola that also challenge the university and its students, staff, and faculty to address inequalities today? That is to say, how do we make such histories evident on campus in the places where we eat, learn, teach, socialize, and live in ways that eschew facile explanations? The essays in this volume refute two common claims: first, that slavery and racism happened in a distant, irrelevant past; and, second, that conditions have improved to such an extent that the injustices of the past no longer exist. Today's Loyola has benefitted from that slave trade and subsequent structural and social racism. Instead of allowing us to fall into the trap of guilt and shame, these essays demand we initiate difficult conversations about the significance of this past and the racist legacies that remain ensconced at Loyola.

The descendants who contribute to this volume directly with their essays and indirectly with the wisdom, experience, and insights they shared with students provide a model for how to approach the past with a critical eye without succumbing to the paralysis of analysis.[29] With transparency regarding the horrors of slavery and injustices of racism, they celebrate enslaved people's foundational contributions to U.S. educational institutions and point to agency, strength, and resilience amidst brutal marginalization, as Nehemiah, Short-Colomb, and Kevin Porter so eloquently capture in recounting and celebrating their rich family narratives against the backdrop of institutional practices of white power and ignorance.

In addition to taking a stance of brave curiosity, the student researchers refused to succumb to easy conclusions—even though sensational findings can be particularly enticing in archival research. When Brandon

Nefferdorf, whose essay provides poignant insight into the personal effects of such research, found two incidents in Loyola yearbooks where students were identified as the members of the "klassy kut klothes" (see figure on p. 118, description of H. Calloway Harrison, Jr.), he surmised that these were veiled references to the KKK. After consulting with an expert in the field— historian Dr. Thomas Pegram—Nefferdorf and his colleagues concluded that because the reference was made during a time when the KKK persecuted Catholics, it was unlikely that Catholic students would have identified with it. Such careful analysis lends credence, validity, and legitimacy to these students' research more broadly. In turn, students labored mightily to uncover and tell the stories of the free and enslaved Black men and women who worked at Loyola despite there being little evidence of their voices in the archives. In his work with the Georgetown University and Maryland Province of the Society of Jesus archives, historian Adam Rothman uncovered only one document written by an enslaved person: Thomas Brown. Trafficked to Missouri by Jesuits, Brown wrote back pleading to be allowed to purchase his freedom.[30] Black voices remain similarly muted in Loyola archival holdings. Indeed, sometimes their names are elided when they appear in photographs where whites are identified (see figure p. 109).

Instead of meeting such absences in the archives with silence, we invited response from our students. We asked them to dig deeper to fill in these archival absences by recovering and piecing together additional histories. We asked them to analyze carefully by questioning previously written historical accounts and by investigating rhetorics of racism and white power in historical artifacts such as Jesuit correspondence, yearbooks, and course descriptions. We asked them to take a stand and to present arguments on how Loyola can begin to reconcile and heal from the insidious, pervasive, and persistent stain of slavery.

We also asked them to draw creative inspiration from the research generated over the past year. Taking a cue from novelists like Octavia Butler and Toni Morrison, for example, students Justine Amedson, Jacolby Lacy, and Israel White write speculative short stories that capture the generational legacy and trauma of enslavement. Camille Barrón contributes a poem that

11

explores the intersections of race and gender as she simultaneously maps the history of feminism onto one Black woman's life. Such creative engagement with the archives provides a different way of grappling with history, one that allows freedom to expand into historical silences while respecting the historical record. Creative writing borne out of the archives is a powerful way to animate history, to put expression on the face of history.

The student-driven research and writing in this volume compellingly demonstrate that Loyola College was founded and maintained at the expense and exclusion of Black people. Loyola's land acknowledgement suggests that was true for indigenous communities too. Relational repair demands that descendant (and indigenous) voices guide the process and outcomes. Given our history, missteps, mistakes, and discomfort are inevitable as we move toward a more just and transparent institution that holds itself accountable to its anti-racist rhetoric and goals. Humility, self-reflexivity, and empathy (as President Terrence Sawyer calls for in his Epilogue) will be crucial attributes for all those engaged in this work.[31] Repair, restoration, and restitution require changing the culture at Loyola. We can begin by ceasing to miseducate students about their past, privilege, and society in which we live.

Encompassing histories, scholarly analysis, argument, and creative works, this volume, we hope, is diverse and rich enough to open conversations and to pave pathways forward, both for our campus and for other institutions committed to anti-racism. We have walked alongside the students in this research journey—from a summer of archival research, to a full semester of further research and writing, to the completion of this volume—and we are grateful for the institutional support that has allowed this book to come to fruition. What happens next must be, however, more courageous. Braver decisions have yet to be made, by our university, and by many other universities. Will we change our colors, as Noah Hileman suggests, because of the connection to the Confederacy, and change the names of Jenkins Hall and the Andrew White Student Center as Faison demands? What will repair look like? How will descendants shape those discussions and allocation of resources? In short, it is one thing to acknowledge our past;

it is quite another to do something about it. We remain hopeful that this is one step before many more.

1 A special thanks to Matt Mulcahy, Tom Pegram, Allen Wells, Jenny Kinniff, and Dr. Lynn Locklear Nehemiah whose expertise and comments and critiques on earlier versions of this essay have significantly strengthened and sharped its final iteration.

2 Thomas Murphy, *Jesuit Slaveholding in Maryland, 1717-1838* (New York, 2001), 15-17, 45-46. The 1717 deed is reprinted in Adam Rothman and Elsa Barraza Mendoza, eds. *Facing Georgetown's History: A Reader on Slavery, Memory, and Reconciliation* (Washington, DC: Georgetown University Press, 2021).

3 Rachel Swarns, "272 Slaves Were Sold to Save Georgetown. What Does It Owe Their Descendants?" *New York Times*, April 16, 2016.

4 Staff and wire reports, "Georgetown University to Give Admissions Preference to Descendants of Slaves Sold by the College," *Baltimore Sun*, September 1, 2016.

5 Bernard C. Steiner, ed., "The South Atlantic States in 1833, as Seen by a New Englander: Being a Narrative of a Tour Taken by Henry Barnard," *Maryland Historical Magazine*, 1918, Volume 13, Issue 3, 290.

6 Archives of the Maryland Province of the Society of Jesus; Christopher J. Kellerman, *All Oppression Shall Cease: A History of Slavery, Abolitionism, and the Catholic Church* (Maryknoll, NY: Orbis Books, 2022); Rachel L. Swarns, *The 272: The Families Who Were Enslaved and Sold to Build the American Catholic Church* (New York: Random House, 2023). During their time in British North America, Jesuit priests had acquired property including from James Carroll, who upon his death in 1729, bequeathed his land and slave holdings, which included more than two thousand acres and what would become the White Marsh forced labor camp. With a 1792 charter that shifted Jesuits' personal property to corporate ownership, the Corporation of the Roman Catholic Clergymen assumed control of three hundred and twenty-three enslaved men, women, and children, and nine properties that spanned some thirteen thousand acres. That consolidation made the Jesuits one of Maryland's largest owners of enslaved peoples. In 1833, the Maryland Province became the first province of Jesuits in the United States. See Adam Rothman, "The Jesuits and Slavery," *Journal of Jesuit Studies* 8 (2021): 1-10; Murphy, *Jesuit Slaveholding*; Joseph Zwinge, S.J., "The Jesuit Farms in Maryland. Facts and Anecdotes," Woodstock Letters XXXIX, no. 3 (1910), 379; Bernard Cook, "Maryland Jesuits and Slavery, Pt. I," *Cura Virtualis*, September 8, 2021, available at https://www.curavirtualis.org/post/maryland-jesuits-and-slavery-pt-i#viewer-4igta; Charles M. Flanagan, "The Sweets of Independence: A Reading of the 'James Carroll Daybook, 1714-21," Ph.D. Dissertation, University of Maryland, College Park, 2005; Thomas Hughes, *History of the Society of Jesus in North America: Colonial and Federal* (London: Forgotten Books, 2009).

7 Archives of the Maryland Province of the Society of Jesus, MPA Box 40 Letter to JR Thompson 01.27.1859 RJC HL. Since his name was on the mortgage, Mulledy enjoyed the power of attorney for any modifications to the agreement.

8 In Maryland, the enslaved population grew from roughly 1,600 in 1680, to 3,200 in 1700 to more than 43,000 by 1750, when enslaved people comprised 31% of the population. Although the transatlantic trade continued, by the mid eighteenth century a native-born population of African Americans predominated the Chesapeake region. From 1820 to 1860, Maryland's free Black population grew as the enslaved Black population decreased. By 1860, free Blacks outnumbered their enslaved counterparts everywhere except for Southern Maryland. See Elsa Mendoza, "Catholic Slaveowners and the Development of Georgetown University's Slave Hiring System, 1792-1862," *Journal of Jesuit Studies 8* (2021), 57, 59; Barbara Jeanne Fields, *Slavery and Freedom on the Middle Ground* (New Haven: Yale University Press, 1985), 62; Richard Bell, "Border State, Border War: Fighting for Freedom and Slavery in Antebellum Maryland," in *The Civil War in Maryland Reconsidered*, ed. Charles W. Mitchell and Jean H. Baker, 16-45 (Baton Rouge: Louisiana State University, 2021), 20, 31; Ira Berlin, *Generations of Captivity: A History of African-American Slaves* (Cambridge, MA: Belknap Press of Harvard University Press, 2003).

9 Archives of the Maryland Province of the Society of Jesus, Cash and Day Book, July 1855, March 1856, May 1857, and December 1860.

10 Mendoza, "Catholic Slaveowners and the Development of Georgetown University's Slave Hiring System," 59.

11 U.S. Slave Schedule (number 2) for Baltimore City, Ward 11, 1860. Since the 1860 census explicitly sought to count slave owners (in contrast to the 1850 census), the enumerator who listed an enslaved Black woman with the Order of the Jesuits was almost undoubtedly indicating that the Jesuits were her slaveowners. In light of the five to ten percent of enumerations that incorrectly listed individuals or

corporations as slaveowners, we have decided to use the term slaveholders when referring to this evidence of Baltimore Jesuits' engagement with slavery in the 1860 census. See "1860 Census: Instructions to Marshals," at https://usa.ipums.org/usa/voliii/inst1860.shtml (last checked January 24, 2023) for instructions to census takers. Our gratitude to historian J. David Hacker for helping us and our students understand this nuance.

12 Loyola Notre Dame Library (LNDL) Archives, Loyola University Maryland Office of the President records (LUMD.003.001), Box 1, Diary of Reverend John Abell Morgan, 1862-1867; Charles W. Mitchell and Jean H. Baker, eds. *The Civil War in Maryland Reconsidered* (Baton Rouge: Louisiana State University Press, 2021).

13 At the insistence of popular movements in recent years, that collection of statuary and public art has been removed in many places. Some pro-Confederate art in statues and bas-reliefs remain in Baltimore, such as the Sidney Lanier tribute that is visible from Charles Street near Johns Hopkins University's Homewood campus.

14 *Baltimore Sun*, August 12, 1902; Nicolas Varga, *Loyola's Baltimore, Baltimore's Loyola, 1851-1986* (Baltimore: Maryland Historical Society, 1990), 99; David W. Blight, *Race and Reunion: The Civil War in American Memory* (Cambridge, MA: Belknap Press, 2001), 33; Frank Williams, "Abraham Lincoln, Civil Liberties, and Maryland," in *The Civil War in Maryland Reconsidered*, ed. Charles W. Mitchell and Jean H. Baker, 139-59 (Baton Rouge: Louisiana State University, 2021), 153; Fields, *Slavery and Freedom on the Middle Ground*. Established in the 1880-1881 academic year to celebrate student poetry, the Ryan award was given to the freshmen with the highest academic standing beginning in the 1910-1911 academic year and continued (with one exception) to be awarded through at least the 1967-1968 academic year. See Jenny Kinniff, Aperio Research Report, unpublished manuscript, 2023.

15 Enoch Pratt Library, MS6: Richard Malcolm Johnston Papers, 1841-1935; LNDL Archives, Loyola University Maryland Office of the President records, LUMD.003.001, Box 1, Diary of Reverend John Abell Morgan, 1862-1867.

16 Archives of the Maryland Province of the Society of Jesus, GTM-000119. Georgetown University Manuscripts, Baltimore (16 of 25), 1911 - 1915, 53_16_11, Box: 156, Folder: 9; LNDL Archives, LUMD.002.006 Scrapbook Collection Box 9, Loyola scrapbook, 1942-1946, Leo A. Codd, "Clansmen," *The Loyola: A Semimonthly Published by the Literary Societies of Loyola College*, 1, no. 2 (November 3, 1913), 6-7.

17 LNDL Archives, "Loyola College: Parents Day Celebration, May 9, 1943," 3; Craig Fox, *White Protestant Life and the KKK in 1920s Michigan* (East Lansing: Michigan State University Press, 2011).

18 LNDL Archives, Loyola College Land Deed, November 30th, 1921; Paige Glotzer, *How the Suburbs Were Segregated: Developers and the Business of Exclusionary Housing, 1890-1960* (New York: Columbia University Press, 2020), 12.

19 Karen Olson, "Old West Baltimore: Segregation, African-American Cultures, and the Struggle for Equality," in *The Baltimore Book: New Views of Local History*, eds. Elizabeth Fee, Linda Shopes, and Linda Zeidman (Philadelphia: Temple University Press, 1991), 73-74. Loyola previously had admitted Black students to its night program partly because enrollees in the night school were not considered "regular" students. By 1945, Black students were taking classes in Loyola College's night school "without causing any comment," according to Father Zacheus J. Maher. See Jesuit Archives, Residence of St. Claude La Colombière, Baltimore, MD, Report by Zacheus J. Maher to the Province of Maryland, Society of Jesus, April 2, 1945.

20 Paul Smith, "Southern Sentiment," *Evergreen Quarterly* (Winter 1954), 26.

21 Varga, *Loyola's Baltimore, Baltimore's Loyola*, 387-89. The federal government (and armed forces) desegregated on July 26, 1948, when President Harry S. Truman issued Executive Order 9980 "Regulations Governing Fair Employment Practices within the Federal Establishment."

22 Into the 1990s, Loyola College held its annual fall event honoring new faculty at the Baltimore Country Club, which did not desegregate its membership until 1995. In 2008, the Board of Trustees decided to change the name of Loyola College to Loyola University Maryland. The following year the Maryland Higher Education Commission approved the change, which took effect on August 19, 2009.

23 Varga, *Loyola's Baltimore, Baltimore's Loyola*, 358-59.

24 Heather McDonald, "The Long Road to Learning," *The Baltimore Sun*, July 30, 1961; Corrinne Hammett, "Champ Commuter to Get New Degree," *News-Post* (Baltimore), June 4, 1959.

25 William G. Thomas III, *A Question of Freedom: The Families Who Challenged Slavery from the Nation's Founding to the Civil War* (New Haven: Yale University Press, 2020), 120.

26 LNDL Archives, SC.057, the Sainte-Marie among the Hurons archaeological collection. The Mohawk were

(and are) part of the Iroquois (or Six Nations) Confederacy.

27 Dr. Lynn Locklear Nehemiah personal archive, Ruth Harmon Walker letter to President Truman, May 15, 1946.

28 Adam Harris, *The State Must Provide: The Definitive History of Racial Inequality in Higher Education* (New York: Harper Collins, 2022); Craig Steven Wilder, *Ebony and Ivy: Race, Slavery, and the Troubled History of America's Universities* (New York: Bloombsury, 2013).

29 A special thanks to Dr. Lynn Locklear Nehemiah and Meli Short-Colomb, for sharing their time and expertise with students during 2022 summer research and fall courses and beyond.

30 Adam Rothman, "Archives and Historical Storytelling at Georgetown University," Paper delivered at Conference on Slavery and Johns Hopkins, Johns Hopkins University, Baltimore, MD, 2021.

31 Sharon Stein, *Unsettling the University: Confronting the Colonial Foundations of US Higher Education* (Baltimore: Johns Hopkins University Press, 2022); Sharon Stein, "Beyond Apologies," *Inside Higher Ed*, January 19, 2023.

Undergraduate Research: Truths and Insights

Era One:

Foundations of Loyola
(1852 – 1921)

Historical Documents:
Portraits

Father John Early (1814-1873), founder and first president of Loyola College, Baltimore. Image courtesy of Loyola Notre Dame Library Archives. (Loyola University Maryland Photograph Collection, Box 64, Folder 15).

Father Abram J. Ryan (1838-1886), freelance chaplain to the
Confederate army, lodged with Loyola Jesuits, gifted money to the college, ca. 1875.
"Fr. Abram J. Ryan, ca. 1875." Courtesy of the Doy Leale McCall Rare Book and
Manuscript Library, University of South Alabama.

Richard Malcolm Johnston (1822-1898), author influential in developing Lost Cause narrative and friend of Loyola College President Father John Abell Morgan, 1894. "Richard Malcolm Johnston," in Mildred Lewis Rutherford, *American Authors: A Hand-book of American Literature from Early Colonial to Living Writer*s. (Atlanta, GA: Franklin Printing & Publishing, 1894).

Structures

Evergreen Campus, Humanities building and Jenkins building. Image courtesy of Loyola Notre Dame Library Archives. (Loyola University Maryland Photograph Collection, Box 1, Folder 24)

Loyola College, Calvert Street, nd. Image courtesy of Loyola Notre Dame Library Archives. (Loyola University Maryland Photograph Collection, Box 1, Folder 4)

(a) An 1882 photo of St. Francis Xavier Church, a small wooden cabin, and the Newtown manor house; (b) Sandstone foundations of the cabin's chimney; (c) Eighteenth and nineteenth-century artifacts— shoe buckle fragment, bone button backs, tobacco pipe stem, century nail, ceramics, and wine bottle glass—from above the cabin. (a) Image from Beitzell's Jesuit Missions of St. Mary's County, 1976. (b-c) Photos courtesy of Laura Masur.

Letters, Censuses, and Land Deeds

January 27, 1859 letter to J.R. Thompson from Jesuits explaining they could not grant him an extension on the 1838 loan because they needed money for a college [Loyola] in Baltimore. Image courtesy of Maryland Province Archives at Georgetown University. (MPA, box 62, folder 20)

Georgetown College Jan 27th 1859

Mr. J.R. Thompson
My Dear Sir,

Yours of the 31st Dec. was received some days ago on my return to the college from the country where I was detained by bad weather. In reply [...], I am sorry to inform you that it is quite out of our power to accede to your first proposition viz: to lend you $30,000. As we yet owe a very large amt for a college built in Baltimore a few years ago. Last year as you have no doubt learnt from the papers was a most disastrous year for the farmers of Maryland. The wheat crop on our farms was almost an entire failure and the other crops fell very short of our average. In consequence I have already been under the necessity of borrowing from Bank to meet current expenses and shall be obliged to go into Bank again before **[End Page 1]** another crop can be brought into market. As to your second proposition we are willing to accede to it; if you still desire it. But Gov. Johnson wrote to us last fall to ascertain the amt. due on his notes yet unpaid & in replying to him I took occasion to state that you had punctually paid the interest and would pay off the balance of the notes in 1860. And finally that it was only know [sic] to ourselves and to no one else, in those parts, that we still hold a note of his & I think it more than probable that my letter had the effect to quieting his [...] on the subject. Should I [several words crossed out] be correct in this inference it would scarcely be worth your while to incure [sic] the expense and trouble of a new mortgage. [Four and a half lines crossed out] **[End page 2]** You will please write again to let me know your wishes on the subject.
P.S. If the mortgage amt be changed you had better enclose the Power of Att. You can describe the property better. The Power of Att. has to be executed by Rev. Tho. F. Mulledy in whose name the mortgage is **[End page 3]**

Transcription of January 27, 1859 letter to J.R. Thompson from Jesuits. Transcription courtesy of Richard Cellini.

SCHEDULE 2.—Slave Inhabitants in *11th Ward Baltimore City* in the County of *Baltimore* State of *Maryland*, enumerated by me, on the *5* day of *June*, 1860. *C C Dunn* Ass't Marshal.

NAMES OF SLAVE OWNERS.	No. of Slaves	Age	Sex	Color	Fugitives from the State	Number manumitted	Deaf & dumb, blind, insane, or idiotic	No. of Slave houses	NAMES OF SLAVE OWNERS.	No. of Slaves	Age	Sex	Color	Fugitives from the State	Number manumitted	Deaf & dumb, blind, insane, or idiotic	No. of Slave houses
Sophew F Hitchcock	1	15	♀	B					Charles Howard	1	22	m	B				
James C Conn	1	21	♀	B						1	21	♀	B				
Robert G Wilson	1	36	♀	B					Charles H Hey	1	60	♀	B				
	1	19	♀	m						1	18	♀	B				
William W McClellan	1	45	♀	m						1	12	♀	B				
John D Daniels	1	60	♀	B					Emily M Parish	1	60	♀	B				
	1	22	♀	m					William Hough	1	25	m	B				
Spear Taylor	1	35	♀	B					Robert Hough	1	24	m	B				
Samuel A Harrison	1	35	♀	m	1	2			Thomas S Alexander	1	50	♀	B				
	1	9	m	m					Peter Herman	1	30	♀	B				
John Y Day	1	60	m	B					Oder of Jesuits	1	60	♀	B				
James S Cottman	1	8	♀	B					Mary L Ridgely	1	17	m	B				
John S McKim	1	38	♀	B					Frances N Bell	1	30	♀	m				
Richard Frances	1	27	m	B					James Carroll	1	55	m	B				
Henry Poindexter	1	35	♀	B						1	45	♀	B				
	1	16	♀	B					Harry D C Carroll	1	18	♀	B		•		
Walter Fernandis	1	8	♀	m					James MacNicholson	1	60	♀	B				
Anthony Groverman	1	33	♀	B						1	47	m	B				
	1	28	♀	B						1	34	♀	m				
	1	16	m	B						1	29	♀	m				
	1	12	♀	B						1	5	m	m				
Elizabeth Cockey	1	18	♀	B						1	4	♀	m				
Richard Munroe	1	33	m	B						1	3	m	m				
Virginia Williams	1	23	♀	B					Henry V Plowrance	1	13	m	B				
Robinson N Eator	1	15	♀	B					Jane Perkins	1	40	♀	B				
	1	7	m	B						1	10	♀	B				
Elizabeth Waguerman	1	40	♀	m					Henry Jones	1	16	♀	B				
William W Aubrey	1	12	♀	B					Augustin F Levrin	1	12	♀	B				
Richard S Hardesty	1	30	♀	m					Susan Makepeace	1	60	m	B				
Henry Gough	1	20	♀	m					Henry W Sheffy	1	55	♀	B				
Michael C Griffith	1	40	♀	m					Eliza Hayne	1	20	♀	B				
	1	17	m	B					Robert H Love	1	50	♀	B				
	1	14	♀	B						1	19	♀	B				
Colin Mackenzie	1	26	♀	m						1	11	♀	B				
	1	11	♀	m						1	6	♀	B				
George Hayland	1	25	♀	B					J W Wm Marriott	1	18	♀	m				
John H Heald	1	21	♀	B						1	19	m	B				
Thomas W Levering	1	40	♀	B					Lavina Hopkins	1	20	m	B				
	1	30	m	B					William Crichton	1	50	♀	B				
	1	40	m	B					Maria Porter	1	35	m	B				

No. of owners, 27 + 25   No. of male slaves, 22   No. fugitives,   No. deaf and dumb,   No. insane,
No. of houses,   No. of female slaves, 55   No. manumitted,   No. blind,   No. idiotic,
Total slaves, 28

U.S. Census Slave Schedule listing Loyola Jesuits as slaveholders of a 60-year-old enslaved woman in 1860 (line 11 2nd column). 1860.U.S. Census Baltimore (Independent City) Maryland, Ward 11, Slave Schedule page 1, Ancestry.com.

hereby conveyed that is to say FIRST The said premises shall be improved used and occupied
by the said The Associated Professors of Loyola College in the City of Baltimore its succes
sors and assigns only for the purpose of conducting a private educational institution for the
university Collegiate or high school education of white persons including in said purposes

ground (e) That at no time shall the land included in said tract or any part thereof or
any building erected thereon be occupied by any negro or person of negro extraction This
prohibition however is not intended to include occupancy by a negro domestic servant or
other person while employed on or about the premises by the owner or occupant of any land
included in said tract IT IS hereby covenanted and agreed that any of the foregoing res

Loyola College Land Deed, Nov. 1, 1921. The Deed specified that only "white persons" could be educated at the College (first excerpt) and that neither the land nor the "buildings erected thereon be occupied by any negro or person of negro extraction" unless they worked there (second excerpt). John W Garrett & Co to Associated Professors of Loyola College, Deed and Agreement, 1 November 1921; Land Records of Baltimore City, Liber 3796 Folio 513, Maryland State Archives, MDLANDREC (https://mdlandrec.net/), Nov. 1, 1921.

Historical Student Publications

MINSTRELS AT LOYOLA

College Athletic Association To Give Entertainment.

The members of the athletic association of Loyola College will hold a minstrel show on, October 25 in the college theatre for the benefit of the athletic association. Rehearsals have already begun under the direction of Mr. Oliver P. Ziegfield, Jr. A musical program will be given by the College Glee Club.

The committee in charge is composed of Messrs. L. Frank O'Brien (chairman), William M. Nevins, Joseph A. Wozny, Thomas J. Wheeler, Joseph Tewes and Edward L. Leonard.

Many improvements have already been made in the college gymnasium this year. Lockers and special apparatus have been moved to a separate room and a new system of shower baths installed. Rev. W. G. Read Mullan, the new rector of Loyola, is giving every encouragement to athletics.

The October 25, 1907, Loyola College minstrel show was performed "to benefit . . . Athletic Association" since Loyola's rector gave "every encouragement to athletics." *The Baltimore Sun*, October 5, 1907.

LOYOLA STUDENTS' MINSTRELS

Entertained Large Crowd With Negro Songs And Dances.

The students of Loyola College presented a minstrel show yesterday afternoon in the college theatre, and the performance will be repeated tonight. The hall was filled by the friends of the performers, who were 40 strong. The little orphans of St. Vincent's Orphan Asylum were present in a body under the care of Rev. John DeWulf, and with the children of the other parochial schools seemed to take great interest in the performance.

Mr. James S. Murphy was interlocutor, with Messrs. Harry Galligher, Joseph Voeglein, William F. Braden, L. Frank O'Brien, Frederick C. Lee and Martin McNulty as end men. Mr. Braden made a big hit when he sang "Handle Me With Care," and the effort of the entire company, "Is Everybody Happy," received great applause.

The performance was directed by Messrs. Oliver P. Ziegfeld and C. F. Ranft. The proceeds of the performances will go to the athletic association of the college.

Loyola students "Entertained Large Crowd with Negro Songs and Dances" to benefit Athletic Association, October 25, 1907. *The Baltimore Sun*, Oct. 25, 1907.

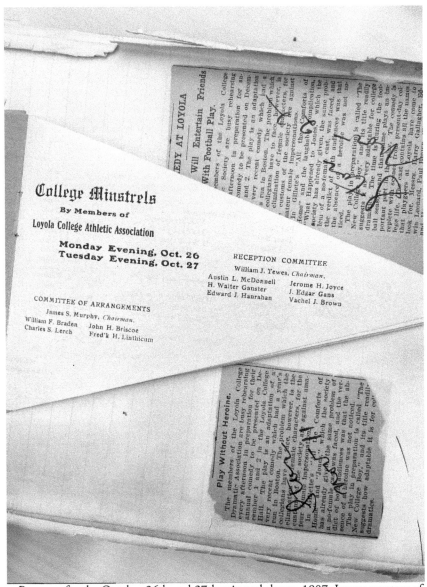

Program for the October 26th and 27th minstrel shows, 1907. Image courtesy of the Loyola Notre Dame Library Archives (Mask and Rapier Society Records; LUMD.010.023 Box 2; Volume 1; 1907).

IN MEMORIAM.

The days we spent together were so few—
　Yet happy ones that ne'er shall be forgot;
The days we yearned have faded as a dream;
　To be with us—was not his lot!

A man of God and man of men was he;
　A soul that knew the worth of earthly
　　place;
A priest who gave to God his all—
　To aid the weakness of our carnal race!

Oh! would that Time had stayed its heavy
　　hand,
　And left him here until reward was won;
But 'twas his wish when heart-throbs lin-
　gered long:—
"Not my will but Thine be done!"
　　　　　　　　　　L. A. C.

———◊———

CLANSMEN.

They tell of yore of a bloody war that was
　waged by the Ku-Klux Klan,
When the peace of home and the peace of
　bone was robbed of man by man—
That out of heart of the dying South
The cry was carried from mouth to mouth,
That men were needed and men from the
　South,
Enrolled in the Ku-Klux Klan!

Oh, the fight was long, but the men were
　strong—these men of the Ku-Klux
　Klan;
And they fought for home and they fought
　for bone as only a Southerner can!
The sons they loved had joined the fray;
The mothers sobbed and passed away;
Their daughters, too, were taken as clay
From the men of the Ku-Klux Klan!

'Tis hard to fight, to fight and lose, like the
　men of the Ku-Klux Klan—
They lost their home and they lost their
　bone, but the bloody race they ran!
And years, long years, have since passed
　by;
The South has wept with a heavy sigh
For the men of the Ku-Klux Klan!
　　　　　　　　　　Leo A. Codd.

———◊———

A DREAM.

In dead of night when all was still without,
When men and things of men were steeped
　in dreams;
Suddenly there passed into the ken of one—
An aged man who studied worlds beyond and
　worlds above—
A brilliant orb, on which there was inscribed
　Love!

And while he looked and thought and pon-
　dered on its mean,
The air about was filled with sweet-toned
　songs,
As though the angels had come down from
　homes above,
And now sang melodies, sweet melodies of
　Love!

And, gazing close, he saw this peopled globe
Pass slowly from this sphere of sight, and
　then
The voices were like unto the cooing of a
　dove,
And faintly died the melodies, sweet melo-
　dies of Love!
　　　　　　　　　　Leo A. Codd.

6　　　　　　　　　　　　　　　7

Loyola student poem praising the Ku Klux Klan in *The Loyola: A Semimonthly Published by the Literary Societies of Loyola College*, Nov. 3, 1913. Image courtesy of Archives of the Maryland Province of the Society of Jesus at Georgetown University (Box 156 GTM000119, Folder 9).

LOYOLA CLUB

BALTIMORE, MD.

3

AN OLD-FASHIONED WIFE.

I want to be a good, little wife
In the good, old-fashioned way.
I'll honor and obey
From home I'll never stray
Although the thing that's smart is
To be out all night at parties,
I'll be sitting with my knitting
In the good old-fashioned way

6

SAILIN' AWAY ON THE HENRY CLAY.

Sailin' away—sailin' away—Sailin' in the moonlight on the Henry Clay—
Just hear that barber shop quartet a-harmonizin' While that coon band is improvisin'
Slidin' along—glidin' along—Dancing till the break of day
Up on that upper deck —just see those darkies spoon,
Hug and kissin' 'neath the Dixie moon, Oh boy oceans of joy—
When you're sailin' on the Henry Clay.

26

MOTHER, DIXIE AND YOU!

Just a picture of the Swanee shore, Where I spent my childhood days,
With Mammy Jinney's young Pickinninies, Just a scene a-round a cabin door,
Where I used to play ev'ry day, To pass the time away.
Each recollection brings affection, Fields of cotton make me think of snow white hair,
Skies mean your dear eyes of blue,—Just three things I live for,
All my life I'll give for Mother, Dixie and you!

Loyola Club song sheet excerpts with racist, sexist, and Confederate-sympathizing lyrics, 1900-1930. Image courtesy of Maryland Province Archives at Georgetown University (Box 156 GTM000119, Folder 6; 1900-1930).

35

Student Essays

'Strong Truths, Well Lived': The Truth Behind Loyola University Maryland's Ties to Slavery

Alysa Krause

Loyola University Maryland, initially Loyola College, was funded and established in 1852 by the Maryland Province of the Society of Jesus, a Jesuit order. Before the construction of the college, the Maryland Province's main concern was Georgetown University, a Jesuit university struggling to stay afloat financially. In order to continue and expand Jesuit education in the United States, the Maryland Province sold 272 of their enslaved people. This paper will argue that the Maryland Province's profit from selling 272 slaves directly resulted in Loyola University Maryland and that the sale of these 272 enslaved people singlehandedly furthered the continuation of Jesuit teachings and institutions in America. By analyzing diary entries, obituaries, letters, and financial ledgers, its apparent that not only is Loyola University Maryland a direct result of the sale of 272 slaves by the Maryland Province in November of 1838, but that the institution is tied to slavery in myriad ways.

"Strong Truths, Well Lived" is the slogan of Maryland's renowned Jesuit college, Loyola University Maryland, emphasizing that staying mindful, connected, self-aware, and happy is of the utmost importance to the Jesuit way of life. Even though some will encounter difficult questions and choices, their Jesuit-instilled "strong moral compass" will guide them through their life. But when will this Jesuit university use its "strong moral compass" to deliver their strong truth to the world? By analyzing diary entries, correspondence through letters, and financial ledgers, its apparent that Loyola University Maryland is tied to slavery through the Maryland Province of the Society of Jesus, who funded the University following their sale of 272 enslaved people in 1838, as well as through the institution's early private donors.

In a letter dating to 1859 responding to a request for funding from a Louisiana slaveholder, the Maryland Province stated that they were not in the financial position to lend a significant amount of money, as they owed, "a large amt of money for a college built in Baltimore a few years ago." That college was Loyola, and this letter from the Maryland Province archives is evidence of Loyola's direct ties to slavery. From its very inception, Loyola was therefore connected to slavery.

In April 2016, Georgetown University announced their connection to slavery and acknowledged that due to financial struggles, the Maryland Province had sold 272 enslaved people, an action later labeled the GU272. Georgetown University historian Adam Rothman argues that "the university owes its existence to this history," and it can be argued that Loyola should admit the same.[1] Since Georgetown University announced their direct ties to slavery, many universities across the nation began grappling with their own histories including Brown, Columbia, Harvard, and the University of Virginia.[2] When Loyola University Maryland was approached by the *Wall Street Journal* to clarify if the institution was involved in the GU272 sale, Loyola's spokesperson Nick Alexopulos stated that "the university is deeply committed to human dignity and equality [...] we have no reason to believe that slavery or the slave trade has ties to Loyola."[3]

In this essay, I will explore how slavery and the slave trade have multiple ties to Loyola. Loyola automatically became tied to slavery once the

---

1 Rachel L. Swarns, "272 Slaves Were Sold to Save Georgetown. What Does It Owe Their ..." *New York Times*, April 16, 2016. https://www.nytimes.com/2016/04/17/us/georgetown-university-search-for-slave-descendants.html.

2 Ibid.

3 "Georgetown University to Give Admissions Preference to Descendants of Slaves Sold by the College," *Baltimore Sun*, May 28, 2019.

Maryland Province trafficked enslaved people, and therefore should have acknowledged that truth to news organizations. Yes, it would be difficult to tie Loyola directly to the 1838 sale of the 272 enslaved people since information regarding how the proceeds were utilized is unavailable. But Loyola's very foundation by the Maryland Province is in itself is a direct tie to slavery, as the mission held nearly three hundred enslaved people across their six properties in the state of Maryland.

In the Maryland Provincial Archives, there are documents regarding the sale of the 272 enslaved people to former Governor of Louisiana, Henry Johnson, and his associate, Jesse Batey for $115,000.[4] Within the Maryland Province Archives, the payments Henry Johnson made to the Maryland Province are documented as a part of the 1838 deal, describing them one such receipt as "October 2nd, 1839, for purchase of 140 servants on November 10th, 1838, payable in notes due on the following terms…".[5] This particular entry shows how the Maryland Province will be receiving monthly payments from those who purchased the 272 enslaved people. It is this purchase and those payments from Johnson and Batey that helped the Province become financially stable, and aided in their endeavors of creating more Jesuit universities within the United States. Leading up to the 1830s, the Maryland mission was suffering from severe financial hardships due to their plantations not returning.[6] The Maryland Province operated six plantations, where the Jesuits did not owe money for the land and were debt free, however, they were not accruing the amount of revenue needed to fund the entire Province of Jesuits as well as the universities they helped build.[7] An internal investigation of the Maryland mission, ordered by officials in Italy, proposed that the Province should free their slaves. Some, however, considered selling the enslaved people. Father Mulledy, a young priest at the mission, believed that the Jesuits' debts in Maryland resulted from trying to be both slaveholders and priests. This limited the ability of both the farmlands

4 Archives of the Maryland Province of the Society of Jesus, GMT 000119, Box OS7, Folder 2.
5 Ibid.
6 Adam Rothman and Elsa Barraza Mendoza, *Facing Georgetown's History: A Reader on Slavery, Memory, and Reconciliation* (Washington, DC: Georgetown University Press, 2021), 41.
7 Rick Boyd, "Many in Slave Sale Cited by Georgetown Toiled in Southern Md." St. Mary's College of Maryland, October 3, 2016. https://www.smcm.edu/about/wp-content/uploads/sites/34/2018/03/Enterprise.-Many-in-slave-sale-cited-by-Georgetown-toiled-in-SoMo.pdf.

and universities to flourish.[8] Failure to reach a decision regarding their plantations and the fate of their enslaved peoples meant their debts would continue to grow and they might be forced to sell everything. In the end, the Jesuits decided to sell their enslaved people. The decision, however, was not without controversy and coming to terms with the sale of their enslaved proved difficult for the Jesuits. In a letter to Father William McSherry, the president of Georgetown at the time, Superior General of the Province in Rome Jan Roothaan wrote, "it would be better to suffer financial disaster than suffer the loss of all our souls with the sale of the slaves."[9] Many of the Jesuits in the mission believed that it was more harmful to sell the slaves than to continue to be slaveholders, arguing that they were called to serve the spiritual welfare of their slaves.

After the Maryland mission finalized their decision to sell both their land and enslaved people, they decided that the money from these transactions would be used to create colleges and missions in cities like Baltimore and Philadelphia.[8] The Jesuits had been planning to open a college in Baltimore, and with the new influx of cash, this plan came to fruition. The college that the Maryland Province built would later be known as Loyola.

Due to his role in spearheading the initiative to sell the slaves of the Maryland Province, Father Mulledy was tasked with finding a buyer as well and making sure that the sale met all conditions set by the Society of Jesus in Rome. In a letter to Father John McElroy, a Jesuit in Frederick, Maryland, Father Mulledy stated that "I find it difficult to dispose of our servants to persons who live in a Catholic neighborhood."[9] He goes on to ask the advice of Father Elroy, inquiring if he believed that instead of pricing every enslaved person differently based on age and gender, he should use a round average of $400 "per head," with a separate price for enslaved people over the age of sixty and count babies under the age of one as one with their mother.[10] The language used by Father Mulledy in his letter to Father Elroy shows how insensitive he felt about selling the enslaved people and finding another master for them.

8 Ibid.
9 Archives of the Maryland Province of the Society of Jesus, ""I would be willing to take $450": Fr. Mulledy to Fr. McElroy on pricing people, June 12, 1838," *Georgetown Slavery Archive*, accessed December 15, 2022, https://slaveryarchive.georgetown.edu/items/show/100.
10 Ibid.

It was on November 11, 1838, that Father Mulledy wrote to Father McElroy "Thank God I have succeeded," stating that he had found two buyers for the Maryland Province's 272 slaves and that the first boat full of enslaved people had left the dock en route to Louisiana.[11] Mulledy goes on to express how difficult the past few weeks had been for him, as he had traveled many miles in order to negotiate a sale, reflecting that "I never want to experience this again."[12] Again, the language used by Father Mulledy is insensitive to the situation at hand, where he is in charge of engaging in 272 counts of human trafficking.

It can be inferred from the 1859 Maryland Province letter that they used the money from the sale of their 272 enslaved persons to create colleges in Baltimore and other metropolitan cities throughout the northern part of the United States. In financial statements from the Maryland Province Archives, it is evident that Loyola University Maryland is indebted to the mission. From 1880 to 1904 Loyola is listed as a college that provided rent to the Province, and as of 1904, it had a remaining grounds rent of $75,329.69.[13] Loyola was only one of eleven universities that were indebted to the Maryland Province as of 1904. The financial ledgers of the Maryland Province Archives were used for the internal accounting purposes of the mission and revealed Loyola's debt to the Maryland Province. The mission's investment in the education of all those that have attended Loyola since its founding in 1852 funded the Maryland Province through Loyola's grounds rent payment, meaning that Loyola is paying the Maryland Province back for the land that the University occupies.

In early volumes of the *Baltimore Sun*, donations made through obituary advertisements can connect Loyola University Maryland to a long history of slavery, the Confederacy, and treason to the United States of America. For instance, on June 6, 1882, the obituary of Anna C. Kane notes her donation of $500 "to the Associated Profs. Of Loyola College."[14] Mrs. Kane had inherited the estate of her husband, George Kane, when he died in

---

11 Maryland Province Archives, ""Thank God I have succeeded": Fr. Mulledy completes the sale of 272 slaves to Louisiana, November 11, 1838," *Georgetown Slavery Archive*, accessed December 15, 2022, https://slaveryarchive.georgetown.edu/items/show/288.
12 Ibid.
13 Archives of the Maryland Province of the Society of Jesus, GMT 000119, Box OS7, Folder 2.
14 Charitable Requests," the *Baltimore Sun* (June 6, 1882).

1878. George Kane was a prominent man in the city of Baltimore, as he was the twenty-seventh mayor and the first Chief of Police to be arrested while actively holding the position.

In February of 1861, it was revealed that George P. Kane was an integral member of the Baltimore Plot, a plan to assassinate President-elect Abraham Lincoln as he drove from Harrisburg, PA to Washington, D.C. for his inauguration. As Chief of Police, Kane was in a unique position to provide security to President-elect Lincoln as his motorcade drove through Baltimore to reach the nation's capital.[15] The Baltimore Plot shows how strongly Kane felt regarding the Confederacy and their values: not only would he be committing murder by assassinating President Lincoln, but also treason against his country. The unveiling of this plot, investigated by Allan Pinkerton, led the President-elect to drive through the city of Baltimore secretly and at night and not divulge his whereabouts to Kane.[16] After Lincoln's no-show during his inaugural motorcade, political officials in Baltimore became wary of Kane, correctly believing he had become a part of the growing population of Confederate sympathizers in the city.[17]

There was a growing population of Southern sympathizers in Baltimore, so much so that it could be compared to the amount of Southern pride that is evident in Richmond, Virginia.[18] This made law enforcement extremely cautious, to the point where they were not allowed to drink water given to them by civilians out of fear it could be poisoned. The Mayor of Baltimore in June 1861, George Brown, began rounding up prominent figures that were suspected Confederate sympathizers. Kane was among them, arrested in the middle of the night by Union soldiers and sent to Fort McHenry, then transferred to Fort Warren, serving a total sentence of fourteen months.[19] Once Kane was released, he began working alongside Confederate General Robert E. Lee, receiving a commission for his aid, and would visit Confederate

---

15 Society, B. P. H. (2023, January 13). *Marshal Kane*. Baltimore Police History. Retrieved January 13, 2023, from https://baltimorepolicemuseum.com/en/k2/marshal-geo-p-kane.html
16 Ibid.
17 Ibid.
18 Rasmussen, F. N. (2021, September 30). *Early Civil War Battleground*. Baltimore Sun. Retrieved January 13, 2023, from https://www.baltimoresun.com/news/bs-xpm-2006-04-01-0604010133-story.html,
19 Ibid.

President Jefferson Davis in North Carolina. After the war, Kane settled in Virginia and became a part of the tobacco manufacturing industry.[20]

Due to Kane's prominence, it is unlikely Loyola College was unaware of the donor's history. With deep-rooted ties to the Confederacy, it can be inferred that the Kanes were supporters of slavery, due to how strongly they sympathized with the South. Through donations similar to the Kanes', the early donations that helped Loyola College prosper were tainted by association with support for slavery, the Confederacy, and treason against the United States. By accepting Anna Kane's donation, Loyola became indebted to those who support the trafficking of humans; it is just one example of the many ways Loyola is connected to slavery.

Loyola University Maryland, under the guidance of the newly inaugurated president, Terrence Sawyer, has launched the Presidential Task Force to investigate the university's ties to slavery. This is a step in the right direction. Just because the university includes people of color, it does not mean Loyola University Maryland is inclusive: the University is able to offer education to its students through systems that are exploitative, without including the histories of people of color. One way that Loyola University Maryland could be truly inclusive is by telling the story of how the university came to be and its foundational connection to slavery.

Before arriving at Loyola, students should know that Loyola University Maryland has ties to slavery in more ways than one. Knowledge of how the university was founded by the Maryland Province of the Society of Jesus in 1852 using funds from the 1838 sale of 272 enslaved people. Neither does the connection end there, as the university continued to accept donations from Confederate sympathizers and those who conspired to assassinate a United States president. Loyola University Maryland owes its history to those who were enslaved, the 272 enslaved people who worked on Jesuit land in 1838, and every single person trafficked since the mission's origin in 1642.

On their website, Loyola claims that "to this day, we remain committed to the ideals embodied by the members of the Society of Jesus throughout its

---

20 Ibid.

rich history".[21] The "rich history" of the Maryland Society of Jesus includes the "discarding" of 272 humans, and a history of leaders who strongly believed in the "rural tradition" that is slavery. Indeed, Jesuit education as a whole was made possible by slavery. Leading up to the 1830s, the Maryland Province was experiencing severe financial hardships and could barely afford to make the monthly payments to keep Georgetown University afloat. Without the sale of the 272 enslaved people from the mission's land, it is probable that Jesuit education would not exist in the twenty-first century. And if Jesuit education did not exist after the 1830s, neither would Loyola University Maryland. Every student who has walked through Boulder Garden Cafe, taken a test in Maryland Hall, or prayed at Alumni Memorial Chapel has benefitted from the Jesuit slaveholders of the Maryland Province and the early donations of Confederate sympathizers. This needs to be recognized by Loyola University Maryland and known by all students.

21 "History and Traditions." Loyola University Maryland. Accessed December 14, 2022. https://www.loyola.edu/about/history-traditions.

After Contrition

Evelyn (Evy) Ryan

Roman Catholic Act of Contrition

O My God, I am heartily sorry for having offended Thee,
and I detest all my sins, because I dread the loss of heaven and the pains of hell,
but most of all because they offend Thee, my God,
Who art all good and deserving of all my love.
I firmly resolve, with the help of Thy grace,

to confess my sins,

to do penance,

and to amend my life.

Amen.

When I was a senior in high school, researching and applying to colleges that would be my home for the next four years, three of the five private institutions I considered were Catholic. Two of those Catholic institutions, Loyola University Maryland and College of the Holy Cross, were Jesuit-founded. The emphasis that Catholic churches, especially Jesuit branches, place on education is well-known and well-recognized, even by people outside the Catholic faith. Jesuit colleges and universities are hundreds of years old, established almost in tandem with the first appearances of Catholic people in North America. Their pedagogy surrounding education emphasizes

45

helping the disadvantaged through access to learning. When I chose Loyola, I did so because the value of education has been an integral part of my life since the moment I learned to read.

And so, imagine my dismay when I discovered that the Jesuits, the founders of the school I chose and have come to love, have a longstanding tradition of exploiting those disadvantaged communities they claim to be aiding. As a Catholic, this information was disturbing and disheartening. Even more disturbing was learning that the Catholic Church continues to contribute immensely to the disenfranchisement of African American people through consistent and constant evasion of responsibility.[1] It was hard to reconcile the school that has given me so many opportunities with the institution that has contributed to immense hatred and harm. The Jesuits, through the power of silence, the implementation of a biased education, and the perpetuation of an incorrect foundational story of Catholicism in America, enact harm on people that they are called as Catholics to love, respect, and cherish. But there is a small yet persistent glimmer of hope. I believe that encouraging healing, forgiveness, and mutual respect for each other through true understanding can help us reconcile past atrocities.

Major reform is necessary to atone for the damage that we have caused. Through a revitalized commitment to educating ourselves and others on the true story of our Catholic institutions, by addressing the current silences that are eroding truth, and by expanding our understanding of what it means to be Catholic, we can begin to accept our role in the continued harm of American minorities. If we miss this opportunity for reconciliation and healing, a legacy of hurt will continue to thrive in communities of marginalized people all over the United States.

Failing To Tell the Whole Story

From the very beginning of European presence on American soil, colonizers (which include the Jesuits) exploited and oppressed Black and Indigenous people for their own gain.[1] English law dictated that political participation was linked to property ownership—men who owned land. Individual Jesuit priests were entitled to land grants and donations and

---

1 Thomas Murphy, Jesuit *Slaveholding in Maryland, 1717-1838,* 1st ed. (New York: Routledge, 2016), xv, 25.

over time built up large landholdings.[2] They first used indentured servants as laborers but over time shifted to enslaved Africans.[3] They first acquired African peoples as gifts from laymen, and eventually hired out enslaved labor directly from their owners.[4] All over the country, Black enslaved people were forced to labor without compensation and were subjected to intense and despicable violence from the people who specifically defined themselves as educated. A member of the Society of Jesus, Thomas Murphy, recently wrote about Jesuit enslavement of Black people in *Jesuit Slaveholding in Maryland, 1717-1838*. In this book, Murphy's tone is maddeningly misleading, offering assertions that, "Catholic slaveholding was universally and inherently more benevolent than Protestant slaveholding" or "Jesuit slaveholding... resembled general slaveholding in many respects, but it was conducted for additional reasons and according to additional norms than other variations of the practice."[5] Statements like these dismiss and distance the actions of the Jesuits from the debilitating effects they had on Black communities. These present-day attempts to wash over the violence, racism, and oppression that enslaved people faced are real and crippling.

The story doesn't stop there. Christian religious sanction of enslavement was encouraged by a society that was economically dependent on the labor of the enslaved, which, combined with fundamentally racist governmental structures filled with white supremacist laws and theories, is the true history of early Jesuit action in the United States. Contrast this with the Jesuit-circulated story detailing an intrinsic focus on education and aid of the disadvantaged through the creation of schools since the moment they arrived in America.[6] Founding these schools, though, costs money – a lot of money. After the Jesuits had used their enslaved people to gain a voice in government, which they then utilized to uphold oppressive and racist practices, it became necessary for them to continue owning their enslaved people

---

2 Murphy, *Jesuit Slaveholding in Maryland,* 15.
3 Ibid.
4 Ibid.
5 Ibid.
6 Jesuits.org, "Education," July 21, 2020, https://www.jesuits.org/our-work/education/.

to keep functioning as a diocese. A standard had been established, one that the Jesuits found easier to blindly defend rather than attempt to change.[7]

After their arrival in Maryland and immediately after establishing Georgetown University, the Jesuits were in debt.[8] They sunk money into funding schools, which cost a fortune to own and operate. In discussing the Jesuit's 1838 sale of 272 enslaved people, consistently referred to as "the end of Jesuit slavery," the need to address that debt is cited as the fundamental reason why enslaved people were sold rather than manumitted (freed), despite ongoing interreligious conversations about the morality of owning other human beings.[9] This debt angle, however, is inaccurate and unproductive because it shifts the blame away from the Jesuits and toward the economic state of the U.S. *The Jesuits always had a choice.* They made the decision to sell—rather than free—their enslaved people so that they could continue gaining power and influence, spreading their version of the story of Catholicism, and quietly sweeping their relationship with the slave trade under the rug instead of confronting it.

The schools that benefited directly from the Jesuit use of slaves still exist today, including Georgetown University and our own Loyola University Maryland.[10] The students who have attended both of these universities benefit from the original sale of the 272 men, women, and children that were sold by the Jesuits in 1838.[11] The money gained by that sale, equivalent to $3.3 million dollars today, allowed Georgetown to remain open by paying off debt, which in turn led to its current status as a premier U.S. university.[12] The funds from the sale also allowed for the expansion of Jesuit educational institutions, particularly the founding of Loyola University Maryland.[13]

---

7 Murphy, *Jesuit Slaveholding in Maryland,* 94.
8 Archives of the Maryland Province of the Society of Jesus, GMT 000119, Box OS7, Folder 1.
9 Murphy, *Jesuit Slaveholding in Maryland,* 136.
10 Archives of the Maryland Province of the Society of Jesus, MPA Box 40, Letter to JR Thompson, 01/27/1859
11 Murphy, *Jesuit Slaveholding in Maryland,* 164.
12 Georgetown University, "Report of the Working Group on Slavery, Memory, and Reconciliation," Summer 2016, accessed January 2, 2023, Appendix C, 85-86.
13 Murphy, *Jesuit Slaveholding in Maryland,* 192.

The Power of Uninterrupted Silence

Loyola's campus has been home to many stories that employ white supremacist stereotypes and racist ideals. Student-run publications from the yearbook to the weekly newsletter to dramatic performances are full of blatantly racist written works, white supremacist jokes, anti-minority sentiments, and white students in blackface.[14] All this evidence is available online, and yet these stories that comprise a bulk of Loyola's history are not widely known, understood, or acknowledged. This silence on the serious harm caused by celebrated members of the Loyola community in the past and present has led to an uninterrupted legacy of racism and oppression.

Staying silent has historically been the chosen mode of operation for the Jesuits and the Catholic church. The Maryland Jesuits owned enslaved people from their beginnings in the U.S. until less than twenty-five years before the Civil War.[15] In the 1770s, as debate around slavery increased, Jesuits thought that "to make no change for the time being" was "the best way to handle an uncertain situation."[16] This silence, interpreted here as due to the *uncertainty* of Catholic clergymen regarding human rights, pervades through hundreds of years of Jesuit thought and action. History repeats itself continuously within the Society of Jesus – and the decades of stationary thought and action prove it. Evidence of this stagnation is laid out before us, and yet there seems to be no real drive from within to make any changes to the current course. Georgetown University, for example, offers legacy admissions status for descendants of the original 272 enslaved people who the Jesuits sold. Loyola Maryland, though still in the beginning stages of investigating its own connection to slavery, could also adopt this practice.

During the 1940s, Loyola quietly decided to integrate its classrooms, offering admission to African American men despite land records stating that Black people were forbidden to set foot on campus as students, a land record that remained unchanged until 2020.[17] In records of consultors' meetings from mid 1949, one member of the board writes,

---

14 Loyola University Maryland Archives, Yearbooks, 1948, 49.: Ibid, 1950,12.; Ibid, 1956, 40.; Loyola University Maryland Archives, Student Publications, The Greyhound, 1925-1933.
15 Murphy, *Jesuit Slaveholding in Maryland*, 203.
16 Ibid.
17 Evergreen Land Deed, November 30, 1921 - 2020

No publicity will be given by the college as to its policy in respect to the admission of negro students. No announcement of any sort will be issued on the matter by the college. Should objections arise which may not be overlooked, the college will issue a simple statement of its position, and avoid all controversy on the matter.[18]

At every turn, Jesuit school leadership did not take advantage of the opportunity to dismantle systems of oppression. Silence meant that the school, continually in debt, would not risk alienating their white clientele or receive backlash for causing waves in Catholic communities.[19] Jesuits, therefore, chose to uphold their systematic power, even at the expense of the Black and Brown communities living around them. To this day, the legacy of silence in the church continues to affect African American people, Catholic or otherwise, in Maryland and across the United States.[20]

Not only are Catholic churches predominantly located in white neighborhoods, but they also serve predominantly white communities of parishioners.[21] Black communities, discouraged with the lack of representation, empathy, and respect from within the Catholic Church, broke off to form their own dioceses, which further segregated the pews.[22] White males also occupy most of the positions of power in the church, and this absence of diverse perspectives at the church's highest levels has hindered attempts to truly tackle systemic issues such as racism.[23] For instance, in 1958 when the National Catholic Welfare Conference "called for Americans to mobilize against racial discrimination and segregation laws still being enforced," schools and churches were left out of the conversation as places where participants of racist systems of oppression were located.[24] This implies that, conveniently for the Jesuits, religious and educational sites were not seen as

18 Loyola University Maryland Archives, Jesuit Community Records, Box 2, Volume 1, Record of Consultations 1924-1956.
19 Emma Welch, "Catholicism's Role in the Lives of African Americans: From Civil Rights to Today," *Journal of Theta Alpha Kappa* 45, no. 1 (2021), 19.
20 Ibid.
21 Joseph J. Flipper, "White Ecclesiology: The Identity of the Church in the Statements on Racism by United States Catholic Bishops," *Theological Studies*, volume 82, issue 3 (2021): 419-420.
22 Welch, "Catholicism's Role in the Lives of African Americans," 16-17; Enoch Pratt Free Library Collections, African American Room, Vertical Files, Rev. George Stallings and the Imani Church.
23 Ibid.
24 Flipper, "White Ecclesiology," 422.

places of active white supremacist behavior. These kinds of selective silences were tantamount to total silence on the issue of race. Both led to exclusion and denial of minority voices from a platform that would allow them to tell their story.

In statements from the civil rights era up until the present day, the church has framed instances concerning racial disparity, the effects of racism, race relations, or any instances of white power by the Catholic Church in ways that implicitly announce the intense white bias of the clergy and the laypeople. These statements were written by white people in the interest of white people.[25] For instance, the writing style in *Open Wide Our Hearts*, which was released in 2018 to address the impact of racism, utilizes the passive voice "to avoid naming the perpetrators" of said racism.[26] Through these direct or implicit silences, the Catholic church continues to uphold white power through its teachings in religious and educational settings. Not only do we remain silent on issues of the past, but we also remain effectively silent on issues of the present. In our collective conscience, Black members of the Catholic church are excluded, unmentioned, and ignored in the history books.[27] Exclusion is another means utilized by Catholics to keep themselves benefiting from systems of oppression while simultaneously doing enough to avoid direct criticism. By excluding those directly affected by systemic racism, white people separate themselves from the prejudicial effects of intolerance and do not witness the harsh consequences, making it much easier for them to ignore social issues like abolition and civil rights.[28]

Those Catholic clergymen who did speak out on issues of racism and white power appear in the record as isolated, individual priests whose actions were many times condemned by their peers and the larger institution of the church.[29] When we are told stories about Catholic participation in the civil rights movement, it was as individual Catholic priests or laypeople who supported the Black community in their struggle for equal rights, not the entire Catholic society. When these Catholic priests did

25 Ibid.
26 Ibid.
27 Ibid.
28 Ibid.
29 Welch, "Catholicism's Role in the Lives of African Americans," 18.

stand with Black communities, they advocated for gradual change, forcing African Americans to continue living longer in a society that did not view them as full human beings.[30] This is because white power was so deeply ingrained in all facets of the religion.[31] Rarely do we see the entire institution of the Church advocate for the collective humanity and respectful treatment of all of God's people.

Choosing not to teach and discuss these specific aspects of our history leads to ignorance, but that ignorance isn't legitimate. It is yet another instance of white supremacist rhetoric creeping into our subconscious. The silence of the church in all areas of teaching allows for white parishioners to pretend as though they do not benefit from the continuation of racist practices within the religion. Individual denial of this privilege leads, therefore, to the societal continuation of injustice.[32] While this ignorance is visible in churches themselves, equally as important is the role that education plays in enforcing these societal beliefs, especially in Jesuit high schools and colleges.

Educating the Future Through Teaching the Past

The educational efforts of the Jesuits were not in vain. Today, across the nation, there are more than 50 Jesuit high schools or preparatory schools and 27 colleges and universities run by Jesuit brothers.[33] Some of these schools are hundreds of years old, hold incredible levels of status and influence, and are responsible for educating thousands of students. As such, Jesuits are positioned to play an important role in developing a style of teaching that combats oppression from within the United States. Jesuit professors across the globe acknowledge that "...pedagogy is fertile ground for more effectively communicating a vision of Catholic higher education today."[34] The first step toward reconciliation for past atrocities is to widely teach the true history of Jesuit colleges and churches to students attending those schools.

30 Karen J. Johnson, "Beyond Parish Boundaries: Black Catholics and the Quest for Racial Justice," *Religion and American Culture: A Journal of Interpretation* 25, no. 02 (2015): 264, https://doi.org/10.1525/rac.2015.25.2.264.

31 Ibid.

32 Flipper, "White Ecclesiology," 435.

33 USA East Province, "Education," September 2, 2021, https://www.jesuitseast.org/our-work/education/.

34 Timothy Hanchin, "Educating for/in *Caritas*: A Pedagogy of Friendship for Catholic Higher Education in Our Divided Time," *Horizons* 45, no. 1 (May 23, 2018): 77, https://doi.org/10.1017/hor.2018.1.

Examining Loyola specifically, the Jesuit staff has historically not lived up to our motto, "Strong Truths Well Lived," especially when past curriculum and teachings are examined. Father Joseph Ayd, for example, was a sociology professor at Loyola from 1928 to 1946 and served as dean of the school from 1927 until 1928. He ran the social science debate club, which argued such topics as "The Eugenics Movement" in 1935, and "The Negro Problem" in 1935-37.[35] Other debating clubs on Loyola's campus argued the merits of lynching in the early 1930s as well.[36] Using these topics so callously exemplifies the privilege found on Loyola's campus: the white male student body could afford to candidly discuss these issues because they were not affected by them and indeed enjoyed relative societal power because of them.

In his classroom, Father Ayd gave final examination questions that further represented this religious and educational disconnect from the outside world. Students were asked to "give the fundamentals of the negro problems in the U.S.A. and outline the various proposed solutions to it. Indicate the most practical solution," or "outline what may be said about Nordic Supremacy."[37] These questions may have been a product of their time, but they paint a picture of privilege – for the students taking the class and for the professor teaching it. From these questions, we can see exactly what was being taught in classes at Loyola. The second question also indicates that professors knew what white power was and had no issue with its implementation in the classroom or at the college.

This one-sided education, filled with religious rhetoric that pandered to its white audience through single-perspective learning, shaped the minds of every student who sat down in Father Ayd's class. The students' prejudices became ingrained, sharpened through their studies. The Jesuit "focus" on education was really a focus on influencing students to uphold racist systemic issues and constructs. We also see this in Loyola's celebration of certain alumni. Students who were loyal to the Confederate cause, who wrote white supremacist and racist works, and who participated in mockery dramatic minstrel shows are celebrated alumni of our school,

35 Loyola University Archives, Father Ayd Papers, Box 4 Teachings, Social Science Club Brochures
36 Loyola University Maryland Archives, Student Publications, the *Greyhound*, December 13, 1933 Issue
37 Loyola University Maryland Archives, Father Ayd Papers, Box 4 Teachings, Sociology Exam Questions

featured prominently in yearbooks, student publications, and even the *Baltimore Sun*.[38]

Thinking about present day Loyola, it is difficult to see where we have really made tangible progress. The curriculum in the classes I take often deem two "diverse" books as enough to fulfill the diversity requirement necessary to graduate. How can an education in the hands of those so famous for emphasizing the importance of learning be valid when we are missing the contributions of so many different members of our society?

In 1522, St. Ignatius developed the "Ignatian Examen," which was a method of reflection designed to bring believers closer to God by "examining" their day and the way that their actions brought them either happiness or regret. Nowadays, Jesuits provide many Examen options for the prayerful: "An Examen for Racism" is the title of one, "An Examen for White Allies" reads another.[39] Members of the church must ask themselves, at what point does this self-reflection lead to outward action? Jesuit enslavers of the past used these same practices to determine if slaveholding brought them closer to God, deciding that, indeed, "slaveholding led both its practitioners and its objects to the Lord."[40] The lack of outward action in conjunction with dialogue and theory about racism and its effects contributes to the perpetuation of injustices against African American and other marginalized communities. Signs in front of churches proclaiming that "Black Lives Matter" and that "Racism is a Sin" mean nothing when they are not supported by direct, feasible actions.

I don't claim to know how to end the systematic oppression that our lives as American Catholics are founded and built on. I do, however, understand that the church needs a radical shift in the way it deals with the issues of racism and white power, past and present. It may start with an "Examen" of behaviors, but it cannot end there. It must continue with a commitment to action regarding racial equality, a commitment to investing in communities of Black and brown people, a commitment to educating individuals on

---

38 Maryland Provincial Archives at Georgetown University, 000119, Box 156, Folders 9-10
   "Loyola Will Confer Award on Him," *Baltimore Sun*, May 30, 1940.
39 Jesuits.org, "The Ignatian Examen," November 4, 2021, https://www.jesuits.org/spirituality/the-ignatian-examen/.
40 Murphy, *Jesuit Slaveholding in Maryland*, 93.

systemic racism, and a commitment to holding the humanity of all people on earth with the respect and love they deserve.

The Catholic Act of Contrition, used by sinners to acknowledge wrong-doing and ask for forgiveness, ends with two pledges: one to do just penance and one to truthfully amend their lives. For us to honestly live by our faith, these same commitments need to be sincerely made by the Catholic Church.

Loyola, the Civil War, and the Long Shadow of the Lost Cause

Brandon Jay Lyda

In many ways, the history of Loyola during the Civil War mirrors that of its mother institution, Georgetown University. Both were Jesuit schools which drew a large proportion of their students from the well-heeled Catholic planter families of the mid-Atlantic; both were hotbeds of pro-Confederate sentiment during the war. Loyola College had only been in operation for nine years before the war broke out. Small as it was in those early days, a large percentage of Loyola alumni served in Confederate units, even though Maryland itself had remained within the Union. Maryland was the classic example of the border state: technically south of the Mason-Dixon Line yet divided internally about ultimate loyalties. A brief discussion of Loyola faculty and staff will show a community broadly supportive of the Confederacy, both during and after the war. Loyola was directly and indirectly connected with both the Civil War and the Lost Cause, and examining this record will provide another avenue for considering Loyola's legacy and informing the discussions about our shared present situation.

In 1860 Maryland tried to have it both ways: to remain in the Union and yet also maintain the "Peculiar Institution" of slavery. That divide was representative of larger tensions. Most Catholics were registered Democrats, with strong misgivings about the newly-founded Republican party. Formed from the remnants of the Whig party and the short-lived nativist and anti-Catholic "Know Nothing" party, the Republicans were deeply unpopular with Catholics and recent immigrants. The decades leading up to the Civil War in Maryland had involved court cases and social unrest that touched on Catholic concerns, such as the use of the Protestant Bible in public schools and the "Know-Nothings" who were openly hostile to the Catholic immigrant populations of Irish and Germans arriving in Maryland. This hostility was not imagined, and it found expression in the seats of power in Maryland. Historian Robert Brugger says of the local 1856 elections, "in the fall of 1855 Know-Nothings took control of the Baltimore city government, filled all the state judgeships up for bid, elected several state commissioners, gained the balance of power in the legislature, and won four of the six Maryland congressional seats."[1] It was the culmination of years of nativist political strength gathered in the face of increased rates of immigration. Nicholas Varga relates that just two years before this electoral landslide, Loyola's president, the Irish-born Father John Early "presented himself in a Baltimore court to declare his intention of becoming a citizen of the United States ... The motives for seeking citizenship now were clear enough. Rising threats from the Know Nothings prompted Father Stonestreet to change the too-obviously Irish names of members of the Maryland province."[2] While the Know-Nothings imploded as an organized party in the late 1850s, the bulk of their members joined with the remnants of the Whig party to form the Republicans. The all-too-recent memories of bad blood between the Know-Nothings and the Catholics would haunt Catholic political calculations and allegiances for decades.

In keeping with broader Maryland demographics, the population of Loyola was largely drawn from those families with some form of economic connection to slavery. Many Jesuits were born into families who had owned enslaved people, as were many of the students. Even those more-recent arrivals with no direct ties to enslavement were non- or anti-Republican due to their experiences with the Know-Nothings. This ambivalence about the Union, or at least a Union preserved by the Republicans, was to

1 Robert J. Brugger, *Maryland: A Middle Temperament 1634-1980* (Baltimore: Johns Hopkins University Press: 1988), 262.
2 Nicholas Varga, *Baltimore's Loyola, Loyola's Baltimore 1851-1986* (Baltimore: Maryland Historical Society, 1990), 35.

demonstrate itself in a dramatic fashion upon the outbreak of hostilities in 1861. Historian Barbara Jeanne Fields notes,

> *When events obliterated the middle ground, the border states appeared at their worst. Denying the obvious at the start of the war, many of their citizens continued to deny the obvious at the end, when the bitterest diehard in the Confederacy had been forced to yield. The period in between found them, as often as not, a carping and querulous body of obstructionists, forced willy-nilly to adhere to the Union and forever thereafter resentful that life could not go on quietly as before.[3]*

So concerned was the Jesuit general over the political dispute within the order that he gave instructions that any "who should so far forget himself as to speak with too much warmth in favor of, or against, either party" were to be corrected by their local provincial.[4] Providing guidance to Jesuits was one thing, controlling the actions of the student body and alumni was quite another, however. When the war broke out, many Loyola alumni made their way to Virginia to volunteer with Confederate units and other graduates already resident in the Deep South volunteered with units in their home states. The following is the complete list of those men associated with Loyola College who can be verified to have taken up arms:[5]

CONFEDERATE

John Akern - Zarvona's Maryland Zouaves

William Fenwick Baugher - 7th Virginia Cavalry

Alexander Brand - 1st Virginia Cavalry

Arthur Brogden - Surgeon, Jackson's Mississippi Cavalry

Bernard Brown - 7th Virginia Cavalry

Albert Carroll - Lieutenant, Signal Corps, Staff of General Ewell

R. G. Carroll - Lieutenant, Aide de Camp, Staff of General Ewell

3 Barbara Jeanne Fields, *Slavery and Freedom on the Middle Ground: Maryland during the Nineteenth Century* (New Haven: Yale University Press, 1985), 91.

4 Varga, *Baltimore's Loyola*, 67.

5 Daniel D. Hartzler, *Marylanders in the Confederacy* (Silver Spring: Family Line Publications, 1986) and L. Allison Wilmer, J. H. Jarrett, George W. F. Vernon, *History and Roster of Maryland Volunteers* (Baltimore: Guggenheimer, Weil & Company, 1898).

Alexander Clendinen - Surgeon, 5th Virginia Cavalry

William Cowardin – 3rd Virginia Infantry

Robert Crowley – 4th Maryland Light Artillery

Phillip Elder – 21st Virginia Infantry

John Gross – Lieutenant, 15th Louisiana Infantry

Edward Jenkins – Confederate Navy, Flag Officer's Secretary

Samuel Kennedy – 1st Maryland Infantry

Bernard McGlone – Zarvona's Maryland Zouaves

Randolph McKim – Lieutenant, Aide de Camp, General Steuart's staff

Richard McSherry – Signal Corps

Arthur Milholland – Unknown CSA unit

Charles Morfit – Confederate Navy, Assistant Surgeon, CSS Raleigh

Wilford Neale – 1st Maryland Cavalry

Henry Roby – 1st Virginia Cavalry

Charles Wilson – 1st Maryland Infantry

UNION

Henry Inloes – Assistant Surgeon, 3rd Potomac Home Brigade

Thomas Jenkins – 2nd Maryland Infantry

William Mayre – Lieutenant, Ordinance Corps

Francis Meehan – 13th Maryland Infantry

Edward Moale – Unknown Union unit

As can be seen from these two lists, a clear majority served in Confederate units. Neither is the record complete: since many entries lack middle names or initials, it was impossible to verify service records and definitively tie it to a named Loyola student. As it stands, the list includes 22 Confederates and five Unionists, a ratio similar to that of Georgetown's. Many of the names are familiar to students of Maryland history, such as the Carroll brothers. Grandsons of Carroll of Carrollton, these men were born into one of the oldest, wealthiest, and best-connected families in Maryland. Their social prominence no doubt contributed to their being placed on the staff of General Ewell. One would come home after the war ended, one would not. Another Loyolan who perished during the war was only located by chance, as he was mentioned in the Sodality records of 1863 as "William Fenwick Baugher, left college in 1858, died 1863, Confederate service."[6] His middle name perhaps indicates that his mother was a Fenwick, a name that recurs in Loyola's history. White Fenwicks appear on the student rolls into the twentieth century, and Black Fenwicks are recorded as working at Loyola. Another notable surname was that of Jenkins, a family that appears to have provided sons to both sides. More information on the Jenkins family can be found in Alexis Faison's essay in this volume. Finally, the inclusion of a McSherry on the Confederate rolls is unsurprising, as his relative Father Richard McSherry was intimately involved in the 1838 Jesuit slave sale.

In November 1863, five men residing at Loyola College were called up for the local militia draft. Daniel Fortescue, Patrick McGlone, John Mahoney, Thomas Casey, and Archibald Fishall were listed in the *Baltimore Sun* listed as required to report for local guard duty, as there had been Confederate cavalry raids in the area at the time.[7] Because Loyola College was not yet lodging students, these men must have been priests and/or scholastics. Since these men were not put into Federal service in the army, they were not included in the earlier list. Faculty member and future Loyola president Father John Abell Morgan was drafted in June 1864. His diary states:

Made several applications and at last received a note from the Secretary of War, wherein I am told that my appearance awaits further orders from the Provost Marshall General or from the War Department ... Went to the Provost Marshall's this morning and showed my note from Stanton. The Major and an assistant did not seem to like the note, but had to respect it anyhow.[8]

Secretary of War Edwin Stanton had provided the note after receiving a request from his friend, Father John Early, on behalf of Father Morgan.[9]

---

6 Loyola Notre Dame Library (LNDL) Archives, Sodality Records, 1852-1911, LUMD.010.019, Folder 1.
7 *Baltimore Sun*, November 28, 1863.
8 John Abell Morgan, quoted in George M. Anderson, "The Civil War Diary of John Abell Morgan, S.J.", *Records of the American Catholic Historical Society of Philadelphia* 101, no.3-4 (1990): 33-54.
9 Varga, *Baltimore's Loyola*, 70.

Apparently, Father Early had used his good offices to secure a release from the draft for his young protégé.

In a letter written in 1868 relating the history of Loyola over the previous five years, the unidentified author says of 1864:

July was marked by the ravages of Civil War. The enemy – that is the Confederates – made an extensive raid into Maryland, destroying property – capturing rail-road trains, and taking off prominent characters as prisoners. The whole city was placed under arms, defences were made on the outskirts, the Citizens were called into service, and some of our fathers and scholastics were called to the Militia, an inconvenience which gave much trouble and annoyance to us. However after our first appearance we were no longer molested.[10]

Some of the word choices are telling, especially that the author felt the need to clarify just who 'the enemy' was for his reader.

Some activities during the war were purely pastoral and should not be construed as particularly partisan. Regardless of their personal opinions on the war, their duties as priests required them to minister to all who sought their guidance and intercession. A section of Loyola College was used as a temporary hospital for Union soldiers after the Second Battle of Bull Run in 1862 and the priests were engaged in ministering to and comforting the wounded in their care.[11] Northern-born Loyola president Father Joseph O'Callaghan was transferred from Loyola to Frederick, Maryland in the fall of 1863, and served as a priest at the hospitals there. Frederick was rapidly filling up with wounded soldiers, Union and Confederate, and he heard confessions and performed last rites to all regardless of their political affiliation. His diary, unlike that of Father John Abell Morgan, contained no overt signs of sympathy to the South.[12]

---

10 Loyola Notre Dame Library (LNDL) Archives, Jesuit Community Records, LUMD.008.001, Box 5, Folder 1.

11 *Baltimore Sun*, May 24, 1873.

12 Archives of the Maryland Province of the Society of Jesus, Georgetown University, Diary of Father Joseph O'Callaghan, GTM-119, Box 8, Folder 10A, MPA 8.1.

Other pastoral roles staffed by the Jesuits of Loyola were in connection with the 'colored church' that was established for the Black Catholics of Baltimore. Father Talbot wrote in the *Historia Domi*,

On September 20, 1857, the Basement floor of the Church was opened for the use of the Colored Catholics on Sundays and some other occasions until in 1863 the old Universalist Church on Calvert Street was bought by the Fathers of St. Francis Xavier as the first Catholic Church in the United States specially for colored people. Our Fathers had charge of this for years until it was turned over to the Josephite Fathers.[13]

Fathers Miller, O'Connor, and O'Callaghan were particularly involved in the ministry at this parish, and Sister Reginald Gerdes writes of them and the parish, "Father Miller continued as pastor of the black congregation. His parish, St. Francis Xavier, was most active in social as well as religious ministries. They were the primary sponsors in supporting the orphans at St. Francis. This vibrant parish ministered to all the black Catholics in east and west Baltimore."[14] Thus, the Jesuits of Baltimore were divided on the question of enslavement and secession, but carried out religious functions for all as the Church dictated. In this matter of divided opinion, the Jesuits closely mirrored Maryland itself.

For decades after the war, college faculty included those who had been affiliated with one side or the other, generally as Confederates. Many of those who did not wear a uniform or were too young to serve in combat were apologists for the Confederacy. In the immediate aftermath of the war Baltimore was an incubator for the Lost Cause myth, a revisionist attempt to recast the South as the victim of so-called unconstitutional Northern aggression. Fleeing the states under direct Federal control, many Southern authors moved to Baltimore, which had escaped the direct impact of wartime destruction. Before long, Maryland played a large role in the reconfiguring of Southern memory.

---

13 Loyola Notre Dame Library (LNDL) Archives, Jesuit Community Records, LUMD.008.001 Box 5 Folder 8.

14 Sister Reginald Gerdes, "Remembering Baltimore's Black Catholic History," *The Catholic Review*, January 19, 2012, https://www.archbalt.org/remembering-baltimores-black-catholic-history.

One such newly-arrived Marylander was Colonel Richard Malcolm Johnston. Born in Georgia to a wealthy slaveholding family, he was an educator and man of letters and was well-known in his home state. Angered by the imposition of Reconstruction in Georgia and impoverished by the cotton crash of 1867, Johnston decided to move to Maryland. He was not alone in moving to Baltimore in those years; Maryland was not subject to the same system of Reconstruction as the rest of the South, and Baltimore was more prosperous than any other city below the Mason-Dixon line. Johnston's account of his move is revealing:

At this time one of my daughters, Lucy, a child of fourteen, seeming to her parents to be of uncommonly good promise, after an illness of six days from pleuro-pneumonia, died. Prostrated by this loss, and apprehending deterioration of the white race in being thus surrounded by negroes, I and my wife, who was now my chief counsellor, after much reflection, decided to go away from the place. I knew that whithersoever we went, unless it was in an unreasonable distance, I could take my school with me. In time we decided upon Baltimore, and in the month of June, 1867, we removed thereto.[15]

Johnston was active teaching in Baltimore and gave literary lectures to college students and the public. He converted to Catholicism and had a close friendship with Father Joseph Abell Morgan, with whom he shared a common background in plantation life. That nostalgia and his penchant for storytelling led him to write stories of the antebellum period that romanticized plantation life and were key in crafting the myth of benign and pleasant slave life and labor on the plantations. He says:

I said that I began writing after my removal to Baltimore, partly for the sake of subduing as far as possible the sense of homesickness. I might add, of alleviating the burden of misapprehension which soon befell me, that perhaps after all I had made a mistake in coming so far away from the other people

---

15 Richard Malcolm Johnston, *The Autobiography of Col. Richard Malcolm Johnston* (Washington: The Neale Company, 1900), 67-68.

who knew me, and setting out to maintain my large family among strangers,
by practice of my profession, my entire competency for which was not known
outside of my native State.[16]

Johnston was not the only Lost Cause celebrity to have connections to Loyola. Father Abram Joseph Ryan, a sometime freelance chaplain to the Confederate army, so despised Abraham Lincoln that he shortened his own name to Abram. Following the war, he would become known as the "Poet of the South," and gain sufficient renown to be described in Margaret Mitchell's *Gone With the Wind* as "the poet-priest of the Confederacy... [who] charmed gatherings...with his wit and seldom needed much urging to recite his 'Sword of Lee' or his deathless 'Conquered Banner,' which never failed to make the ladies cry."[17] In 1880 Ryan was making final preparations for the publication of a collection of his poems. While conducting business with his Baltimore publisher he lodged with the Jesuits at Loyola, and following a public reading of his work that raised $300, he promptly gifted the sum to the college as compensation for their hospitality. These funds served to endow the Ryan Poetry Medal.

Already by the 1880s, Southern memory and sympathy were merging into a renewed profession of loyalty to the Union, albeit in the guise of military honor. The South was recast as the heirs to Lexington and Concord, fighting honorably against a distant central government. The focus upon battlefield bravery, by design, minimized any meaningful discussion as to why the conflict had occurred. In 1882, Georgetown professor Father Hugh Magevney gave a lecture in Baltimore at a fundraiser for the Confederate Army and Navy Society. The *Baltimore Sun* reported that "the lecturer asked for a true history of the deeds of men who fought in the Southern cause as their enduring monument ... as evidence that their fathers fell on the field of honor. United under the Star Spangled Banner they can be proud of that record. He said Southern men will stand by the flag of the Union against all foes which may hereafter assail it." Father Magevney was a Confederate

---

16 Johnston, 85-86.
17 Margaret Mitchell, *Gone with the Wind* (New York: Macmillan Publishing, 1936), 737.

veteran, and many prominent Marylanders attended this lecture, including Loyola president Father McGurk and Loyola professor Father Ryan.[18]

That same year, Anna Kane, widow of George P. Kane left $500 to Loyola College. While her political sympathies are unrecorded, her late husband was a noted pro-Confederate activist who had refused to allow New York troops passage through Baltimore, advocated for Marylanders to fight for the Confederacy, and was personally acquainted with John Wilkes Booth. While Loyola was not directly involved in Kane's activities, it is another example of the college's financial connection to those who supported the Confederacy.[19]

Loyola itself was the site of many lectures and discussions. As one example, Father Cowardin, a Loyola professor and Confederate veteran, gave a lecture in 1893 titled "Negro Lore in the South." According to the *Baltimore Sun*, "He spoke of the value of studying the folk lore of the colored people and recited several selections in the negro dialect."[20]

By the close of the nineteenth century, some 35 years after the end of the Civil War, it was clear that Loyola College remained a bastion of pro-Confederate sympathy. In this, it was not out of step with the surrounding community. It would be easy to dismiss this as the last gasps of romantic nostalgia from those who had lived through the conflict, but this is wishful thinking. Loyola continued to have student publications lauding the "noble" South and lecturers discussing the "Negro Problem", as well as other racial issues. While not delivered at Loyola College, an example of the content of these lectures can be gleaned from the words of an 1894 lecture at the Bloomingdale Church in New York City.

Why, the South is the only truly American part of our nation today. The South may yet have to be called on to save the North from her reckless immigration, which is now weakening and undermining the foundations of our social order. Rebel? That word must henceforth not be spoken. I believe that the South today grasps the hand of the North in a fellowship which

18 *Baltimore Sun*, November 22, 1882.
19 *Baltimore Sun*, June 6, 1882.
20 *Baltimore Sun*, December 23, 1893.

has in it no misgiving or deceit. The public men of the South are not, as with us 'professional foreigners' who have made public office a public steal. The Southern men in public office are patriotic and devout, conscientiously American and personally the embodiment of integrity. But you say that they do not believe in 'negro domination.' Neither do we... Enfranchising all the negroes immediately after their emancipation was practically one of the greatest mistakes ever made by any free government. In many counties and States the colored people are in the majority, and a majority rule would take that government entirely from the property-owners and place it in the hands of those who, with few exceptions, have no qualifications to entitle them to a voice in the affairs of the government. Negro domination would mean white damnation ... A suffrage limited to an educational qualification is the only solution to the negro problem. But illiteracy is not confined to the South. Our Northern cities are thronged with foreigners as imbecile in their ignorance and degraded in their morals as were the rabble hordes that wrecked the republics of antiquity. Universal suffrage is a menace to free institutions.[21]

The transition of Confederate southerner from rebel to super-patriot was largely complete by the 1890s and remains with us to this very day. Lost Cause thinking and Confederate apologist ideology has continued to swirl around Loyola more than a century later. One recently departed professor of economics published several books with titles needing no explanation including *The Real Lincoln: A New Look at Abraham Lincoln, His Agenda, and an Unnecessary War* and *Lincoln Unmasked: What You're Not Supposed to Know about Dishonest Abe.* He is also on record as describing the Civil War as "The War to Prevent Southern Independence."[22] Another current example is alumnus Michael Peroutka, a former board member of the League of the South and a public figure who ran for Attorney General of Maryland in 2022. Though he graduated Loyola in the early 1970s he espouses some ideas that would not have been out of place in 1870s.

21 *Baltimore Sun*, December 4, 1894.
22 Thomas DiLorenzo, "The Problem With Lincoln," *Abbeville Institute Press* (blog), June 29, 2020, https://abbevilleinstitute.org/the-problem-with-lincoln/.

These examples do not serve to condemn Loyola University Maryland writ large, but are a strong indication that there is more, much more, to be done to examine and confront the long shadow of the Lost Cause. The record is a mixed one, which should surprise nobody familiar with the trends in politics and society, but we can do better. Perhaps it is time to recall Loyola's motto "Strong Truths, Well Lived" as a signpost for further study and reflection.

Spotlighting Loyola College's Foundation of Black Labor

Anna Young

Loyola College's history of Black labor dates to 1855, when the school first recorded the purchase of "servants" under its founding president Father John Early. Five years later, on the 1860 U.S. Census Slave Schedule, one woman was recorded under the Order of the Jesuits in Baltimore. Starting in 1879, Baltimore city directories listed numerous African Americans as waiters and porters at Loyola College. These people, whether they were enslaved or hired servants, belong to a history of exploited Black labor at Loyola even from the college's earliest years. The roles these individuals had during their time at the college helped the school function on a day-to-day basis and allowed it to expand into what it is today. Yet the Jesuit institution has not always accepted them. From a land deed describing a college built for the education of "white people," paying Black workers less than white workers, and the persistent white supremacist undertones in faculty writings, the social climate of Loyola reinforced the perception that Black people were not accepted as anything but labor. Throughout Loyola College's history, the institution has enabled the oppression of Black people as is evident in its financial ledgers, the 1860 U.S. Census Slave Schedule, writings from former president, John Abell Morgan, and the college's land deed.

Observing Loyola's initial ties to slavery provides context for how the college was embedded in an existing slave-holding society when it opened its doors in 1852. The first link between enslaved laborers and Loyola can be found in Georgetown University's Maryland Province Archives. There, the Jesuit's General and Special Accounts Cash and Day Book from 1839-1881 reveals transactions made by Loyola College's first president, Father John Early.[1] In July 1855, $100 was paid to Father Early "for Mrs. H. S. Manning for serv. [servant] hire," the first of five annual payments made. In March 1856 there was a direct payment "To Mrs. H.S. Manning in full for servant wages" for $15.79. Another payment was made in May 1857 "to Mrs. Manning a/c servants hire" for $75, followed by a final payment in December 1860. The December payment was listed as "By cash to Mrs. H.S. Manning in full for hire of servants for 1860" totaling $32. With once-a-year payments made in varying amounts, many questions are left for researchers. Although who was sent to Loyola remains unknown, along with the type of work they completed, the payments show that in the first decade of the college, forced and enslaved labor was a regular practice.

The terminology utilized for the payments, as well as the history of the Manning family, suggest that from 1855 to 1860 Loyola had close ties to slaveholding. The term "servants" used in the payment descriptions mirrors language used for enslaved people from the early nineteenth century. Documents in Georgetown's Slavery Archive from as early as 1803 commonly refer to enslaved people in financial ledgers and Cash and Day Books as "servants" rather than "slaves."[2] Therefore, it is very possible that these people were not servants and instead were enslaved. Furthermore, laborers or servants were typically paid for their work directly.[3]

However, the ledger instead shows Mrs. H.S. Manning being paid for the "servants." Because Mrs. Manning received the money directly, instead of the "servants" themselves, it seems very probable that these "servants" were enslaved.[4]

1 Archives of the Maryland Province of the Society of Jesus, "General and Special Accounts- Cash and Day Book, from 1839-1881."
2 Archives of the Maryland Province of the Society of Jesus, "Several students purchased 'servants attendance,' 1803-1804."
3 Mary Beth Corrigan, Conversation, July 26, 2022.
4 There is an additional possible interpretation of these unclear transactions, as the "servants" may have also been enslaved people working to buy their freedom.

The Manning family was from Baltimore's 15th district, close to Loyola College.[5] Elizabeth Manning, listed on the Jesuit records as Mrs. H.S. Manning, was married to Henry S. Manning, a butter dealer in Baltimore.[6] Together the couple had nine children and in 1850, were recorded as owning one female slave who was ten years old.[7] Without a name listed for this young girl, it is difficult to determine how long she had been with the Mannings or if she ever was manumitted. Similarly, it is also difficult to trace the identity of the enslaved female who was listed as eighteen years old and owned by Elizabeth Manning in 1860. Despite the listed ages suggesting the presence of two different females enslaved to the Mannings at different times, it seems more likely that a recording error occurred and that the same enslaved female was in the household in both 1850 and 1860. The 1860 Census of Free Inhabitants also revealed a free Black eighteen-year-old male named Isaiah Garrett living with the family at their residence. Overall, the censuses and Slave Schedule clearly indicate that the Manning family was part of Baltimore's slaveholding society.

There is thus strong evidence of Loyola College's involvement with enslaved labor from its earliest years, supported by both the Jesuit Cash and Day Book and the Manning family's slave owning history. These findings suggest the college was rooted in slavery and leaves the current Loyola community with the responsibility of acknowledging the university's past.

1860 Census Slave Schedule

Federal government records provide a clear indication of Loyola's connection to slavery. The 1860 U.S. Census and Slave Schedule shows that not only were Jesuits in Baltimore engaged in slave ownership, they were also doing so at a time when the institution of slavery was fading within the city. The 1860 U.S. Census Slave Schedule contains a listing for the "Order of Jesuits" under "Names of Slave Owners." This entry records the Jesuits as the slave holder of one Black female, who was sixty years old. This finding provides more context as to how Loyola College benefited from enslaved labor. While no Jesuits are specifically named, the 1860 entry directly

5 Loyola College changed its name to Loyola University Maryland in August 2009.
6 1860 U.S. Census Free Inhabitants.
7 1860 U.S. Census for Slave Schedule.

involves Loyola College because in 1860 no other Jesuits lived in Baltimore's Ward 11. Therefore, any Jesuits mentioned in the census and Slave Schedule during that year would have been associated with Loyola College.

The 1860 Census primarily focused on capturing how many slaveowners existed in comparison to past censuses and as such is a somewhat unclear source. At first glance this entry would suggest the Order of the Jesuits in Baltimore City's 11th Ward were definitive slaveowners. In the *1860 Census Instructions to the Marshals*, the first section titled "Owners of Slaves" states, "when slaves are the property of a corporation, enter the name of the corporation."[8] According to the instructions, this is how the Order of the Jesuits would be listed. One challenge to naming the Jesuits in Baltimore explicitly as slaveowners, however, arises in section two titled, "**Number of Slaves.**" These instructions also state "the person in whose charge, or on whose plantation the slave is found to be employed may return all slaves in his charge, (although they may be owned by other persons)." Here, it is evident that just because a person or corporation is listed as a "Slave Owner" it does not necessarily mean they formally owned the enslaved people counted because some enslaved "may be owned by other persons." Nevertheless, those who were not actually slaveowners are the minority of cases and experts estimate only a small percentage—about five to ten percent—of the names listed as owners were not. In theory, people who were not slaveowners would have been indicated as an "employer" or with some other designation ("for Mr. Brown", "trustee", etc.) by marshals. Slave holders without such designations were presumably the owners.[8] Although there are no doubt errors in the enumeration, most people and groups listed as slaveowners were. While our research team has not found tax documents or other documents that explicitly demonstrate Jesuits slave owning, evidence including Father John Early's rented "servants" and the 1860 Census suggests that Loyola College and the Order of the Jesuits were, at least, slave holders.

With much heartbreak and frustration that the university has never admitted to this history, our research group became eager to find more information on who this woman was. Unlike the 1860 U.S. Census for Free Inhabitants, where peoples' name, age, sex, race, occupation, and birthplace

---

8 David Hacker, Email correspondence, December 13, 2022.

are recorded, the only identifying information available for enslaved people were their age, sex and "color." With such limited details, finding more information on this woman's story became difficult. Documents such as the census are a reminder of the dehumanization of enslaved people, with their very existence and history visible only through the lives of their enslavers.

Some Jesuit priests in Maryland recorded the names of their slaves in diaries or letters. Direct references to their enslaved was part of the "paternal relationship" priests used as an excuse for having slaves.[9] However, the "benevolent style" used to justify Jesuit slaveholding has proven to be hypocritical. Resistance from people who were enslaved by Jesuits shows that they were mistreated and exploited. Additionally, Georgetown's priests claimed keeping families together was one of their highest priorities, yet to keep families together they were sometimes transported to harsher working conditions. Some of these harsher conditions were located in Louisiana. Although these working and living conditions were worse for children and families in comparison to life at Georgetown, Jesuits believed Louisiana was home to "Catholic masters who were capable of taking on large slave families." Maintaining families was also something of a front: researchers have found evidence where "some children were sold without their parents," and some slaves were "dragged off by force to the ship" during a slave sale involving Georgetown's Jesuits in 1838.[10]

While names were kept and recorded by some Jesuits, it was not necessarily because of close emotional connections.[11] In searching for the name of the enslaved women held by the Jesuits, we discovered that Loyola's priests never referenced an enslaved woman. For example, Father John Early's diaries and sermons, some of the only existing records from Loyola College in 1860, make no mention of a slave working on the premise. Yet the omission of this woman's name does not mean there was no enslaved labor at Loyola. Although there were still people who had enslaved labor at this time, what is significant is how Loyola College utilized enslaved labor so late in the nineteenth century. Using enslaved labor during this time would have gone against the growing number of African Americans and Black people

9 Thomas Murphy. *Jesuit Slaveholding In Maryland 1717-1838* (New York: Routledge, 2018).
10 Rothman and Barraza Mendoza, *Facing Georgetown's History*, (Washington DC: Georgetown University Press, 2021), 253.

who were gaining social and economic mobility in Baltimore. Loyola in the 1860s may have been one of the last institutions in the city to use forced and enslaved labor.

In 1830, over twenty years before Loyola College opened, Baltimore's black population was already "largely composed of those who acquired freedom and were born free."[11] The decade before Loyola opened, 339 out of 710 free African Americans in Baltimore City were born free according to the certificates of freedom between 1852 and 1860. By 1850 almost 90 percent of African Americans were free and just over four decades earlier, more than seventy-five percent had been manumitted. The increasing number of African Americans who were living in freedom meant newer generations were born into their freedom as well, removing them further from slavery. In Maryland between 1800 and 1860, there was a decrease in the number of slaves people owned. By 1860, ninety percent of Maryland slaveholders owned eight or fewer slaves and it was much more common for people to only have one slave. Census data suggests that there were at least 22,600 free Black residents in Maryland and about 4,400 enslaved Black people in Maryland, at least one of whom was connected to Loyola through the Order of the Jesuits.

As we researched the neighborhoods surrounding Loyola College, we found that within the 11th Ward of Baltimore, there were about 2,400 free people of color and an estimated 350 enslaved people. Breaking down the demographic of slaves even further, 252 of the enslaved people in this ward were females, and Loyola held one of these women. Narrowing the number of enslaved women in Loyola's ward may help researchers that look further into who she was.

The growing population of free Black people in Baltimore and Maryland shows Loyola had difficulty evolving to modern society. Loyola's connection to this enslaved woman demonstrates how the college continued to be tethered to slaveholding. With this knowledge, Loyola's community must reflect on and question the college's impact on the local community. For the

---

11 Christopher Phillips, *Freedom's Port: The African American Community of Baltimore, 1790-1860* (Urbana: University of Illinois Press, 1997), 146-147.

enslaved woman and the surrounding Black community, Loyola was stuck in the past.

Wages Earned

Evidence of Loyola's regressive practices surrounding Black labor emerges from expense books from this period. These records show that in 1855 there were frequent payments made out to "Susan" who was first noted as a "washer woman" on January 26.[12] The payment showed Susan earned $8.00 for the month. What made this record even more fascinating was that underneath Susan's name an entry for a payment to a hired servant for $1.50 was listed. Once again, the term "servant," especially in 1854, makes it unclear if the person was hired or enslaved. It is also unclear if Susan herself was also a servant and therefore grouped with the "hired servants." Other payments made to Susan indicate she was paid $5.00 in May and another $5.00 in July. While we do not know for certain Susan's race, we can conclude she may have been a woman of color because she was only listed by her first name, was named in reference to her occupation, and made low wages compared to others. For example, payments made to men listed as laborers at Loyola College in the city directory from 1855, averaged about 16.25 monthly.[13] The names and directory show these laborers were white men, suggesting the pay inequality may be because of Susan's gender, race, and status. The financial ledger is useful because it also lists daily expenses. Susan's monthly payments of $5-8 were less than the amount Jesuits paid for newspapers and wine. During the Reconstruction era Baltimore city directories began listing Black and African American residents as people of color. These directories shine a light on the formal labor of Black workers at Loyola College. The city directory of Baltimore lists Madison Fenwick and George Short as "colored" waiters and porters for Loyola College from 1888-1898. In 1891 a white worker, William Lapsley, whose occupation was not listed, was paid in increments of $3.50, whereas George Short was paid $2.00 throughout the month. Although we do not know why there was a discrepancy between the two wages, it cannot be explained by seniority,

---

12 Loyola Notre Dame Library (LNDL) Archives, Loyola College Financial Ledger, 1855.
13 Matchett's Baltimore Directory, 1855-1856.

since Short had worked at Loyola College longer than Lapsley. While it is possible that Lapsley may have had a job that required more skill, it is equally, if not more likely, that Short's race was the explanation.

Comparing Short's and Fenwick's wages to other workers, not only were they paid less, they were also paid infrequently. While other workers were regularly paid at the beginning and end of the month, sometimes Fenwick and Madison were paid two months' wages in one month making their wages highly variable. For example, in June 1891 Short was paid $11.75 for May's work and then paid $2.00 for June at both the beginning and end of the month. Similarly in October 1891 Fenwick was paid $17.75 for September's wages.[14] Most months Fenwick received $18.00 for a whole month's work however in October he was paid $4.50, $7.00 in November and only $4.50 in December. The varying amounts in his payments are unusual compared to other white laborers at Loyola who received about $16.00 in the beginning of each month. Knowing other workers were paid the same amounts monthly raises many questions as to why Black waiters and porters at Loyola College were treated differently. Researchers also found it helpful to compare Fenwick's and Short's wages to other expenditures, as comparisons with other laborers proved difficult. For context, priests spent about $60.00 a month or more for beer. Directly observing how much more was spent on day-to-day items compared to the salaries people of color, demonstrates how Loyola disadvantaged families like the Fenwicks and Shorts.

Reflecting on Loyola's history of Black and African American workers in positions like waiters and porters during the mid to late 19th century also encourages researchers to understand what labor looked like broadly in Maryland and Baltimore. In looking for the specific breakdown of waiters and porters in Maryland, no information was listed. However, this was not because Loyola was the exception in having these positions. Instead, people who were waiters and porters were considered servants.[15] Overall, this means Loyola College relied on servants for most of its opening years. While it was most likely common for servants and laborers who were people of color to

14 Loyola Notre Dame Library (LNDL) Archives, Loyola College Records of Daily Expenses and Income, 1891-1894.
15 1860 U.S. Census Maryland Occupations.

make less than white coworkers, it is still crucial to Loyola to recognize the part it played in this larger picture. Disadvantaging its own workers shows Loyola was not immune to the racism and discrimination that was, and still is, prevalent in society today.

John Abell Morgan's Diary

Beyond the oppressive and degrading treatment of Black laborers on campus, Loyola's faculty culture was also harmful. To understand campus culture during this period, our research group turned to John Abell Morgan's diary for better insight on professor and student beliefs during the late 19th century.

John Abell Morgan was born in St. Mary's County, Maryland in 1838.[16] His family, like other southern Maryland families, owned slaves. The family's wealth made it possible for Morgan to attend Georgetown University where he later became a priest. In August 1862, Father Morgan moved to Loyola College where he taught arithmetic and French. Despite leaving Loyola, he returned in 1891 as the college's ninth president until he stepped down in 1900. Given that Father Morgan was a Maryland native, a graduate of a Jesuit university and had experience as a professor at Loyola College, he is representative of some of the Jesuit beliefs in Maryland during the time.

In Loyola's archives, there is a collection of Father Morgan's diary entries from 1862-1867. These entries provide a first-hand account of life and culture at Loyola College in its opening years. Throughout his diaries he writes in support of the Confederacy and gives detailed accounts of events in the Civil War. He also outlines some of the relationships the Maryland Jesuits had with Confederate soldiers and generals.

One of Father Morgan's September entries in 1862, within the first two months of his arrival at Loyola College, discusses the Jesuits' relationship to the Confederacy. In his diary on September 11, 1862, he writes, "Fr. Provincial had a kind of interview with General [Robert E.] Lee, who received him with respect. Many of the Confederates came to our house [in

16 George M. Anderson, "The Civil War Diary of John Abell Morgan, S.J.: A Jesuit Scholastic of the Maryland Province." *Records of the American Catholic Historical Society of Philadelphia*, vol. 101, no. 3/4, (1990), 33.

Frederick] and conversed with our fathers. Many confessions were heard. Fr. Maguire saw many."[17] This entry shows how the Maryland Jesuits were sympathetic towards the Confederacy and supportive of the Southern cause at large. Hosting Confederate soldiers and hearing their confessions shows the willingness some Jesuits had to assist and care for them.

On September 22, 1862, the day after President Abraham Lincoln issued the preliminary Emancipation Proclamation, Father Morgan expressed his frustration with the U.S. government. The Emancipation Proclamation declared that as of January 1, 1863, all enslaved people in the states currently engaged in rebellion against the Union "shall be then, thenceforward, and forever free."[18] The document applied only to enslaved people in the Confederacy, and not to those in the border states that remained loyal to the Union. Father Morgan fumed in his entry:

The president has emancipated all the slaves in the rebellious states he has been, gone, and done it [sic]. Judicial blindness seems to be an attribute of the present Administration. They said this war was not for emancipation; many protested against such a movement. The papers and the Conservatives of the North would clamor, were such a rash thing attempted. The fact is accomplished, people will do nothing, giving another example of the inconsistency of American character.

The entry expresses Father Morgan's frustration with the actions taken by the government. Father Morgan also believes America is changing in a new direction, one that upsets him. What is interesting about this entry is that this is the first and only time Father Morgan discusses emancipation. Nowhere else does he mention slavery or state his stance on the issue.

Morgan's stance in support of the secessionists and for the Confederacy mirrors the broader attitudes of people who attended and taught at Loyola College, as seen in Brandon J. Lyda's chapter within this book. John Abell Morgan's diary entries were made while Black workers, possibly enslaved,

17 Loyola Notre Dame Library Archives, Loyola University Maryland Office of the President records (LUMD.003.001), John Abell Morgan Diary, 1862-1867.
18 Abraham Lincoln, Emancipation Proclamation (1863)

indentured, or freed were also working at Loyola College. Since Father Morgan was in a position of power as a professor and eventually president of the college, beliefs such as these made it difficult for Black people at Loyola to be seen as equal. Because Father Morgan describes how other Jesuits shared his sentiments, it becomes obvious how challenging it would have been for people of color to fit in at institutions such as Loyola College.

Land Deed

A final indicator of Loyola's persistently harmful attitude toward Black labor can be found some sixty years after Father Morgan's diary and twenty-two years after he stepped down as president. In November 1921, Loyola purchased a tract of land from the Garrett family. In the early 20th century, much of Baltimore's suburbs were controlled by the Roland Park Company (RPC). The RPC is one of the companies that spearheaded suburban segregation in Baltimore. The group used "stringent and exclusionary practices for their subdivisions, which they saw as potentially becoming model suburbs" for the rest of the U.S. Moreover, the RPC had covenants that used racist language to restrict African Americans from purchasing properties.[19] Although Loyola College's land purchase had no ties to the RPC itself, the Garrett family did. The family adopted one of the covenants used by the RPC and attached it to the land Loyola College bought. The deed stated, "That at no time shall the land included in said tract or any part thereof or any building erected thereon be occupied by any negro or person of negro extraction." This prohibition also stated "occupancy by a negro domestic servant or other person while employed on or about the premises by the owner or occupant of any land included in said tract" was permissible.[20] The stipulations of the covenant were especially harmful considering the number of Black people living in Baltimore during the 1920s.

The RPC's restrictions set the standard for Loyola College and immediately limited who was allowed to make up Loyola's community. As the RPC

19 Paige Glotzer, *How the Suburbs Were Segregated* (New York: Columbia University Press, 2020), 6,8,87.
20 John W Garrett & Co to Associated Professors of Loyola College, Deed and Agreement, 1 November 1921; Land Records of Baltimore City, Liber 3796 Folio 513, Maryland State Archives, MDLANDREC (https://mdlandrec.net/).

developed some of the earliest formal restrictions against African Americans in the suburbs it clearly also marked who was able to receive education and inhabit Loyola College. Restricting Black people from occupying any of the buildings or land except if they were domestic servants or employees of white individuals reinforces the notion that Black people at Loyola College were only accepted as labor. Purchasing land with this type of language demonstrated again how Loyola remained complicit in the oppression of Black people. Accepting this land deed shows the college was willing to expand their campus to an area that restricted Black people despite being in a city with one of the largest Black populations. Loyola's actions proved it envisioned a future that did not include the local Black community. Twenty-eight years later, when the first Black student enrolled at Loyola, this same covenant was still in place.[21]

Conclusion

This essay has attempted to highlight the stories and lives of the earliest Black workers at Loyola College. However, the limited information available in censuses and financial records makes it difficult to trace a fuller version of Loyola's history. The impact of archival silence is seen here. Capturing the lives, emotions, and legacies of Black workers at Loyola is almost impossible to do. Jesuit priests like Father John Abell Morgan are preserved as historical figures while workers like Susan "the washer woman" are left as payments on a financial ledger.

The information gathered throughout this research project demonstrates Loyola College was one of the many institutions that benefited from enslaved and Black labor. The census data, ledgers, diary entries, and the college's land deed are evidence showing Loyola's role as an oppressor. As Baltimore became home to free Black people and many Black communities, Loyola was unable to shift away from slavery as quickly as the surrounding area. The college's actions and inaction prove it was part of the nation's slaveholding society.

For the time being, Loyola can only frame its possible enslaved workers, servants, porters and waiters in the context of their labor. With further

21 Nicholas Varga, *Baltimore's Loyola, Loyola's Baltimore* (Baltimore: Maryland Historical Society, 1990), 358.

research I am optimistic that one day Loyola can properly honor and recognize these people as part of its community rather than just its labor force. Future research should work to expand Loyola's narrative, recognizing how each worker has contributed to Loyola University Maryland today.

Loyola Yesterday: A Look at the Unrevealed Culture of Early Loyola University Maryland

Deidra Jackson

Among the numerous institutions that now seek to acknowledge and reconcile their roles in the forming of modern wounds from historical injuries is Loyola University Maryland. The primary culture of Loyola during the late nineteenth and twentieth centuries is guilty of subscribing to practices and ideologies that perpetuated racism and misogyny. These ideologies can be seen mostly through the attitudes, speech and activities of both students, who attended the college, and its presidents, who led the college during these formative years. Loyolans would often become active participants on the side of the Confederate South and made derogatory comments about other races. They would also make statements about the innate and biological weakness of women while subjecting them to hypersexualisation. This essay links these behaviors to the ideologies of the country at varying points in time.

"All histories are amalgamations of past events… historical truth refers to embracing the messy and often uncomfortable contradictions, gray areas and injustices of the past."[1]

-Malaine Rush

As America now grapples with the consequences of its historical immorality concerning slavery, sexism, and segregation, many institutions have been forced to confront the shame of their complicity and reinforcement of racial and gender-based prejudices. American universities are at the epicenter of this reckoning. Recent investigations have proven that universities were central to the practice and perpetuation of society's use of enslaved labor, as well as ideologies that reinforced racial and gender-based discrimination. As historian Craig Steven Wilder observes, "the academy stood beside church and state as the third pillar of a civilization built on bondage," acting as stewards to and perpetrators of ideals of a society submerged in the depravities of economic lust.[2] Universities did not and would not separate themselves from the transgressions of the outside world; rather, they locked themselves so firmly in society's tight embrace of sin and satisfaction that both cultures became indistinguishable from one another. Loyola University Maryland was no exception to this tradition. From the moment of the university's inauguration in 1852, campus culture could not help but reflect its surroundings and revel in the conventions of its time. Loyola's early culture was characterized by favorable attitudes towards human bondage, racial bigotry, and gender-based biases. Life at Loyola, in many ways, mirrored the antagonistic and apartheid society around it. Like many members of the U.S. society from the 1850s through the Civil War and beyond, Loyola's presidents and students alike were active supporters of the Confederate South and even served in the ranks of the Confederate Army in later years. Students would also host and participate in plays that featured the use of blackface, and routinely dismissed the value of female social participation through

---

1 Melaine Rush. 2020. "Universities and Slavery: An 'Inevitably Inadequate' Movement," History Department of Brandeis University, 4.

2 Craig Steven Wilder, *Ebony and Ivy: Race, Slavery and the Troubled History of America's Universities.* (New York: Bloomsbury Publishing, 2013), 11.

sexist and misogynistic comments during the nineteenth and twentieth centuries.

If one wants to know and understand the nature and values of an institution, one may look no farther than the characters of its leaders. While the presidents of Loyola were pioneers in the school's advancement and success, they were proponents of society's bigotry. Presidents such as Father John Early and Father John Abell Morgan have been discovered to have had strong ties to enslavement and groups that supported the oppression of the Black body. They proved themselves to be typical examples of men of their time, who could not separate themselves from the temptations of traditions, despite the grandeur of their piousness. Instead, their religiosity seemed to be rooted in the slave and post-slave economies and blossomed in the systems' growth.

Father John Early was the first president of Loyola College. He held office twice, first 1852 to 1858 at the college's inception, and again from 1866 until 1870. Whilst fulfilling his presidential obligations to Loyola, archival evidence from the Loyola College Cash Day Book has revealed that Father John Early was involved in the purchasing of numerous "servants" from 1855 going into the 1860s from a Mrs. H.S. Manning. Mrs. H.S. Manning was the wife of Mr. Henry Manning, a butter dealer in Baltimore who died in 1866.[3] As discussed in Anna Young's essay elsewhere in this volume, these "servants" were hired from the Manning family, which was recorded as owning one female slave in the 1850 and 1860 Slave Schedules. One might be quick to argue that the use of the word "servant" seems to be indicative of a position besides enslavement. However, before making such a presumption, it should be recognized that the use of the word "servant" was quite popular during slavery as a sort of euphemism for the enslaved situation.

Additionally, it must also be highlighted that the motivation for Father Early's purchase is not certain. Buying slaves from slave owners for the purpose of manumitting them from their condition was not an uncommon practice, especially in the nineteenth century North. One may assume that this could have been a part of Father Early's religious mandate as a respecter

3 1860 Slave Schedule, 16th Ward, Baltimore County, Maryland, digital image s.v. "Issac Garret," Ancestry.com

of all of God's creation. However, it has also been discovered from a correspondence of Father John Early in March of 1850 that he may have subscribed to the racial stratifications of his society. In this correspondence, Father Early seems perturbed about the potential loss of land. In his anxious writings he mentions being concerned about someone being robbed of "negros and cattle."[4] His language seems to indicate that he too approved of the belief that the enslaved were indeed property, diminishing the likelihood that Father Early's intentions were to manumit the enslaved.

Father John Abell Morgan is another president deserving of scrutiny for his ideologies concerning enslavement and the Civil War. Father Morgan was the ninth president of Loyola University Maryland. His tenure as the college's president was from 1891 to 1900, and he previously taught French and arithmetic at Loyola in 1862. The diary is strongly suggestive of his prejudicial leanings, as he comments frequently on the Civil War and, in July of 1862, remarked that "the news of the South is quite encouraging. Everything seems to be in their favor at present. Congress is foolish, the government is not much better, and the generals (some) in the fields are raving maniacs. Such is the status, no one should be surprised if the South is victorious."[5] This diary seems to be a collection of other thoughts such as the aforementioned and reveals his prejudicial nature.

In his analysis of Morgan's diary, George Anderson observes that Morgan was "born in Southern Maryland" and thus, was a "southerner himself" who "held traditional views of a Southerner of his time with regard to slavery. He himself was the son of a slave owner."[6] This, in part, explains his racial ideologies and support for the Confederate South. While Anderson does reveal that Morgan changed his belief surrounding the Black community at the end of the Civil War, his support of the Confederate Army and his previous attitudes towards the Black community are still worth mentioning,

4 John Early to Reverend Father, March 4, 1850, Archives of the Maryland Province of the Society of Jesus, Subseries 1.1 Correspondence, Chronological 1805-1883, Digital Georgetown: Georgetown University Manuscripts, Booth Family Center for Special Collections, (GTM.119); Box 12; Folder 20, https://repository.library.georgetown.edu/bitstream/handle/10822/1061990/GTM-000119_B12_F20.pdf?sequence=1&isAllowed=y

5 John Morgan, *Diary of John Abell Morgan*, 1862-1867, Loyola University Maryland Archives, (LUMD.001.002), Folder 4.

6 George Anderson, "The Civil War Diary of John Abell Morgan, SJ.: A Jesuit Scholastic of the Maryland Province," Records of the American Catholic Historical Society of Philadelphia 101, No. ¾ (Fall, 1990): 33.

despite his ideological metamorphosis. The attitudes and behaviors of some of Loyola's presidents raise questions about their effects on student life and culture. Given that he was a faculty member of Loyola during the time of the Civil War, one can rightly imagine that students' attitudes were shaped by these ideas of slavery, black oppression and inequality.

Like university leadership, Loyola students conformed to and adopted the segregationist and racially hostile culture of the wider society. There are three significant pieces of evidence for the persistence of discriminatory culture at Loyola: student and alumni participation in the Civil War on the Confederate side; the use of blackface as a form of theatrical entertainment on campus; and the prevalence of misogynist attitudes in the writings of campus leadership. Loyola fell within America's traditions; America's traditions dwelled within Loyola.

There is abundant evidence detailing the Civil War period, allowing us to identify the names of numerous Loyola students and alumni who were overt supporters of the Southern cause and added to the ranks of the Confederate Army. Nicholas Varga's work of the preservation of the school's history in his book, *Baltimore's Loyola, Loyola's Baltimore*, recounts how the Civil War ignited the fervor of Loyola's youth in favor of the Confederate South. Varga states that,

> *In fact several of these [Maryland transfers] had been students from Loyola before transferring to Georgetown [University]. Only one alumnus of both colleges, William Marye, served in the Union forces, but joint alumni Albert Daniel and Robert Carroll, William Bolton Fizgerald, Richard McSherry, Charles Morfit, Eustace and Wilfred Neale, John Daniel Smith and Samuel Raborg joined the Confederate Union. These were not the only Loyolans in uniform, but the tendency to favor the Confederate cause is apparent from even this brief accounting.[7]*

---

7 Nicholas Varga, *Baltimore's Loyola, Loyola's Baltimore* (Baltimore: Maryland Historical Society, 1990), 66-67.

There is not a simple explanation for Loyolans' affinity for the Southern cause. However, Varga does mention that Catholics, of which many went to Loyola, did identify with the cause of the Confederacy. He suggests that,

"They [the Catholics] may have felt some residual attraction for the agrarian, hierarchical, relatively static Southern society, which was believed to represent the natural order. Also it was easy to romanticize a distant milieu when conditions near at hand were strange, harsh and threatening. Industrialization in the Northern states was being achieved through the sweat and humiliation of the Irish. Furthermore, after the demise of their organization, the Know-Nothings had joined the Republican Party and worked eagerly for the election of Abraham Lincoln. The Baltimore Irish, in particular, could not forget the blows they had suffered from these ultra patriots. In reaction to such immediate dangers and irritants, the Confederacy appeared at least as the lesser evil, if not an actual ally."[8]

This "residual attraction" of the Catholics to Southern ideologies is a plausible explanation for Loyolans' support of the Confederacy. The primordialism and non-malleability that characterizes that Catholic faith does explain why Loyolans would be sympathetic to the Confederates who wanted to maintain the status quo, given that Loyola itself was, and still remains, a Catholic institution. This attachment to their faith may have meant that Loyolans believed that it was their duty to defend the ideologies of Catholicism. Thus, in order to fulfill this mandate, joining the Confederate Army seemed a rational, incumbent and, perhaps, even necessary action. This would mean that Loyolans were directly in support of the continuation of slavery and the dehumanization of others, a juxtaposition of the Godly tenets to have mutual respect and love for all his creation.

Moreover, social influences seemed to have been at play in the Loyolan's Confederate sympathies. Maryland, at the time of the Civil War, was below the Mason-Dixon Line, but had not seceded from the Union. In addition to this, there was a cleavage between the Northern and Southern portions of

8 Ibid 67.

the state along economic lines as "Northern Maryland had a largely indus-trialized economy based on free labor by 1850 while southern Maryland remained more wedded to the land and slave labor."[9] It is a possibility that many of Loyola's students, like President Morgan, could have been sons of planters from Southern Maryland and so too, would have shared his ideol-ogies in support of slavery and the marginalization of African Americans. Loyola therefore seemed to have been cornered by the religious, social, and economic temptations of joining the Civil War on the side of the Confederate. The lack of documented dissent from Southern sentiments, contrasted with the broad reception they received, is confirmation that the student body shared an affinity to the motivations of the Confederates Army. James McPherson, in seeking to explain the attraction of joining the Confederate Army emphasizes that,

Unlike many slaveholders in the age of Thomas Jefferson, Confederate soldiers from slaveholding families expressed no feelings of embarrassment or inconsistency in fighting for their liberty while holding other people in slavery. Indeed, white supremacy and the right of property in slaves were at the core of the ideology for which Confederate soldiers fought.[10]

The participation of Loyola in the Confederate Army is a clear man-ifestation of their ideals of separatism and their megalothymia; their need to establish their superiority. It is yet another sad example of "tell me what company you keep and I will tell you what you are."

Loyola's earlier culture was also defined by the use of language and actions that sought to undermine the human dignity of other races, includ-ing, but not limited to, African Americans while simultaneously elevating white power. The student publications at Loyola in the 20th century are lined with references that are racially and culturally derogatory. A yearbook from the 20th century has been found to contain images of students in blackface. In one yearbook from 1948, a white student was photographed with black

9 Thomas Murphy, *Jesuit Slaveholding in Maryland, 1717-1838* (New York: Routledge, 2001):191.
10 James M. McPherson, *For Cause and Comrade: Why Men Fought in the Civil War* (Oxford: Oxford Universi-ty Press: 1997), 106.

paint covering every inch of his face.[11] Other instances of blackface appear in subsequent yearbooks in 1950, where the use of blackface is featured in a "Loyola Night" event, and again in 1956 by the Drama Society.[12]

In another student publication, *The Greyhound*, one can see the attitudes of Loyola students towards Native American culture. In the publication, the writer criticized the traditions of Native Americans as primitive, uncivilized and beastly in comparison to white culture. Reflecting on the trajectory of American music from the arrival of Europeans until 1925, the writer posits in his piece, "American Music," that,

When our forefathers first arrived on this continent, there was, no doubt, a typical American music here. But it was the echoes of savage hearts and minds, reflecting in the monotonous beat of its tom-toms, the lust to kill, the joy of torture, aboriginal treachery and the mononic intelligence. In some of its phases and movements, for instance, for instance the "Deer Dance", it did, perhaps, embody a certain weird beauty. To the European mind, however, the general effect was depression. Therefore, it found no place in the lives of our adventurous forebears and they discarded it quite as ruthlessly as they discarded the Indians themselves.[13]

Given the tempestuous history that exists between the colonists and the Native Americans, it is of no surprise that Loyola's students, themselves being descendants of Europeans, would share in these prejudices. Despite this, it is nevertheless still horrific. Analogous to their ancestors, early Loyolans condemned who and what they did not understand through fallacies, falsities and fantasies for fear that their status would be irrelevant in the face of the world's cultural multifariousness.

These are just a few instances of the manifestations of racial prejudices that characterized the attitudes of the institution's early students. The examples have, by no means, been exhausted, but for the purposes of this essay,

11 Loyola University Maryland, Yearbook (Baltimore, Maryland:1948) 49, Loyola University Maryland Archives, LNDLSC.
12 Loyola University Maryland, Yearbook (Baltimore, Maryland:1956) 40, Loyola University Maryland Archives, LNDLSC.
13 "American Music,", *The Greyhound*, January 16, 1926 Loyola University Maryland Archives, LNDLSC.

only these striking samples have been provided to stimulate the curiosity of the reader.

Divisions in the decade of the 1850s and beyond were not solely confined to racial issues, as the subjugation of women was still a prominent ideology that marked the society of the United States. Many at Loyola were receptacles and conduits of these ideologies. Assuredly, Loyola's men, like many men of patriarchal America, were blind to the worth of women in other spheres of life apart from the home. Moreover, not only were women's views devalued and considered irrelevant, but they confined women's worth to being solely as sources of sexual gratification for men. Consequently, Loyola's culture was also one that heavily featured misogyny and the hyper-sexualization of women. Evidence of misogyny on Loyola's campus can be found in the speeches of presidents, recitations given at the college, student writings and in student publications like the yearbooks.

Father Joseph A. Sellinger became the president of Loyola in 1964. He were a devout Catholic and so often displayed resistance to change. He was particularly disquieted about the changes that were taking place during his time. A year after he had assumed the university presidency, the Second Vatican Council had made a decision to make Catholic colleges co-educational as part of their endeavors to keep up with the ever-increasing transformations in social, economic, political and religious ideologies. With this, Loyola was compelled to merge with Mt. Saint Agnes. Father Sellinger, being a primordialist, opposed the idea, but saw to this to fulfill his presidential and Catholic duties. Sellinger later shared in a school magazine his feelings about the merger stating that, "I was dogmatic that Loyola stay all-male. Those next five years were torture for me, coming from my upbring."[14] President Sellinger admits that his feelings towards the education of women was not based on the rationale that women also had the capacity to be intellectuals that equalled or surpassed their male-counterparts, but was the manifestation of the religious and familial socialization which he endured.

Students too, could not help but also take part in society's opinions on women. An instance of student misogyny cited in the research appeared in

14 Father McCoog, "Loyola's Presidents", *Loyola Magazine*, 1991, 21.

the *Historical Sketch*. It contained a poem given at the school by a student who attended Loyola, John Curlett. Entitled "Chivalry," the work describes aspects of life during the nineteenth century, but the author's views on the roles of women are especially attention-grabbing. He states that:

And more than once she threw aside the weakness of her sex, donned
the skel-bound corslet and learned to fight gallantly when her life or safety
required it… Man is the oak, woman the ivy which twines around its mighty
trunk and umbrageous branches receiving from its support and shade and
gives its picturesque beauty to the monarch of the forest… Like the ivy is the
woman-ornament of prosperity, the solace of adversity.[15]

If these descriptions seem to give credit to women, the message is profoundly condescending. The "weakness of her sex" speaks to the fact that men believed that women were biologically fragile and would have to "throw aside" their femininity—that is, adopt masculine traits to be considered able. The description of men as oak is a symbol of their strength, while the mention of women as ivy seems to point to the fact that women, by nature, are dependent on men. Moreover, women are described as an "ornament… and the solace of adversity." Here, Curlett tries to emphasize the idea that the role of women is to be comforters to men and accessories to them when required.

One can also cite instances of the objectification of women in the school's yearbooks. In a 1952 yearbook, one of the students, Lawrence Rodowsky, was quoted below his yearbook photo saying he was a "Constant believer that women lack order and good sense."[16] In another yearbook from 1969, one will encounter a photograph of a nude woman that is included in the description of Hammerman House, a dorm on campus. The writer describes the purpose of the photo as "decorative results of individual desires."[17] In 1968, when considering that the college then had more females on campus

---

15 John J. Ryan, *Historical Sketch of Loyola College: 1825-1902* (N.P., 1903)."
16 Loyola University Maryland, Yearbook (Baltimore, Maryland:1952) 59, Loyola University Maryland Archives, LNDLSC.
17 Loyola University Maryland, Yearbook (Baltimore, Maryland:1969) 7, Loyola University Maryland Archives, LNDLSC.

a writer muses that "when he examined in the proper perspective, he soon agreed that the girls were a welcome change and civilizing influence."[18] His statement was in response to the college having more females on campus. However, the statement is accompanied by five images featuring the lower half of females' bodies, some of which seemed to have been taken non-consensually. Indeed, Loyola existed in the age of "boys will be boys" where inappropriate behavior towards women was so normalized that it would be allowed in print. This aspect of society seemed especially alluring to the men of Loyola in the twentieth century and with open arms, they embraced society's acceptance and defense of masculine lust.

While this paper does emphasize the role of socialization and environmental influence on attitudes and behaviors, it is not a defense for Loyolans as participants in the offensive orientations of its early existence. Rather, this paper illustrates Loyola's failure to use its influence to catalyze change to a society that would truly represent the will of God. Instead, they surrendered to the seductive hiss of the serpent, beckoning them to join and support the indecencies of the nineteenth and twentieth century. While it is expected that one will be swayed by the leanings of their environs, one must also not discredit the ability of human beings to have free agency. Loyola and Loyolans had agency and could have used their voice to champion efforts for unity and inclusion rather than reinforcing segregationist and misogynist ideas. While Loyola maintained these trends during the nineteenth and twentieth century, it abandoned these ideals for customs of unity and diversity in the twentieth and this is evidence that self-examination and change were possible.

It is true what the Bible says, "train up a child in the way he should go: and when he is old, he will not depart from it." This is a famed scripture from the Proverbs that outlines the power of socialization. In layman's terms, children live what they learn and carry these norms and values with them throughout their lives, many of which are reinforced by religious, social and educational institutions. Children are receptacles into which the doctrines and dogmas of their societal institutions flow and so, strongly

18 Loyola University Maryland, Yearbook (Baltimore, Maryland:1968) 26, Loyola University Maryland Archives, LNDLSC.

influence the chemistry of their composition. Loyola students seemed to be such excellent repositories of the ideologies of its environs that at its 50th Jubilee Celebration, Father Conway delivered a speech declaring that "Loyola is a worthy daughter of the time honored seat of learning and for 50 years she has carried out the designs of Ignatius and fulfilled the wishes of John Carroll," a man whose overt support of enslavement was well-known.[19]

One cannot discount the strength of human autonomy to reject generalized ideologies. Loyola failed to set itself apart from the temptations of the outside world and to be an example of free agency in a world permeated by immorality and ruled by economic avarice, prejudice and partiality. Instead, Loyola basked in the iniquities of the material and succumbed to the summons of the sins of society, belying the piousness the institution had so prided itself on. However, as Loyola seeks to address the erroneous ways of our past, it has thrown off the weight of separationist and sexist opinions, easing its journey into a new age of acceptance and diversity. No longer does the culture reflect these antiquated attitudes discussed here, but now seeks to promote and foster ideas of unity and inclusion. The Loyola of today stands as a complete contrast to the Loyola of its yesteryears…right?

---

19 Ryan, *Historical Sketch of Loyola College*, 219.

Ludeema

Justine Amedson

Move-In Day

"Ha! Different air," Ludeema exclaimed as she took a deep breath.

She was finally on campus, the same campus her mother went to. She took a look around the parking lot bustling with life, first-years moving in, Evergreens assisting (what the campus called the student ambassadors), carts rattling on the brick walkway. This was perfect, a chance to be independent, make new friends, go out without her parents' watchful eyes monitoring her every move.

"I'll be back; I have to go get a cart and Evergreen to help," she said to her dad.

"Do you know where to go?" her dad asked.

"Yes Dad, I can see the green tent. B-r-b." She leaves.

"What does b-r-b even mean? It's as if she's allergic to full sentences," he grunted.

Abram Johnson, Ludeema's dad, was trying to keep his bravado up; he was a man after all. The truth was, he was sad. His little bird was leaving the nest, about to be on her own in a new city that none of them were familiar with, and with so much on the news about that city, he was skeptical. If it

93

were left up to him, his daughter would be homeschooled until after her doctorate. Mrs. Johnson—or as most people called her—Euphrosyne, was staring at her husband, holding back both laughter and tears. She found his forced bravado funny, but at the same time, she shared in his concern. She had taught her pup how to be strong, but as a mama wolf, she wanted to be there to protect her baby.

"I just made a new friend," Ludeema said excitedly, returning with a cart and an Evergreen. "Her name is Emefa or Eme, for short, and she's also Ghanaian."

"Good afternoon Mr. and Mrs. Johnson," Emefa said, turning to Ludeema's parents.

"Very well mannered, this one," Abram said.

"Good afternoon my dear, how're you?" Euphrosyne asked.

"I'm doing good Ma, how about you?"

"I'm doing good, can't complain."

They began loading things into the cart and headed up to Ludeema's room on the fifth floor of Thea Bowman Hall. In the elevator, Ludeema asked Eme, "I heard they changed the name of this building over the summer. Why did they do that?"

"Apparently, it became known that Flannery O'Connor was a racist, and with the BLM in full swing now, the University decided to change the name to Thea Bowman."

"That's horrible! How did the university miss this? You would think they would research before having a racist person associated with their brand," Ludeema lamented.

Euphrosyne, who had been on her phone, looked up and said to Ludeema, "That is indeed horrible, but you need to be careful with your words and how you phrase things Lu. You're new here, you don't want to make enemies before you start this journey."

"But Ma, you always told me to always tell it as it is, and I'm doing just that!"

"I said that, yes, but you need to have a filter as well and know when and where to say certain things," Euphrosyne chastised.

Ludeema sighed. "I guess you're right. I'll keep myself in check."

They got to her door and as Ludeema was trying to figure out which direction to turn the key, someone from inside opened the door wide, smiling. In a split second, there was an eruption of high-pitched screaming. Standing in front of the group was Ludeema's immediate roommate and best friend from high school, Amarachi.

"AHHHHHHH, you're here. Auntie African time. You said you'd be here by 12pm; it's now 3pm," Amy said before she and Ludeema burst out laughing.

"I was ready, but the people who gave birth to me were not ready for my presence to leave that house," Ludeema said laughing.

"Girls, let's keep the shouting to a minimum," Euphrosyne interjected, smiling. "Chichi, how're you doing?"

"I'm doing good auntie, Good afternoon uncle," Amy said, turning to Abram.

"Good afternoon, dear."

They started moving Ludeema's things in. After 3 hours, they were done, and Ludeema was ready to send her parents' home. Just then, their suitemates, Vanessa and Jasmine, came in through the adjoining bathroom.

"Hi guys," they entered, grinning.

Another round of screams, hugs, and introductions ensued. Euphrosyne, reluctant to say goodbye, suggested taking everyone out to dinner before they left Ludeema. Excited, the girls changed and headed over to the Cheesecake Factory over by Pratt St. By about 10, they were back at Thea Bowman dorm. Everyone went inside except Ludeema and her parents. In the parking lot, a tearful Ludeema, Abram and Euphrosyne hugged tightly.

Abram told Ludeema, "Be safe, study hard, be selective with your friends. You seem to have picked the right ones so far. Remember quality over quantity. May God be with you, and I love you very much. Make us proud."

"Okay Dad, I'll make you guys proud of me. I love you too," she said before turning to Euphrosyne.

Still hugging Ludeema, Euphrosyne told her, "I love you so very much, you will be great, you'll have fun, you'll be successful, and if you need anything, just call, and ask. Do not do anything we wouldn't do."

"I love you too Momsy. Now, when you say don't do anything you guys wouldn't do, are you referring to your college selves or your parent selves?" Ludeema asked, laughing amidst the tears.

"Madam, behave," Euphrosyne said laughing.

Mr. and Mrs. Johnson got in the car, waved goodbye, and drove off. Ludeema headed upstairs and met a sleeping Amy. She quietly showered and got into bed. She started going over the day's events, reminiscing about home and imagining what would lie ahead for her, slowly drifting off.

Primo Conscientia

Six weeks had passed since Ludeema moved onto campus, and everything had been going great for her. She found her friend group, she officially got in a relationship with the boy she had been talking to since before the summer began, and was excelling in most of her classes. Everyone who knew her loved her; she was charismatic, friendly, always smiling, and very respectful. She had become close to her professors and the staff she encountered. Although things were going well for her, something in the back of her mind always bothered her: diversity in the student body was lacking; Loyola, built many years ago, was a PWI, short-hand for Primarily White Institution. Ludeema couldn't help but feel out of place sometimes.

One day at lunch with her roommates and her friends Eme, Audrey, Kofi, and Jeanette, she asked them, "Do you guys think this campus is lacking something?"

"Something like what?" answered Kofi.

"Like, I know we go to a PWI, but the diversity is *really* lacking here. If I didn't have you guys, I would definitely feel out of place every time," said Ludeema.

"Oh girl, you ain't lying. I'm like one out of about four Black people in three of my classes," Vanessa said.

"And this doesn't just stop with the students – like, you can see it in the faculty and employees as well. All my professors are white. In fact I heard that about 96% of the professors are white, but look over to dining services, janitorial services and jobs like that and you'll see a lot of Black people working those parts," Eme said.

"I thought I was the only one noticing this. It's a big shift from what I saw in my high school," Ludeema said.

"And I heard the building we live in was changed from Flannery O'Connor to Thea Bowman," Jeanette said.

"You would think they would at least research the person they were putting on the building to represent Loyola, and, like, why did they wait until this year to change the name?" Kofi let out.

"I literally said the same thing to Eme when she told me," Ludeema shouted, popping up from her seat, her eyes wide open.

"Okay take it down a notch madam, so dramatic," Kofi said, laughing. They all started laughing—they knew she was always enthusiastic, but they always found her energy very amusing.

They talked about their weekend plans, the group dispersed, and they all went about their day. Ludeema was still dwelling on the conversation. She was so excited to go to the same university her mom went to but couldn't help questioning her decision with all these discrepancies coming up. Was Loyola the right choice? Did her mom notice these discrepancies, and if so, why did she not transfer or discourage her daughter from applying to the same school? Ludeema had a lot of questions and no answers, but she didn't have time to dwell on this; there were more trivial things to deal with.

Let's Take a Walk

By nightfall, Ludeema had forgotten about the discussion she had with her friends and the doubts that were on her mind. She had had a productive and tiring day, and it felt as though her bed was calling her. She took a quick shower, changed into her pajamas, and settled in bed. While scrolling through TikTok, she dozed off. She looked peaceful while lightly snoring; however, that peace did not last long.

It was dark. There weren't a lot of light poles lit on campus, but something wasn't right. The campus did not look the same, the buildings did not look the same, the atmosphere was different.

"Umm ok this is some matrix-type weirdness. Pretty sure I was in bed a few minutes ago," said Ludeema.

"Sorry, where or what is this place?" she asked a couple of students passing by.

They passed her without answering.

"Ok, rude much? Ughh," Ludeema exclaimed.

She kept asking but everyone she asked ignored her as though she didn't exist.

"You ain't gon' get a reply," someone said from behind her.

Ludeema turned around to see a stout, sheepish woman who seemed like the years had betrayed her. Her clothes were torn in several places and barely clinging on. She had several scars.

"I'm sorry, what?" Ludeema asked.

"You hard of hearing or somethin'? I said, 'you ain't gon get a reply,'" the woman responded.

"Why not?" Ludeema questioned.

"Cause you ain't from 'round here."

"Where is 'here'?"

"Lo'ola."

"Yes, I am, I'm a first-year here at Loyola."

"Good f'ya, you still not from 'round here."

"Ma'am, I don't appreciate what you're insinuating."

"And that is?"

"I don't know…yet."

"Walk with me," said the woman to Ludeema.

"Where? I'm sorry but I don't know you."

"You wan' answers or d'ya want to keep throwing fancy words at me? '*Insinating*.' Hmph," the woman scoffed.

"Um, in..sinuating, and I'm coming."

Ludeema and the woman started walking down the Evergreen campus, and she began noticing more differences: there were more trees than walkways, the buildings were much shorter, and the Starbucks wasn't where it usually was. Unlike everyone else she kept seeing as they walked, the Black workers, the woman she was walking with and herself included were in black and white, while everything else was in color. It was like a movie except she knew what the reality of Loyola was, she had lived it for the past six weeks. She asked the woman, "What do you mean when you say I'm not from around here?"

"I think you know the answer."

"So…So why can't everyone else see me, but you can? And… And why are we in black and white and everyone else is in color and why are you dressed like that and why-"

The woman put her index finger up to stop Ludeema "Chile, hush. You need to talk less and observe. Yo' parents must wish they was deaf. This ain't your Loyola. You not 'posed to be here. The land ain't meant for you or folks like us. If I was you, I'd leave."

"Here or my Loyola?"

"Both."

Just then, a couple of white students passed by. They turned their attention to the woman. "Can you smell that? Something stinks like a dead rat. It's nauseating," said one of the girls.

"I bet it's that wretched Black servant over there. Don't you have some floor you should be scrubbing instead of standing there talking to yourself like a mad person?" one of the guys said.

The group burst out laughing, and a second guy shoved her, saying, "Nigger."

Ludeema looked on, shocked. She couldn't believe what had just happened. This was definitely not her Loyola, or was it? A rage came over her that she couldn't explain. Maybe it was the African in her, but she grew up knowing you never speak to your elders in such a manner. She shouted, "How dare you, you pieces of trash, illiterate nincompoops! How dare you speak to her in that manner? Do you have no home training? You're not even half the human she is. Absolutely no decency, it's outrageous."

The woman looked at Ludeema and burst out laughing, surprised at Ludeema's outburst. "You's hot-tempered. They can't hear you remember?" the woman said, still laughing.

Ludeema became even more outraged. Why was the woman taking this abuse? Why was she laughing and not defending herself or giving those kids the spanking of their lives? Tears started streaming down her round face; she wasn't just sad, she was extremely angry. She couldn't defend the woman as she wanted because the students couldn't hear her, but the woman wasn't defending herself either.

"Girl wipe those tears. You get used to it," the woman said.

"No, no....No one should have to get used to this abuse, it is awful. And I don't understand why they can't see or hear me. You need to report them to someone."

The woman burst out laughing again. "Who you gon' tell? You know why we're in black and white and they're in color? They can't hear us unless they speak to us, and we can't talk unless they talk to us first. Ain't none of 'em lookin' out for us except us. But who among us gon' talk? We all got family to take care of and God knows they ain't paying us enough, but we need the little we can get. So, you keep quiet, keep movin' and do what you told to do."

Sadness slowly drowned out the rage; Ludeema started to realize what kind of Loyola she was in. Not the version that welcomed her the first day but the version where Black people could be abused and attacked, and nothing could be done about it. The two were in front of Thea Bowman by now, or Flannery O'Connor, as the name showed. Ludeema looked up and realized that this Loyola really wasn't meant for her, or people like her. She turned to the woman, but she was gone. Is this really the Loyola she wanted to be a part of?

One Step Forward

The alarm woke Ludeema. It was 7:30 a.m. She was covered in sweat, her pillow was wet as well, and her cheeks dry with tear stains. Ludeema pulled the comforter over her head and just laid there. Her alarm went off again at 8:45, and her roommate, Mara, tried to wake her up, but she wouldn't budge. She told Mara she was under the weather, and Mara told her she would get her some chicken noodle soup from Boulder on her way back from class.

Ludeema was left with her thoughts, but her thoughts seemed to be fighting against her. What had transpired while she slept; did she have superpowers? What was this vivid memory that was haunting her? It was unclear but, at the same time, clear. She broke down crying, this time not from outrage but from the fact that she couldn't make sense of what had happened or the memory she had. She knew what she saw; she knew what she heard. But did what she saw and what she heard happen? Or was that just a torturous dream from her subconscious? She started laughing amidst her tears. She had finally gone mad, she thought. She was imagining things that didn't exist. "I need to stop watching TikTok before bed," she mumbled.

Or, maybe it was real, maybe this nightmare did happen. This nightmare where she could not be seen or heard, this nightmare where she couldn't speak up, this nightmare where she couldn't fight against an injustice that occurred on the land on which stood the school where she was getting an education.

"How much is too much abuse and oppression that you get so used to it and give up defending yourself? At what point do the lines of dignity and survival get blurred together? Was it really worth the cost of being subjected to this sort of treatment?" Ludeema pondered. She could still hear the insults of the students and the woman's laughter.

Then she remembered the question the woman asked: "Who will you tell?" "Who do you go to when your representation is far outnumbered? Perhaps we have more diversity and organizations in place to help and maybe listen," she thought, "But who was this voice for Black people at Loyola in the past? Who could defend against the disparities and give Black people equal footing and solid ground to be heard and given their due accolades at Loyola?"

Second Time's The Charm?

It was a rough night, and it took a toll on Ludeema. She didn't realize it, but her body and mind hadn't exactly rested. While still in bed with the comforter over her head, she dozed off again. She must have dozed off for maybe 10 minutes, but it felt longer. She went back. She was back at Loyola before it was the Loyola she knew, but it seemed different than the first time. There were less trees, more light poles, and the buildings were not the same. Of course, everything was different from what she knew, but, at the same time, it was different from her first encounter with past-Loyola. The buildings seemed to have been renovated because they were much taller.

"Can't stay away, I see," the woman from before said.

"Wait, no. I'm not sleeping, I'm awake. Is this what sleep paralysis feels like?"

"Sure, and I make $80 dollars a month," the woman replied sarcastically.

"Ok, um, that's really low, like extremely," Ludeema said.

"Well, you would know and again, not the same Lo'ola, remember?" the woman chuckled.

"What happened to the place? It's different from when I was last here...I think."

"Times are changing, no?"

"Oh, most definitely...What happened with those insolent kids from last time?" Ludeema questioned.

"Chile, ain't nothin' happen to 'em. What d'ya think would happen?" More sarcasm.

"I...I don't know, something to teach them a lesson," Ludeema said.

"Oh, you's a teacher now? Ain't nothing changing. Times are changing but the flow staying the same," the woman chuckled.

"Some things are actually changing; that Flannery O'Connor building was changed to Thea Bowman," Ludeema said.

The woman hesitated for a minute. She looked deep in thought.

"What's wrong?" Ludeema asked.

"Why you think they did that? That seem like the right move?"

"Well…they found out that Flannery was racist, so… I don't know, they are trying to make some long overdue changes."

"No, I'll give you a minute to think about it…why?" The woman quizzed. "A leopard can never change its spots. It can bleach its fur, but them spots always gon' be part of its identity. That's the same with Lo'oya. The names of a thousand buildings can be changed, but that don't change what they ancestors doing or, in your case, what they did. If that were possible, you not gon see me here working like a dog for chicken change. I can't even speak unless spoken to! That any way to live!?" The woman broke down crying.

Ludeema just watched as tears streamed down the woman's face unsure of what to say or how to react. There was nothing good to say and no right reaction because she wasn't in the woman's position; she grew up with many advantages that she never considered to be privileged. Her thoughts were interrupted.

"Er'body wants to help eat the food from the pot, but no one wants to help cut the vegetables or wash the pot afterwards. Problem? Oh, let's send a letter out showing unity. Oh, let's change the building's name. But, no, God forbid we actually question the roots of the problem or start an action plan that will last a long long time. Every single building on this land that forbids our identity, heritage and skin color has a foul history behind it, but ain't nobody asking the right questions or looking in the right places."

Just then a man's voice echoed behind them, "What are you standing here for woman? The floors won't clean themselves. Get to it."

Before the woman could reply, a gust of wind surrounded Ludeema. The woman turned to face Ludeema instead, handing her a picture. "Ask the right questions, and get you a spade cause you got some digging to do." The woman laughed and Ludeema woke up in bed.

The Closeted Skeletons

Ludeema woke up confused and dazed, but she did not have time to process what she had seen in her astral projection form because she felt something in her hand. It was a really old picture of the woman from the past Loyola, a child on her hip. On the back, it said the names, Bazile Akosua Lawson, and Euphrosyne Ama Lawson. Ludeema recognized the names but refused to believe what she was reading. She turned to the front of the picture and studied it carefully. She saw the "Gye Nyame" symbol on the woman's foot, as well as the kid's. She burst out laughing like she was starting to run mad. Maybe she was. She had the same symbol on her left foot, as well as her mom, but there was no way. Right? Amidst the laughter she called home and broke down when her mother picked up the phone. She needed to talk to someone right away, even though she wasn't sure what exactly she wanted to talk about. She told her parents everything and sent them a picture of the picture she woke up with. Euphrosyne broke down in tears uncontrollably.

"The woman in the picture is your great-grandmother and the kid is your grandmother," Euphrosyne let out.

"How do you know for sure?"

"You see that Gye Nyame symbol? It's a distinct birthmark that runs in our family. It distinguished us from other tribes back in Ghana," Euphrosyne explained.

"I'm not sure what to do with all this information. I did not sign up for this. Why me?" Ludeema lamented.

"Because you're the right person to start doing something about it. First start by looping your friends in, and a good place to start is the school library. It must have some sort of information about the university's history," her dad replied.

"You always know what to say. I think Mom needs you right now, I'll call you tomorrow morning. Love you."

"We'll come see you tomorrow after work, Sweetie. Try to get some rest, and we'll see you tomorrow. I love you so much, my warrior," Abram said and hung up.

Ludeema still couldn't believe the revelations but she had decided she would do something, start somewhere. She hadn't been out of her dorm in over 48 hours, so she took a shower, dressed up, and went out for a walk.

As she walked around the Loyola campus, many thoughts ran through her mind. The words of the woman from old Loyola echoed in her head, "Ask the right questions, and get a spade." She texted her best friends and roommates on campus and asked to meet with them at Starbucks. She didn't know how she was going to start the conversation, but she was going to at least try to start somewhere, ask the right questions and hopefully find the right spade to dig for the truth. It was the start of a long journey, but a very necessary one.

Era Two:

Building Architecture, Developing Cultures (1921 – 1970)

Historical Documents:
Portraits

CAFETERIA STAFF: Miss Doris Washington, Mr. Edward Calhoun, Miss Fanny Caesar, Mr. Louis Cherry.

Photograph of Black cafeteria staff in Loyola yearbook, 1955. Image courtesy of Loyola Notre Dame Library Archives. *Evergreen Yearbook*, 1955, page 18.

Yearbook page depicts cafeteria staff while excluding Black staff's names, 1956. Image courtesy of Loyola Notre Dame library Archives. *Evergreen Yearbook*, 1956, page 18.

Structures

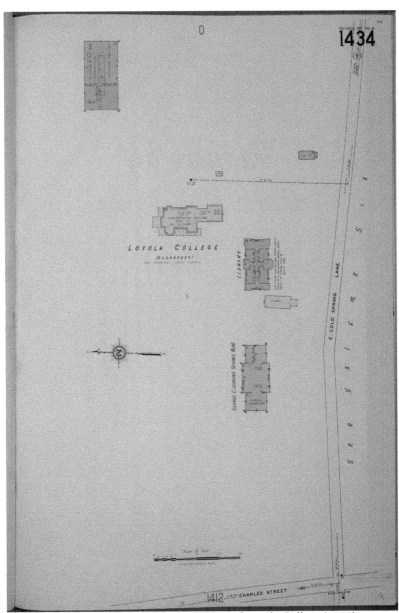

Library of Congress Sanborn Map of Loyola College (1929)

111

Faculty on
Race Relations

A December 20, 1942 *Baltimore Sun* article captures the paternalistic racism of Dean of Studies Dr. James d'Invilliers, S.J., even as he denies U.S. imperialism: "As far back as 1898 the Philippines, always a liberty-loving nation, wanted their independence, but they were not prepared for it. . . . at no time were they exploited for the aggrandizement of the United States." *Baltimore Sun,* December 20, 1942.

EDITOR SEES WORLD CRISES

Rev. John LaFarge Gives Final Lecture In Series At Loyola College

---

Post-War Planners Must Be Fully Aware Of The Problems, Speaker Says

Fearful physical and spiritual crises will confront the nations of the world even before the war is over, the Rev. John LaFarge, S. J., executive editor of *America*, said yesterday in the final lecture of a series on world unity at Loyola College.

He warned that "before we can reach solutions or venture on plans concerning the post-war world, we must be fully aware of the problems."

The physical crisis, he said, will come "as the grim picture of Europe's starvation unfolds."

Degeneration Predicted

With the invasion of Europe, he said, "the closer we shall find the peoples of the occupied countries pushed to the abyss of physical annihilation or complete degeneration of the coming generation."

· An even deeper problem, he said, is that of the spiritual crisis which will "take the form of extreme pessimism as to humanity itself,

partly as a result of the physical miseries of the war, partly as an escape for the feelings of frustration and humiliation with which the defeated Axis will turn in upon itself."

Father LaFarge stated that pessimism as to mankind is a powerful means of escape, and one of the most psychologically effective and appealing forms that such pessimism can take is that of racism: the view that certain groups of people or nationalities must be kept in subjection because of their racial inheritance.

Warning Is Sounded

Although the policies of the United Nations at present completely disavow any such doctrine, which is officially sigmatized as being the dominant concept of Hitler, he visualized the sinister prospect opened up if any extension of that racist pessimism is allowed to influence the policies of the United Nations with the post-war world.

"As long as a racialist philosophy controls our political thinking, no solution can be found for the eternal question of national and cultural minorities," he said. "As long as such minorities are dealt with on a racial basis they will respond, make claims and agitate upon a racial basis. If they suffer wrongs because of their race they will claim rights upon the basis of race; they will claim, that is to say, racial rights."

"There can be no solution of the minorities problem unless the solution is based upon the consideration of the individual person, seen in his natural worth, his acquired character and his real relation to society. The strength of the Christian position, as expounded in recent years by the social encyclicals of the Popes and utterances of many Catholic bishops, lies precisely in the plain recognition of this fact."

Rev. John LaFarge, S.J., former Loyola professor and author of *Interracial Justice: A Study of the Catholic Doctrine of Race Relations* (1937), examines pessimism's link to racism and denounces racialist philosophy in a lecture at Loyola College, April 5, 1943. *Baltimore Sun*, April 5, 1943.

LOYOLA COLLEGE
EVERGREEN
BALTIMORE, MARYLAND

4501 NORTH CHARLES STREET

Midyear Examination in Sociology – 1938   Jan. 25 –

1) Define Sociology and classify it.

2) What is meant by heredity? Environment? Do they play equal parts in the making of an individual?

3) What is meant by "race"? Mention the criteria of classification.

4) What is meant by racial purity? Is it a myth?

5) Can any arguments be based on mental tests for the intelligence of the various races? Explain.

6) Describe the fundamentals of the negro problem in the U.S.A. and its practical solution.

7) What is meant by population? Is overpopulation the menace to-day?

8) What is meant by sterilization? Are all types of sterilization forbidden by the Church?

9) Why is birth control forbidden.

10) What basis have the Neo-Malthusians for their urgency of population restriction?

Examination questions of sociology professor Rev. Joseph Ayd revolving around race and eugenics, such as "What is meant by racial purity? Is it a myth?" and "Describe the fundamentals of the negro problem in the U.S.A. and its practical solution," Jan. 25, 1938. Image courtesy of Loyola Notre Dame Library Archives. (Father Ayd Papers; Box 4; Jan. 25, 1938).

Historical Student Publications

Recent Lynching Activity Is Subject of Bellarmine Debate

Society Re-established After Period Of Several Weeks Of Inactivity

After several weeks of inactivity, the Bellarmine Debating Society comes to the fore with the timely and interesting discusison on lynching. This was in the form of an open-forum discussion.

Favor Lynching

The chief speakers in favor of lynching were Messrs. Kammer and Peach, who held doggedly to the argument that, since the Courts fail in their end, namely, the rendering of prompt justice, it is only right that the people accomplish what the law does not. Since it is the people that constitute the state, then the people have a right to act when the state fails.

Furthermore the delays in past trials have driven the people to this act and if justice is not more efficient in the future, then more lynchings are bound to result. Lynching, then, accomplishes a good, inasmuch as it will cause the courts to respond to a demand for better justice.

Among those who opposed lynching were Messrs. Ahearn, Kane, and Phelan.

(Continued on Page 4, Col. 4)

Recent Lynching Activity Is Subject of Bellarmine Debate

Society Re-established After Period Of Several Weeks Of Inactivity

(Continued from Page 1, Col. 1)
They contended that common sense and ethical principles stamp such an act as unjust and detrimental to society. The people have no right to take the law in their own hands, because it is only the constituted authorities who have the power to carry out the law.

Lynching, they continued, leads to mob rule and contempt for law. Under no conditions is lynching justified.

When a vote was taken on the question, it was found that all the members of the Society were against lynching except, Kammer and Peach who, as remarked above, spoke in favor of this measure.

The Bellarmine Debate Society addressed lynching on December 15, 1933. In a debate society, the team that argued for the topic was called "the affirmative," and the team that argued against the topic wass called "the negative." In the lynching debate, "the affirmative" argued the people had a right to accomplish "prompt justice" that Courts failed to deliver; "the negative" argued that lynching lead to "mob rule." All except two members determined that "Under no circumstances is lynching justified." *The Greyhound*, December 13, 1933.

AUTUMN 1943

GORDON C. GRAU
B. S. 1

Sodality 1, 2; Chemists' Club 1, 2, 3, 4; Math
Club 1, 2; Mendel Club 1, 2, 3, 4; Intramurals 1,
2, 3.

"Mr. Paramount" . . . University of Maryland Medical School . . . leather brief case
. . . "Meet me at the Coffee House" . . . a
pipe that has taken root between his molars
. . . smooth line . . . clothes made the man . . .

JOSEPH E. GRENINGER
B. S. 1

Sodality 1, 2; Chemists' Club 1, 2, 3, 4; Math
Club 2, 3, 4; Mendel Club 2; Social Science Club
3, 4.

"Joe" . . . wide-awake Joe . . . bicycle
pedals—caught in the act . . . Sociology
beadle . . . Sears-Roebuck employee . . .
Physics librarian . . . amorphous personality
. . . Stepin Fetchit II . . .

H. CALLOWAY HARRISON, JR.
Ph. B

Social Science Club 3, 4, (Sect'y 4) ; Lacrosse 3;
Intramurals 1, 4.

"Flash" . . . man of mystery . . . Loyola's
prodigal returned . . . "Devil driver" . . .
klassy kut klothes . . . sheepherder from
Reisterstown . . . subjected to many jibes
about it . . . hates his acquired cognomen (see
above).

Page Fifty-Nine

Reference to "klassy kut klothes" in description of H. Calloway Harrison Jr., which student-researchers initially flagged as a reference to the Ku Klux Klan, but further student research suggested that was not the case, 1943. *Evergreen yearbook*, 1943; page 59.

118

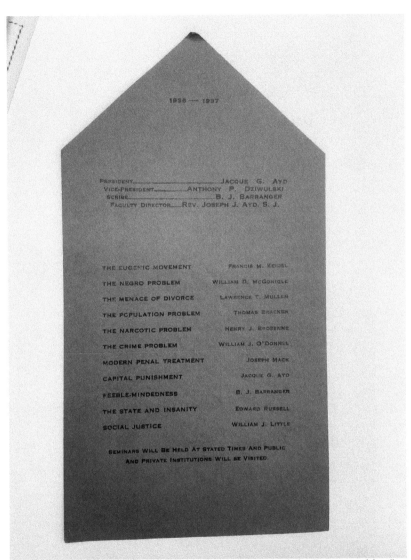

Loyola Social Science Club brochure lists eugenics and the "negro problem" as planned seminar topics (1936-1937). Courtesy of Library Notre Dame Library Archives (Father Ayd Papers; Box 4; 1947)

1947

SOCIAL SCIENCE CLUB

LOYOLA COLLEGE. BALTIMORE

PRESIDENT
FRANK G. ODENHEIMER

VICE-PRESIDENT
JAMES C. SWEENEY

SECRETARY
FRANK RODGERS

MODERATOR
REV. JOSEPH J. AYD, S. J.

SEMINARS

The Immigration Problem To-day
—TERRENCE E. BURKE

The Negro Problem and Current Legislation
—RICHARD C. KEMP

The Modern Approach to Juvenile Delinquency
—VINCENT DiPAOLO

The Present Status of Parole and Probation
—ALBERT SEHLSTEDT, JR.

The Labor Problem To-day
—CHARLES H. KECK

Public and Private Institutions will be
inspected under the supervision of the Moderator.

Social Science Club program lists "The Negro Problem and Current Legislation" as seminar topic (1947).

120

GOOD-BYE RUBY

Come Ruby, golden rule I knew
Before you vanished and your voice was spent
Echoing back to me among the monuments
And gilded halls, resounding back to me
The age and song of a love forever gone.

Come Ruby, goodness knows it's time
To count our losses; you and I are old:
The face in the Istrian sun is forgotten
The hum of your voice to be forever remembered
Comes cold, and not willing tells me we are old.

Judge not of me too harshly, Ruby
Now it's time. We were very young
We thought the face in the Istrian sun would be forever remembered;
That the light in the sky or the leaf on your hair
Were apart from the setting sun.

You must have known, Ruby, even though the time
Forbade our meeting in the gilded hallways
The monuments we built into the West;
You must have known Ruby how our gentle causes
In kind no longer meant the best.

The monuments we built into the West,
The cares we gave old Aesop for his fancy;
An ordered world, for even Uncle Remus and Aunt Nancy:
These forms of a past misspent have turned to snow
In the shape of a heart I loved and couldn't know.

I see you Ruby now in time I knew
Before you vanished and your voice was spent
To echo back among the monuments
And gilded halls, recalling back to me
An age and a song, and a world forever gone.

This student poem depicts the past as having monuments that "we" built *into* the West. The speaker then portrays the past as having an "ordered world" for "even" Uncle Remus and Aunt Nancy. Uncle Remus refers to a nineteenth-century Black character with only "pleasant memories of the discipline of slavery" who tells folktales for a white child, and Aunt Nancy refers to an Americanized version of Anansi, a mythological figure originating in Ghana whose cultural functions diversified when brought to the Americas with the Transatlantic Slave Trade. *Evergreen Quarterly* Vol. 5 No. 1, 1948, page 11. See also Joel Chandler Harris, *Uncle Remis: His Songs and His Sayings* (Gutenberg Project, 2020), https://www.gutenberg.org/cache/epub/2306/pg2306-images.html#link2H_PREF.

Loyola yearbook contains photographs of students in blackface, praising the performance, 1950. *Evergreen Yearbook*; 1950, page 12. The first full-time Black student, Charles Dorsey, enrolled at Loyola in 1949, and thus it was during his first year in college that the 1950 yearbook was published. The performances documented above were staged weeks after he began classes.

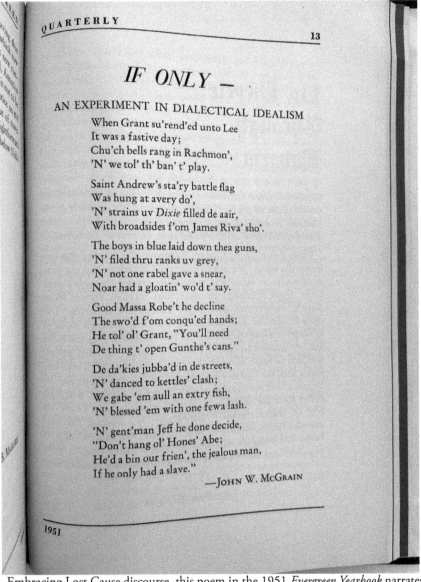

IF ONLY —

AN EXPERIMENT IN DIALECTICAL IDEALISM

When Grant su'rend'ed unto Lee
It was a fastive day;
Chu'ch bells rang in Rachmon',
'N' we tol' th' ban' t' play.

Saint Andrew's sta'ry battle flag
Was hung at avery do',
'N' strains uv *Dixie* filled de aair,
With broadsides f'om James Riva' sho'.

The boys in blue laid down thea guns,
'N' filed thru ranks uv grey,
'N' not one rabel gave a snear,
Noar had a gloatin' wo'd t' say.

Good Massa Robe't he decline
The swo'd f'om conqu'ed hands;
He tol' ol' Grant, "You'll need
De thing t' open Gunthe's cans."

De da'kies jubba'd in de streets,
'N' danced to kettles' clash;
We gabe 'em aull an extry fish,
'N' blessed 'em with one fewa lash.

'N' gent'man Jeff he done decide,
"Don't hang ol' Hones' Abe;
He'd a bin our frien', the jealous man,
If he only had a slave."

—JOHN W. McGRAIN

1951

Embracing Lost Cause discourse, this poem in the 1951 *Evergreen Yearbook* narrates the end of the Civil War with derogatory and racist language such as "Good Massa Robe't" and "De da'kies." *Evergreen Yearbook* 1951, vol. 6, no. 3, page 13.

It was dark now; one of those cool clear nights when Ephraim liked to sit back and smoke his cob pipe. He was doing just that when he saw the distant flickerings of fires. Every time he saw that, Ephraim became uneasy. "That always spells trouble," he thought, "when fires burn on Swamp Island." Suddenly there was confusion: the noise of a small mob, a crash on the door as it swung wide to frame a white-shrouded figure that spoke with the voice of a leader. "Green, people who put crosses in their back yard gotta be taught a lesson. Some people think you might even be going to that Papist Church on the sly. We aim t' show you it ain't worth it." Ephraim, realizing it would be futile to explain that the cross-like structure was a clothes pole, whispered a word of comfort to Daisy who stood crying and hysterical at his side.

Quickly he was snatched from his cabin-home by the white-shrouds, beaten, and shoved along the modern but very narrow highway that ran through the swamp ahead. As the weird crowd came within ear-shot of the howling, shrieking animal voices of the marsh, Ephraim saw his little son following the mob at a distance. Glancing back, at first with a painful frown, he summoned up all the anger he could and shot it out of his eyes with a fierce look at the crouching little colored boy. At the edge of the swamp Ephraim could see that his attempt to send the boy home had failed. The little form still could be seen, now and then, creeping through the dark brush at the side of the road.

The flat-bottom skiffs pushed through the black waters of the swamp and occasionally would frighten a pair of glowing jade-green eyes from the knees of a cypress into the muck below. They reminded Ephraim of the nocturnal hunts he had made; nothing in the decaying swamp was more weird than those cottonmouth eyes. He was stirred from his thoughts by the bright lights on the swamp island and the sudden scrape of

Excerpt from Frank C. Vogel's short story about a Black man attacked by the Ku Klux Klan, the man's son who finds help, and a white man who saves them, 1951. *Evergreen Quarterly* Vol. 6 No. 4; 1951; page 35.

Night School and
World War II

Scarborough, Katherine
The Sun (1837-); Jan 17, 1943; ProQuest Historical Newspapers: The Baltimore Sun
pg. CH6

Confusion In The Colleges

By KATHERINE SCARBOROUGH

WITHIN the next few weeks announcement will be made in Washington of the selection by the War Manpower Commission of the 350 American colleges in which the proposed military-educational program will be carried out for the army and navy.

Under this system young men selected by the army from its trainees and existing ROTC groups and by the navy from its personnel and from civilian life, will receive specialized instruction in technical subjects with military value. It is also reported that, later on, the Manpower Commission intends to assign a number of colleges for civilian science study, but this is not yet authoritative.

To date no intimation has been given of the schools to be chosen. Their selection, it has been announced, will be made on the basis of data on plant and teaching corps obtained from college and university presidents by a joint committee of the armed services and the Manpower Commission.

Hard To See Ahead

Uncertainty concerning their probable status under this program, the loss of teachers and students to the armed forces and Government service, the prospect of further inroads consequent upon the draft of 18-year-olds and increasingly acute financial problems have combined to throw universities and colleges, except those exclusively for women, into unprecedented confusion.

At the moment no college president knows whether or not he will be called upon shortly to operate a new school for the army within the one he is now trying to pilot. Assuming that his institution may be chosen for the army plan, he does not know whether he will be able to muster a faculty sufficiently large and competent to instruct both military and regular classes or not. He does not know how many students not yet in uniform may be pulled suddenly out of the classroom, giving thirteen weeks' basic military training, then sent back to school for technical instruction lasting from three months to two years and not necessarily on college level. He does not know whether the system of deferments in operation before the draft age was lowered will continue.

Financial Problems

Assuming that his institution will not be chosen, a college president faces most of the same difficulties and several others as well. Loss of tuition fees will not be offset by Government money. Additional faculty members may be lost. Students wishing to prepare ahead of time for military advancement after induction may desert to an institution where the army program is in operation.

Army and navy plans for college training differ materially. No student, under the army program, will be called up before completing the semester or quarter in which he was working on January 1 last. This varies in Maryland colleges from February 1 to about March 19. Upon completion of this term, however, he is inductible material the day he is 18.

Navy Plan Different

The navy which is now recruiting through the selective service, reverses the army process to secure leadership. Building up its reserves from the ranks of high-school seniors and college students, it is keeping these youths in classroom and laboratory until they are ready for strictly naval training, thus eliminating the educational hiatus involved in the army plan. A tentative date of "about July 1" has been fixed for the inauguration of its plan for navy reservists.

Occupational Bulletin No. 10, issued by the selective service headquarters and effective immediately, instructed draft boards that a registrant in training for engineering and entitled for deferment upon successful completion of his first college year if he gave promise of acquiring skills needed for the war effort. At the same time it was announced that bacteriologists, chemists, geophysicists, mathematicians, meteorologists, naval architects, physicists, astronomers and psychologists were also eligible for deferment under certain circumstances.

Receipt of this bulletin has done much to bolster the hopes of college presidents whose students are preponderantly in these fields. At the Johns Hopkins between three-fourths and four-fifths of all students are now majoring in engineering, chemistry or physics, or are taking the pre-medical course. At the University of Maryland there are about 750 students in engineering, about 150 taking the pre-medical or pre-dental course, hundreds more majoring in chemistry, physics and bacteriology.

Preparing For War

Similarly, according to the Very Rev. Edward B. Bunn, S. J., president of Loyola College, most of the students at that institution "are in some course preparing for the armed services or for industry." At Western Maryland a recent survey made by President Fred G. Holloway showed a like condition, with enlarged chemistry and physics laboratories. At Washington College twenty-five or thirty students, says President Gilbert W. Mead, are in the army's enlisted reserve. with "twice that many in various branches of the navy.

At St. John's College, Annapolis, eighteen students are in the Air Corps, which calls its men up one by one, but most undergraduates are in the army's and navy's enlisted reserves. The one hundred best books still are basic at this college, which has always heavily emphasized mathematics, astronomy, physics and chemistry. Navigation and shop work have been increased on an extra-curricular basis.

B. S. Course Only

Liberal-arts studies inevitably will be eliminated or drastically modified in consequence of the army-navy college program.

At Loyola, Father Bunn has announced that the Bachelor of Science course will be the only one offered to freshmen matriculating February 1, but this course contains a healthy proportion of cultural subjects.

Facing what it regards as inevitable crippling of its liberal arts program, Western Maryland College is trying to set up a one or two-year curriculum designed especially for matriculates who expect to enter the armed services. The college will now accept, on the basis of individual review, students who have completed three-and-a-half years of high-school work.

Teaching Chinese

All of the liberal arts courses are still being given at Washington College, but there is a pronounced emphasis on science and mathematics. Modern languages, including Chinese, Russian and Portuguese, will continue to be taught at College Park, says President H. C. Byrd, of the University of Maryland, but he anticipates the loss of numerous specialties in the liberal arts field.

The present upheaval in the schools is attributed by some executives to Government independent report to the trustees of the Johns Hopkins, educators had been "told emphatically . . . that everything had been worked out in the way of national reorganization, with respect to research, industry and manpower in anticipation of M-day." Now, he points out, "if the 18 and 19 year old students are taken, /college/ training, with uncertain deferment or no deferment, might be stopped altogether, except in the case of the physically unfit or those admitted from secondary schools at an earlier age and on lowered admission requirements. . . . All and any training now devised need not be called education at all, but rather training for war."

Altogether, the situation has reached the point where it constitutes what one educator calls "a cross between confused organization and regimented chaos." What will come out of it is anybody's guess.

LOYOLA GRADUATES CLASS NEXT WEEK

77 To Be Given Degrees' At 91st Commencement, First Under War Plan

Seventy-seven graduates will receive degrees at the ninety-first commencement of Loyola College, which will be held in the gymnasium at Evergreen at 3 o'clock next Sunday.

The graduation is the first under the accelerated war plan which allows students to receive their degrees in a shorter period of time than in pre-war years.

Many Will Leave For Service

Approximately half of the graduates already have enlisted in the armed services and will leave immediately after the graduation for officers' training schools.

Raymond Gram Swing, radio commentator, will be commencement speaker. Degrees will be conferred by the Very Reverend Edward B. Bunn, S. J., president of the college.

Jubilee medals will be awarded to three members of the class of '93: J. Edwin Murphy, former managing editor of *The Evening Sun*, Albert B. Hoen and W. Seton Belt.

Award To Dr. O'Connor

Dr. John A. O'Connor will receive the Carroll award for being the most active alumnus in the preceding year.

Commencement activities will begin next Wednesday evening with a dinner for the class of '18 in the faculty residence. The baccalaureate mass will be held at St. Ignatius Church at 9 o'clock next Sunday and a breakfast for the graduates will follow at the Belvedere Hotel.

Sollers Point School Contract Is Awarded

Award of a contract to William F. Sutter, of Nescopeck, Pa., to construct a one-story school building at Sollers Point, in the Sparrows Point section of Baltimore county, at a cost of $58,576, was announced yesterday by the Federal Works Agency.

The structure, designed by Hilyard R. Robinson, Negro architect, of Washington, will accomodate children of Negro families living in a 304-unit war-housing project on a site removed from existing school facilities.

It will contain five classrooms and a large multi-purpose room, providing facilities for approximately 175 pupils. Of brick and frame, it conforms to standard plans for war-emergency types of construction, with the use of critical materials restricted to a minimum.

Loyola's Class of 1943 received their degrees under an accelerated war plan to allow for faster enlistment in the armed services. *Baltimore Sun*; Jan. 24, 1943.

127

MEN STUDENT ENROLLMENTS SHOW BIG DROP

Officials Of Maryland Colleges Perturbed Over Situation

With the opening dates for Maryland colleges a week to a month hence, many college officials are perturbed to find that their enrollments of men students appear to be approximately two-thirds less than in normal years.

With the announcement that drafting for the armed services will continue at the rate of 63,000 a month, they say it is evident the situation will not improve very rapidly unless something is done to permit some of the more promising youths of the country to return to college and start their training for a lifetime of peace.

The Very Reverend Edward B. Bunn, S.J., president of Loyola College and chairman of the Maryland Education Conference for Postwar Organization, yesterday said college heads everywhere were beginning to wonder when they would be given back some of the boys the services took in the period of emergency which existed from April, 1944, to the end of the war.

Building Up Another Emergency

"At that time," Father Bunn said, "we of the education field realized that the nation was facing a grave emergency. We gave in to the drafting of young men of scientific and professional promise into combat service, and in substance permitted the Selective Service law to become a draft law, something it was never intended to be.

"Knowing that technologically trained brains have become a commodity of supreme importance to military and social well-being we had hoped to keep the nation's supply well filled even though a war was being fought, but when the emergency arose, we, as good Americans, realized it, and acquiesced, trusting that the armed forces would see their way clear to returning the 18-19-year-olds to the classrooms as soon as possible.

Atomic Bomb Cited

"It now appears that some do not realize that they are building up another emergency—that of making it impossible for us to supply the demand for sufficient technically trained men to meet the nation's needs in the future.

"To me the emergencies in the Pacific and those caused by the battle of France and the Ardennes breakthrough no longer exist sufficiently to hold back the training of leadership for peace."

Among other things, it was point-

(Continued on Page 7, Column 3)

MEN STUDENTS MUCH FEWER

Officials Of Maryland Colleges Perturbed

(Continued from Page 22)

ed out, when everyone is singing the praises of the atomic bomb here are no men either in training or trained to become the successors of those scientists who made the discoveries which made the bomb possible.

It was said, further, by most of the heads of Maryland colleges and universities that there already had been a setback of several years in the education of trained men and, that since it takes from six to eight years to train professional men and scientists, the nation was heading for a period of scarcity among these vocations.

"Not Keeping Pace"

The danger, according to the Maryland educators, lies not only in grave lack of trained Americans at some time in the future but also means that we are not keeping pace with other nations of the world in this field. They point to a survey made by the American Council of Education which shows that at Massachusetts Institute of Technology in March, 1945, there were only 65 American graduate students as compared with 173 from foreign countries. In 1940 here were 675 American and 48 foreigners in the same classes.

The total enrollment at M.I.T., undergraduate and graduate, in 1940 was 2,914 American, 224 foreigners, and in 1945 it was 871-302.

The consensus of most Maryland college heads is that they and the other American colleges have been most generous with the armed forces in giving their facilities and services during the period of emergency, and now they do not feel that another emergency should be created for the nation through shortsightedness on the part of the Selective Service laws.

Male enrollment decreased due to war drafting. *Baltimore Sun*, Aug. 28, 1945

which 131 students of the February and May Classes will receive diplomas, Mr. John L. Sullivan, Secretary of the Navy, has graciously agreed to give the Commencement address, and to accept the honorary degree of Doctor of Laws. For the second Commencement on July 2ⁿᵈ (?), the present Prime Minister of Canada, Mr. St. Laurent has indirectly at least agreed to be present. Fr. Rector stated that this last speaker's presence is a national event, and may prove to be the occasion of an historic speech to the American and Canadian people. At this Commencement there will be graduated 183 students of the July class. However, Fr. Rector wishes that all the graduates, including those of the February and May classes, should be on the platform when Mr. Laurent rises to speak.

5) Rev. Fr. Rector, with the help of the Consultors, formulated the policy of Loyola College in regard to the acceptance of negro Catholic students. It is simply that Loyola College does accept negro Catholic students. While this basic principle was admitted by all, some amendments were added on which all the consultors did not agree. The first amendment was that in keeping with our principle of receiving no transfer students from other colleges, no negro seminary students can be admitted should they wish to stop studying for the priesthood. A second amendment was that it should be made clear to a negro student here that he is not expected to attend the college dances. A third amendment proposed by Fr. Dehaut was that only negro students from Maryland should be accepted. Fr. Rector was not in favor of any restrictions on such students which would limit them more than white students. All agreed however to the following points a) negro students are subject to all the regulations of the college as regards academic standing, discipline, with the proviso that they are not to receive special favors but must be treated fairly by all, b) the manner of admission will be in accord with the regular procedure of admitting white students. c) No publicity will be given by the college as to its policy in respect to the admission of negro students. No announcement of any sort will be issued on this matter by the college. Should objections arise which may not be overlooked, the college will issue a simple statement of its position, and avoid all controversy on the matter.

There being no further business, the meeting adjourned with

Policy on admitting "negro students" noting "that they are not to receive special favor but must be treated fairly by all" (March 14, 1949). Image courtesy of Loyola Notre Dame Library Archives. Jesuit Community Records, Box 2, Volume 1 Records of Consultations 1924-1956.

Student Essays

Building White Success & Preventing Black Prosperity

Alexis Faison

"The said premises shall be improved used and occupied by the said Associated Professors of Loyola College in the City of Baltimore its successors and assigns only for the purpose of conducting a private educational institution for the university Collegiate or high school education of white persons."
—Loyola College Land Deed, November 30th, 1921.

Introduction

When Loyola College relocated in 1921 from Calvert Street in Baltimore, Maryland, to the Evergreen campus there was an explicit exclusion of Black people who had no area of campus dedicated to their potential to grow, learn, and be educated. This was demonstrated through the covenants set in place with the transfer of the property. This exclusionary foundation was documented in the land deed, cited above, which utilized language from the Roland Park Company covenants.

When asked about the language of the land deed and whether there had been an update to rectify the language, current Chief Financial Officer John Coppola responded via email that the deed had not been updated as of December 2020, and still was an active legal document. This discovery, just over one hundred years after the relocation came through the efforts of Jenny Kinniff, head archivist at the Loyola Notre Dame Library.

Loyola College was not intended for people of color to inhabit the modern-day spaces that exist for education or social-growth experiences. Black staff, faculty, and students still struggle to this day to navigate the institutional barriers of discriminatory white influence among building names and the lack of acknowledgement when it comes to Loyola's foundation. Loyola University Maryland's buildings emphasize racist historical ties with names honoring white supremacists, colonizers, and racists. These buildings were not created to facilitate learning, success, and advancement by students of color. Even when Charles Dorsey Jr., the first full-time African American student, was admitted in 1949, Loyola's willful ignorance towards this larger history along with the exploitative labor of maintaining the campus demonstrates that the school's legacy is tied to slavery.

Constructing the Evergreen Campus

Initially, the college was to be relocated to a site in Guilford in 1915. The deed for that site indicates that Loyola is bound to the "Nuisance" restrictions for Subdivision II of the Roland Park Company's property. The restrictions stated:

At no time shall the land included in said tract or any part thereof or any building erected thereon be occupied by any negro or person of negro extraction. This prohibition however is not intended to include occupancy by a negro domestic servant or other person while employed on or about the premises by the owner or occupant of any land included in said tract.[1]

Thus, not once, but twice did Loyola allow for exclusive language to be written into their land deeds to prevent the presence of Black people, except for servants and workers. However, the first relocation effort did not come without pushback from community partners. A letter to a priest at Loyola in the 1920s noted that "the new locality, on account of its proximity to Johns Hopkins University, will force a comparison between our school and Hopkins, or will emphasize the contrasts between our school

1 Roland Park Company Deed &c to Edward H. Bouton; Land Records of Baltimore City, Liber S.C.L. No. 2829, Folio 1-16, Maryland State Archives, MDLANDREC (https://mdlandrec.net/).

and the University."[2] The concern was that based on the size of Loyola's population and buildings, along with Loyola's Jesuit education compared to Johns Hopkins University. By measuring up the two schools, there was a distinction that Johns Hopkins was perceived to be more 'acclaimed' in appearance and offerings. These concerns from the archdiocese ultimately kept Loyola from building on the property, and the Guilford property was sold by Loyola College in 1931 to the Hospital for the Women of Maryland of Baltimore City. This land deed for that sale stated:

"At no time shall the land included in said tract or any part thereof or any building erected thereon be occupied by any negro or person of negro extraction except as a patient in a hospital or clinic provided however that such patients will not exceed at any one time twenty five per cent (25%) of the total number of patients in said hospital or clinic. This prohibition however is not intended to include the occupancy by a negro domestic servant or other person while employed in or about the premises by the owner or occupant of the land included in said tract."[3]

Even in selling the property, therefore, Loyola continued the practice of excluding Black people from existing anywhere near Baltimore; in this case, in proximity to the college.

On the eventual Evergreen campus, the first building to be built after acquiring the land was Beatty Hall in 1922.[4] Since then, twenty-two buildings have been built on Loyola's campus. However, the story of how the campus came to be begins with the Garrett family mansion. Known today as the Humanities Building, it initially sat on the dirt road that was Charles Street. The mansion, originally called Evergreen Junior, was initially built as a wedding present for Horatio Garrett and his wife Charlotte Garrett, the son of T. Harrison Garrett & Alice Whitridge Garrett.[5] Tragically, Horatio

2 (Baltimore, Maryland, n.d.).

3 Associated Professors of Loyola College in the City of Balto. Deed to Hospital for the Women of MD; Land Records of Baltimore City, Liber SCL 5221 Folio 465-469, Maryland State Archives, MDLANDREC (https://mdlandrec.net/).

4 "Facilities and Campus Services," Buildings - Facilities & Campus Services - Loyola University Maryland, accessed December 19, 2022, https://www.loyola.edu/department/facilities-campus-services/buildings.

5 (Baltimore, Maryland, n.d.).

died of leg cancer on his wedding trip abroad in October 1896.[6] Charlotte never lived in the home, however, and it was ultimately rented to Mr. Wilbur Miller, a close family friend of Horatio's brother, Robert Garrett, from 1912 to 1917.[7] The house was then renovated in November 1917 to be a U.S. Army General Hospital as a donation by Mrs. Garrett, and then transitioned to a center for the American Red Cross inside of the estate.[8] Given that World War I had left more blinded veterans than anticipated, the Red Cross opened various rehabilitation centers across the nation. In 1921, the Garretts sold the Evergreen property, including the mansion to the Jesuits of Loyola. The mansion then served as a residence for Jesuit priests from 1924 to 1992, prior to their relocation to the Ignatius House on Millbrook Road that was purchased by the university in 1956.[9] Yet it was the initial purchase of the mansion that marked the new campus's foundational racism, because it was this transaction that enshrined the 1921 land deed.

Maintaining the Campus[10]

As the Evergreen campus developed, the racism of the land deed manifested itself through the treatment afforded the Black laborers who built and maintained the new college. Black men and women were paid significantly less than their white counterparts, and received no recognition for their work.

In one example of discriminatory treatment, Donald Summerville, a black boy working on the campus in June of 1943, was "arrested by police today… after several articles had been stolen from the rooms of various Fathers while they had been away. A wrist watch… several rare gold coins… a couple of flashlights… After several hours of questioning, the boy confessed," according

6 Lori Beth Finkelstein, "Evergreen Obscurus #2: The Hidden History of Charlotte Bellairs," The Sheridan Libraries University Museums Blog, May 26, 2020, https://blogs.library.jhu.edu/2020/05/evergreen-obscurus-2-the-hidden-history-of-charlotte-bellairs/.

7 (Baltimore, Maryland, n.d.).

8 Lori Beth Finkelstein, "Evergreen Obscurus #2: The Hidden History of Charlotte Bellairs," The Sheridan Libraries University Museums Blog, May 26, 2020.

9 Loyola University Maryland, "Facilities and Campus Services," Buildings - Facilities & Campus Services - Loyola University Maryland, n.d., https://www.loyola.edu/department/facilities-campus-services/buildings.

10 Construction companies that were noted for buildings discussed in this piece include Renwick, Aspinwall, and Russell, the Gant Brunnet Architects, Henry Smith and Sons, and other companies that contributed to the construction of Loyola University Maryland. These companies are bound to be researched in coming years as the narrative regarding potential exploitation is explored.

to William Moloney, S.J, the Father Minister.[11] The minister's diary goes on to detail Summerville's arraignment in Juvenile Court without any follow-up regarding his fate. Summerville's arrest also could not be located in Baltimore records. The Evergreen campus had other Black men and women workers including Ellen Mahoney, Dominic Butler, Alexander (Alex) Briscoe, Madison Fenwick, Matthew Fenwick, George Short, George C. Bush, Thomas C. Burke, and Richard Thompson. All these individuals were either porters, cooks, janitors, servants, or butlers. There are many more individuals in the twentieth century whose stories are lost, and in this erasure, there is a stark contrast with the naming of the buildings at Loyola University Maryland to recognize racists and colonizers. The ideology responsible for this demonstrates how the university was built for white success but not for black appreciation.

The Buildings We Inhabit Today

At the time of his death in June 1930, George Carrell Jenkins was Loyola's largest benefactor.[12] George was the son of Thomas Courtenay Jenkins and Louisa Carrell Jenkins, and Thomas was the director of the Savings Bank of Baltimore and the Merchants-Mechanics' National Bank before his death in 1882, at which point George succeeded him as director.[13] Prior to the younger Jenkins' directorship, he was a soldier in the Confederate army and in his obituary in the Loyola *Greyhound,* was cited as saying he supported the "lost cause."[14] The Lost Cause refers to a retrospective Southern justification for the Civil War, emphasizing that slavery was not one of the main reasons for the conflict; rather, the South sought to protect states' rights and benevolent practices of slavery. George Jenkins today is honored through the name of Jenkins Hall. The space was initially the library of Loyola College. Today, it serves as a space for offices and The Study, where students have a quiet space to review course material.[15] Jenkins also helped to fund the

11 Vol. III, Diary of Fr. Minister, June 28th, 1993, Loyola University Maryland Archives, 66.
12 There is a discrepancy between George Jenkins middle name being 'Carrell' or 'Carroll' based on various city records and Loyola records.
13 "George Carrell Jenkins (1836-1930) - Find a Grave...," Find a Grave, accessed September 2022, https://www.findagrave.com/memorial/104654551/george-carrell-jenkins.
14 "Builder of Loyola's Science and Library Building Ends Long Career of Charity," *The Greyhound,* June 9, 1930.
15 Loyola University Maryland, "The Study," The Study | Loyola University Maryland, n.d., https://www.loyola.edu/department/the-study.

building originally known as the George C. Jenkins Science Center. This building was renamed Beatty Hall after a renovation, and today serves as "a center for career planning and placement offices, for the education department, and for several of the social science departments."[16] Jenkins' donation of this building was made possible by his wealth. While an education could be earned by white persons in this building, there was no similar opportunity for Black students; not until Charles H. Dorsey Jr. was admitted to the college. While the name "Jenkins" harms Black people by celebrating the success of a Confederate sympathizer, Black students still walk alongside and inhabit the building that originally would have never allowed them to step inside. Loyola College chose to accept the turn of a new tide with Dorsey's arrival, but it chose to maintain the legacy of suppression by keeping the name of this building. This ambivalence echoes Loyola's century-long tolerance of the land deed's original racist covenants from 1921 to January 2021. There was a bubbling tension between Dorsey's presence on the campus and the existing white dominance that festered throughout.

Today, George Jenkins is still recognized through the establishment of the Jenkins Society which is "a giving society named for George Carroll Jenkins, one of Loyola's first benefactors."[17] The society promotes this individual without holding him accountable for how his wealth was acquired and how he continued to defend a lost war based on slavery. George Jenkins is only one of at least three problematic building name dedications on the Evergreen campus.

Another controversial figure with a name dedication is Andrew White, a Jesuit missionary who sought to convert native populations in the Maryland colony in the 17th century; the Maryland colony was home to various native peoples that ebbed and flowed as time and circumstances progressed.[18] White was described as "the British Jesuit who landed on Saint Clement's Island in the Potomac, March 25th, 1634, with the first band of settlers in Maryland." His time in the Americas ended when he was

---

16 Varga, *Baltimore's Loyola, Loyola's Baltimore*, 517.

17 "Advancement," Donor Recognition Societies - How to Give - Advancement, accessed December 2022, https://www.loyola.edu/department/advancement/give/recognition-societies.

18 Joseph Banvard, Pioneers of Maryland and the Old French War: With an Account of Various Interesting Contemporaneous Events Which Occurred in the Early Settlement of America (Boston, Massachusetts: Lothrop, 1875).

eventually "arrested and transported back to England in chains," due to the tensions of the English Civil War that had English Catholics working under the Gunpowder Treason Plot to destroy areas of the colony and to suppress the Society of Jesus.[19] The nuanced argument is that Andrew White's colonial practices were horrible, his arrest created an environment of tension due to the lack of peaceful infrastructure through his missionary work, forcing groups to relocate north, or subjecting them to be impacted by disease, along with intertribal and colonial warfare. Andrew White's bigotry and his white saviorism undermined peace for Native Americans, which ultimately cultivated a culture of white dominance that oppressed Native Americans and many other marginalized groups.

Loyola College recognized the Jesuit missionary by dedicating the Andrew White Student Center, a space with four levels that allows for students to gather, learn, and work towards their education. Ironically, Loyola's land acknowledgement is sometimes read aloud at public events in the Andrew White Student Center. The student center was constructed and completed in 1958, 300 years after Andrew White committed his atrocities against natives. The name dedication was based off his work when he "arrived in Maryland aboard the Ark with Lord Baltimore's founding party in 1634 to teach in the Indians." The center was described by former president Vincent F. Beatty as being "the focal point of all campus life and provid[ing] opportunity for better development of understanding between our undergraduates and alumni."[20] The building, initially called the 'Loyola Center,' was funded through a $750,000 dedication from the college.[21] There was no particular finding as to why Andrew White was chosen, other than his association with Lord Baltimore's party and his Jesuit affiliation. White's missionary work, documented in his *Annual Letters of the English Province*, spoke to how Indigenous people "[surrendered] themselves like lambs."[22] While Loyola students did not necessary surrender themselves to

19 "Gunpowder Plot," Encyclopædia Britannica (Encyclopædia Britannica, inc.), accessed December 2022, https://www.britannica.com/event/Gunpowder-Plot
20 Loyola College Alumni Association, "Fr. Andrew White Center Dedicated," n.d.
21 John D. Hackett, "Loyola Student Unit Being Dedicated Sunday: Center Is Named For Jesuit In Lord Baltimore's Party," *Evening Sun*, January 27, 1960, sec. Family, p. 31.
22 "Records of the English Province of the Society of Jesus," Internet Archive (London: Burns and Oates, January 1, 1875), https://archive.org/details/recordsofenglish00fole/page/334/mode/2up.

a Jesuit education, they assimilated into a culture that promoted the success of a colonizer. Students have been taught to "care for the whole person," or Cura Personalis as the phrase is referred to. However, Andrew White is a Jesuit who only cared for the average white Jesuit person.

The findings regarding Andrew White's actions were initially passed on to Loyola's former interim Chief Equity and Inclusion Officer, Dr. Rodney Parker, on March 23, 2022, by a member of Loyola faculty. Regarding this aspect of campus, there has not been an investigation put into motion by the administration.

The concern with the slow-moving investigation into the student center's name was the university's comparatively speedy response to a first-year dormitory named after [Mary] Flannery O'Connor, a Catholic, Southern Gothic author who used racist language in the 1940s, including the word "nigger."[23] Originally, Flannery O'Connor hall was named East Residence Hall for at least two years, presumably 2007-2009, and then was dedicated to the author around 2009 or 2010. It subsequently came to light that in O'Connor's rhetoric, she documented her exposure to the Ku Klux Klan, and even spoke upon her perspective on Black people, stating "I don't *like* negroes. They all give me a pain and the more of them I see, the less and less I like them."[24] In July 2020 Loyola students protested, demanding the removal of her name from the building and the renaming of the building to commemorate a figure with a less controversial past.

Nevertheless, it appears the university was keen on preserving Jesuit figures that may have a controversial past. Arguably from another perspective, it may have been easier to remove the name of a white woman compared to a Jesuit priest. Former university president Father Brian Linnane S.J. (2005-2021) spoke to the National Catholic Reporter in July 2020, stating that "they [students] don't take into account any evolution in her thinking."[25] While Linnane ultimately advocated for a name change, this did not come without his own hesitance and hesitation of those around him. Former

23 Paul Elie, "How Racist Was Flannery O'Connor?," *New Yorker*, June 15, 2020, https://www.newyorker.com/magazine/2020/06/22/how-racist-was-flannery-oconnor

24 Ibid.

25 George P. Matysek, "Amidst Charges of Racism against Flannery O'Connor, Loyola University Maryland Renames Residence Hall," Catholic Review, April 29, 2021, https://catholicreview.org/amidst-charges-of-racism-against-flannery-oconnor-loyola-university-maryland-renames-residence-hall/.

Loyola professor Angela Alaimo O'Donnell was neutral regarding the name change but noted "O'Connor grew up in the virulently racist culture of the American South and could not help but be influenced by that culture."[26] Over 80 individuals along with a Fordham professor signed a petition to retain the Flannery O'Connor name.[27] This blatant, deep-rooted racism is justified by Jesuit individuals as a sign of the times, that a past culture justifies contemporary hate.

Most students from Loyola University today, an institution built and still surrounded by the influences of racism, have not felt inclined to perpetuate racism in their education or actions. Yet, there is some evidence that some students are integrating racism into their education and social actions through their willful ignorance of the policies of the Community Standards that may be ambiguous. For example, students who are educated about the intolerance of the Confederate flag and still have this form of hatred hung in their dorm. There is still an excessive use of derogatory language such as 'white lives matter' and the n-word in public campus spaces, and the Community Standards do not mention the term 'racism' or 'racist,' in any capacity. The 'Bias Related Behaviors Policy' section of the standards states:

"Negative actions against an individual or group because of their actual or perceived race, sex, color, national or ethnic origin, age, religion, disability, marital status, sexual orientation, genetic information, military status, gender or gender identity, any other legally protected classification, or other targeted aspects of one's identity."[28]

Negative actions could range from a variety of behaviors, including giving a person a dirty look or tripping them on the sidewalk. This does not explicitly list out verbiage or language for which people should be held accountable.

Ironically, during President Linnane's tenure, the population of students of color increased, which the president recognized was essential. "About a third of the undergraduate population is made up of minorities," President Linnane stated to the *Catholic Review*, acknowledging that "we can't be a

26 Ibid.
27 Ibid.
28 Loyola University Maryland Community Standards, 2022.

viable university unless we attract a very diverse student population."[29] Yet the presence of the names of racists and colonizers on the campus discounts and undermines the experience of students of color. The overarching concern is that when faced with public shaming by the protests, the university responded quickly, however, internal and private discussion of Andrew White's wrongs did not require a rapid response.

I interviewed Dr. Rodney Parker on December 13, 2022, regarding the process of renaming the first-year building, Flannery O'Connor, to honor Thea Bowman. The goal was to understand the perspective of an administrator when it comes to addressing historical affiliations with racism. The first question focused on the restoration component, asking if the university has ever established a renaming committee to conduct audits on not only Thea Bowman, but for the rest of the buildings on the Evergreen campus. Dr. Parker indicated that he has not heard of one, but that does not mean that it did not exist; there was an allusion to a potential committee with cabinet members but there was no confirmation that one was ever in existence. According to Dr. Parker there was also a lot of transition, interim positions, and shifting, as the administration's focus on keeping the university afloat dominated the pandemic years of 2020 to 2022. When it comes to renaming buildings in general, Dr. Parker emphasized that context is important. Looking at the renaming of Flannery O'Connor, a petition on change.org was published in July 2020, at a time where America was experiencing a tense racial divide following the murder of George Floyd. Broadly, the Black community felt ousted as citizens of the nation. The renaming of the building was reactive, in terms of the quickness of the process, but proactive and responsive because the university could have chosen to take an alternate course and justify not renaming the building. Despite Father Linnane being urged by Angela Alaimo O'Donnell along with signatories of the counter-petition to not rename the building, Father Linnane still spearheaded the initiative and followed through on the decision.

Changing the building name to Thea Bowman is significant because she was a Black Catholic whose work was dedicated to racial and gender

---

29 George P. Matysek, "Amidst Charges of Racism against Flannery O'Connor, Loyola University Maryland Renames Residence Hall," *Catholic Review*, April 29, 2021.

justice in a predominantly white system. A follow-up question to Dr. Parker included why this renaming took place quickly and why a similar urgency was not felt regarding the renaming of the Andrew White Student Center given that the information was passed along on March 23, 2022, and Dr. Parker once again emphasized context of the situation. Dr. Parker's initial tenure as the interim Chief Equity and Inclusion Officer ran only from July 2021 to June 2022, with no guarantee of renewal, and thus prevented him from undertaking projects that would stretch beyond that term. With that, the information provided to Dr. Parker was not credible enough to pass along to the Board of Trustees. Dr. Parker suggested kickstarting a university wide committee that would be dedicated to scanning the diversity, equity, and inclusion environment of Loyola. A prior conversation with President Terrence Sawyer also indicated that he was very open to the proposal, but both Dr. Parker and President Sawyer acknowledged that this was not an administrative priority though there was a willingness to eventually tackle the renaming of buildings. Dr. Parker also emphasized that he wanted to gather more research with the assistance of students and other credible sources to present a concrete proposal that would allow for the initiative to be taken seriously. All in all, there is a call to right the wrongs when it comes to recognizing the environment of Loyola and that this is being taken seriously by President Sawyer's administration.

Conclusion

Over the years Loyola University Maryland has existed, the integration of racism within the construction of the campus has rarely been examined. The truth lies in the walls of the buildings, in the land deeds that had no intention of allowing Black and indigenous populations on the property. Buildings named after George Carrell Jenkins, Andrew White, Mary Flannery O'Connor, and others raise concern as to whether Loyola's advertising of a welcoming, open campus is earnest, as the school fails to do the bare minimum of renaming buildings that honor individuals with ties to the Confederacy, assimilation with indigenous people, and discriminatory rhetoric. Loyola University Maryland needs to rename these buildings and stop perpetuating a culture of exploitation by failing to recognize the staff of today and the staff of the past that worked in low-level jobs with less compensation. By allowing white supremacy to be entwined within the bricks and historic representation, the Evergreen campus cannot be deemed a place of equity and inclusion.

Columbia's Rising

Israel White

Then they said, "Come, let us build ourselves a city, with a tower that reaches through the heavens, so that we may make a name for ourselves; lest we be scattered on the grounds of the earth and the Lord" **– Genesis 11:4**

Given my place in the tower, I admit that I was quite surprised to find that the man I was speaking with, who introduced himself as the "resurrectionist," was religious, as only rationality could have allowed a man to climb such a great height. Instead, he seemed like the type to take pride in manual labor, as his personality was buoyant despite his appearance being sweaty, disheveled and overused. Then again, it was only a floor or so below that a child – a violent, street-urchin one at that – had been able to approach me.

When I saw the poor child, I had been balancing on the line between my face appearing gaunt and revealing any fat, a desirable place to be, an admirable feat. I had managed to lose 20 pounds, at the least, which was fine because I had my lab coat on covering my arms, and my jawline was growing even more pronounced than it was before, my nose more chiseled. However, my skin was unnaturally pale, and I was dehydrated, which had made the climb slightly more difficult. Plus, the halls had soggy floors and were uphill, often filled with bodily fluids up to my hip. The poor child, fat – too fat to expect women to coo over, though his eyes a redeeming pure blue – in torn jeans, a hoodie and a raggedy bowler hat, offered me a bottle of water for my boots and a few dollars. The little maggot of a child was shrewd, eyeing my tongue as it stuck to the inside of my mouth and whitened lips when I told him I would pay him but would not give him my boots. Still asking for them, he doubled the price. $16.

I smiled, partly out of my growing respect for him, partly out of my irritation at his conviction that he could beat me. He grew too eager, casually comparing my hands to the skeletons' around the tower we were in, and as I glared at him, he snatched the $20 bill from me, ripping it. I could have talked him down to $5, so there was a hint of disappointment in my laugh as he ran, tripped over a spinal cord protruding from the staircase, and fell. The cord, along with another to which it was seemingly welded at the base, spun like the two mimicked leaves that would spiral when dropped. Helicopter leaves, I think they were called. The shoddy floor fell through before the poor child had a chance to land, and so he fell through the hole. He kept falling, his scream dying away; the tower was quite the entertainer. I remember staring for a while, then picking up the sharpened bone that the poor child had been carrying, a shank. Turning towards the stairs to continue my ascension, I caught a glimpse of a running man's silhouette. It was unsettling.

"Floor" was not quite accurate; "mass" was more fitting, as the tower – a collection of narrow halls and stairways – was constructed from the decomposing bodies of every negro. The ground, the walls and ceilings of every level as well, all of it. Many parts in different stages of the decay process. For instance, during one attempt to find a way out, as I had momentarily forgotten my purpose for being in the tower, I snapped a stiffening thigh beneath my boot, but on my next step, pressed down into another's chest, still very warm, which fired a teakettle's whistle. It must have been during that temporary retreat that I lost my left boot, as it remained caught between the ribs like a bear trap, and the hissing of the chest continued. I do not remember the sound ever softening however, even as I limped further down the stairs, feeling the strengthening force of the tower's back-and-forth sway. Rather, it felt as though the sound eased into the river of the rest of the towers' moans, adding to the incessant chorus. The hiss punctured any potential the bodies had of harmonizing correctly, but they were out of tune anyway. A waste.

But I was impressed with the builders' work. It was airtight; I had yet to see a crack in the structure revealing any glimpse of outside. I had long since forgotten the feeling of the sun and had come to forget ever seeing it at all, but I was still able to see within the tower. There was generally a warm lighting present, though with no apparent source, which made me uncomfortable. Nevertheless, given the faint lighting, it was rather impressive that I maintained an understanding of how high I had climbed. For some time, I had made sure to note the strength of the tower's teeter, as any structure could be expected to sway farther with an increase in height, of course. This method caused an anxiety, however; mainly because it was too inexact. But my complementary approach was novel, as I instead made note of who I had seen on my way, rather than viewing the tower as a ruler in which to estimate my progress against like the other men. They worried about what floor they were on; this alone informed me of how lowly they were, for only rationale would allow a man to ascend.

The resurrectionist was interesting in that he cared nothing of where he was yet had managed to make it that far. In fact, he could not even remember when exactly he started digging the shallow ditch in the hall from which he spoke to me. Covered in bodily fluids like a butcher or a newborn maybe, holding the broken-off blade of a shovel, he told me that he was digging for a pair of singing slaves, "Carolina Twins." He offered to sell them to me at a discount when I lied and told him that I was a surgeon, my specialty neurology. In truth, I was a medical researcher – though, I made just as much money and had the opportunities to become a surgeon but decided to turn them down. I looked back at him, his head coming up to my boots, his hair wavy, full of faded-orange flakes, and I said nothing. Still offering, he halved the price. "Two-for-one," he joked.

I smiled.

"Come on, brother. Shake on it," he joked once more, reaching his hand out. I flinched, and he then tried to hide his smirk, changing the subject. "So, if you're not in here to buy, what are you here for, Doc?"

"I'm leading a medical team – ambitious younger gentlemen like yourself, actually – to carry out examinations and follow-up procedures on the towers' builders. I was asked to lead on account of a potential viral outbreak among them."

"Hell of a team ya got there." He chuckled but was eyeing me.

"Someone has to carry the equipment."

"And that slows them down. Right, right. But y'all don't stay together? Brother, teams stay together, like a pack, a family. Protects us from the lone."

"I'm not *on* the team. I'm leading it."

"Sorry Doc, I'm a straight shooter-"

"From the hip."

He laughed, shaking, flakes falling from his hair. "From the hip? I haven't heard that, I like that. Shooter from the hip. That's alright. I'll shoot: no offense, but why'd they send a white doctor to go fix some rottin' niggers?"

"They didn't. I was asked to lead check-ins on the builders, not –"

"Exactly, niggers." We stared at one another, and an awkward grin crept across his face. I could tell the bastard was trying not to laugh. "The builders aren't white, Doc. Why would they be white? Genesis says, 'the children of men built the tower'. Does that sound like white men to you?"

"'Genesis'?"

"Oh, Doc...You are lost," he said, genuinely concerned.

The foreigner to sanity was accusing me of being lost. I was not lost. I smiled, "How long have you been digging? If I may ask."

"Well, um, if I had to guess," he paused and peered around him. "Not too sure, um...Let's see, dug nearly half my height, meaning – but no because the ground's been switching from warm and moist to cold and dry." He leaned back on the rim of the ditch, and when he did, I caught a sudden movement above. A chain of loose braids hung from the ceiling, curving downward before curving back up into the mass, and a pair of purple and light-brown feet, a pendant, swung from the chain. "Um...Maybe–"

"No rush, brother," I said. "Grave robbing takes a toll, I know. The time must just fly."

He whipped his head around to look at me, his face reddening. How amusing it was to watch him decipher if I was being spiteful or was simply ignorant. He could not even bring himself back to shoveling entrails. "Now, listen here: the word's 'resurrectionist.' I'm not some damned grave robber; there's respect in what we do, honor and sacrifice even. Whether for professors or postcards, I'm reviving these bodies' potential for purpose, ya hear? Giving life to the dead and helping the living. Plus, way I see it, any buried nigger dead worths more than any lazy nigger alive. But all this time I spend hauling that weight: honest work. And all those slick grave robbers just snatch and go, disappearing quick as a darkie. Grave robbers? Oh no, there's no respect in being them. Bunch of damned vultures playing like coons. Stealing and selling and shit, move to one of their neighborhoods with all that. Hell, you wouldn't have to pay for it. Grave robbers. Would leech off their own if it came to it, the cannibals. Why don't you be a man and get a real fucking job, huh? It's madness. No honesty, no dignity. Nothing. 'Thieves cometh not, but that he may steal, kill, and destroy.' John 10:10. Lord knows."

"Ah yes, a man of faith? I could feel it," my tone charismatic, my smile ingratiating as the man stood in the ditch of intestines proudly.

His innocent nature had returned, "That's the spirit in me, brother. We all got it. Yes, we all got it, even if we don't know it yet." He gave a reassuring smile. "The lost won't be lost for long. God'll put you right where he wants you."

"So you're right where you're meant to be."

"Yup, no doubt about it. We all got a role here, and God led me to this spot," he tapped the rim of the ditch with the shovel head, chipping a protruding ear, "and told me that this is where they are – the Carolina girls. The voice of God, I tell ya, it was something."

He continued, "I must have been wandering for – well, I don't know for how long, and I don't know from where, but I guess it doesn't even matter now. He came to me. I was lost, Doc. Stomping, sloshing around in all these halls. Brother, I'm sure you know the toll. Just all looks the same, the same bodies, the same women, the same crackling sounds, the same smothered screams or howl or whatever the hell that is, and that same sharp smell. Damn, that smell. All of it. Just felt like I was going nowhere. But I wasn't, because when I got here, He told me to stop. Just like that, 'Stop,' He said. I was just surrounded in His voice, almost like a fog or something. But I froze. Damn near had a heart attack. And that's when he told me, 'Relax my son, I am here. They are here.' By 'they' he meant the twins. And I was shuddering, crying my eyes out thanking Him. I asked him if they were still together, and He said, 'Yes, my son. But your shovel will give, your hands will give, your body will give, your mind will give, but let not your soul follow suit. Let your soul follow me. Find them as you have found me, through faith, and let that faith produce works: dig.' Haven't left since."

I let a silence pass, one that seemed meaningful. "Right where you're meant to be."

He nodded, "And it's really just a miracle." The man was an echo chamber of delusion and conviction, but he was useful because of this: such echoes were common among people. He was like a case study I could generalize.

"About as much of a miracle as the freak of nature I'm 'bout to find, brother. A surgeon like yourself, I'm sure I don't have to tell you how much a case like this is worth. Could help a lot of folks. God's plan. God's work. Turned a mutation to a miracle, a freak to a fortune. Hell, that could give even the ol' faggots some hope. You ever cured one of them, Doc? Of the 'disturbance' I hear's the 'polite' word for it now."

I winced, clutching the shank in my pocket; it irritated me that he thought I was in psychology, and it disgusted me that he thought I worked with homosexuals. I corrected him, slowly, "I'm a surgeon, no. And they're too risk-"

"Right. Devil's doing. Can't treat that sick shit. But even then, you know, I try to keep faith in that whole 'kill the gay in him and save the man' thing, but brother, where do you draw the line between illness or whatever and personal responsibility? Way I see it – hell, the way it is, a diagnosis is not a pass."

While it was true that I had not dealt with any homosexuals personally, I would go on to encounter two, one young and lost, the other old and paralyzed. When I met the young one, effeminate, he approached me in the stairwell leading into my flooded dead-end hallway. I had been floating on my back for a while, in and out of a sort of sleep. One might say unconsciousness, but even buried in this respite, I found no escape from that dog-whistle hiss of the tower, nor its beastly stench. When I would wake, I lied still, staring up through the gaping hole in the hallway's ceiling, a view not unsimilar to one's view from the bottom of a well or the bottom of a trash chute. Of a grave? No, more like the view from the inside of a throat, possibly.

Gray and mustard-yellow specks at the other end, teeth possibly, stared down at me, the tower's sway rocking me back and forth, and I stared back, floating. How far the tunnel led, I felt I could never be sure.

But, one particular time, at the teeth's end of the tunnel, the silhouette of a man—of a desirable height and well-built—shot out looking down on me, and he reached his hand over the pit, dropping something. It took over a minute to reach me, so while I eventually could tell that it was a piece of paper, some time had passed before I could make out any specifics. The silhouette disappeared, the scrap fluttered into my hand, and it was the other half of my ripped $20 bill.

I then heard the echoes of the young one's patter and squishes falling down the stairs, and I swam towards the bottom step where my lab coat lay, still clutching the bill. The left sleeve was covered in blood, largely dry, but I could simply tell him that it came from the tower. I considered severing one of the bodies' arteries and bathing the entire coat to evade suspicions concerning why it was only on the sleeve, and only one sleeve at that. However, reaching down to pick up the coat made me dizzy, and I wanted to pass out when I merely thought of the effort needed to break the thick skin with the shank. He was sniffling, 16 maybe, a match in hand and a mammary vest almost as pale as himself tucked under his arm. "E-Excuse me sir, excuse me. Good d-day. How are you?"

"Fine. You?"

He was trembling, wide-eyed. It was unseemly. "Sir, you don't ha-happen to know where the exit is, do you? I've been here for– I've honestly no idea. But-but I fear my wa-wardrobe may rot too soon, and I really can't lose this. I've already lost my-my hat to some kid with this white knife thing –"

"It wasn't a rhetorical question," I said, emotionless. I drew my finger along the shank in my pocket, flakes of dry blood falling off the blade; it was still cold. Nothing of my demeanor had changed from the time I began listening to him to then. I felt hollow, hollow with an air of faint sadness. He, and everything he said, was just so helplessly unimportant. But I also did not want him to leave, which revealed to me a growing, familiar disgust inside. And the familiarity of this disgust healed, though slightly.

"Wha-excuse me?"

"I'm fine. *How are you?*"

"Oh, I'm well? I'm sor-apologize. I'm well. I apologize. My name's Harris."

"Thank you. Now, you were saying?"

"Y-yes, of course. If I lose the wardr-drobe, everyone's gonna be mad at me. I've been losing everything though, my g-group, my hat, and – and I don't know what's wrong with my smell – my sense of smell – it's gone too. Forgive my stuttering. It's sim-simply just too cold. But sir, do you know where the exit is?"

I was scowling, weakly, and he must have noticed as he quickly began to explain, fiddling with the vest, "Oh, sir no, no. This is for a show; I'm wearing it *for a show*. I don't do that type of stuff, sir," he said, chuckling nervously. "I mean, not that-not that there's, like, anything wrong with that? But for me it's just for a minstrel. For the little or-orphans, the St. Vincent Asylum ones you know? It's our second annual one. A pretty big deal. I'm playing – well I wouldn't want to take up your time with de-details," he said with a hint of shy excitement soon drowned in childish panic. "But yes, the exit, do you know where I might find the exit?"

I stared at the little hysteric in silence. "Sir, please, Mr. Ziegfield might replace me if I'm not back in time! Hey, wait, I'll prove it to you actually. Almost forgot," he tried to hand the match to me, but I backed up, partly because I did not want to make contact, partly because I did not want to risk him spitting on me speaking. He instead tucked it between a gap in the teeth of a part of the wall, before digging into his trench pocket and pulling out what seemed to be the shadow of a droopy circle. He held it up to the fire. It was a thick-lipped, mustached face with decently-stitched dark skin. The nose was upturned, which I thought was funny, though I doubt the irony was on purpose given the young one wasn't nearly as shrewd as the literature had made his type out to be.

But what made it even funnier was the mixture of confusion, relief, and hope draped across the young one's face as I began grinning at him, saying nothing. The sheer silence of the moment was just picking on him too – it was a joy, it felt like the silence was in on this little game.

"My dear boy, you're a performer. I'm convinced. A *performer*: a fine young man."

"Yes, thank you sir! Now, the exi-"

"My dear boy, might I ask you a question?" and I couldn't help but smile wider at the teary-eyed pity.

"Of course."

"My dear boy, why do you know how to sew?"

Despite how it may have appeared, I was pleased to have him perform for me. It was interesting, a warm taste to contrast the clanging frankness of the resurrectionist. Both sheep to different gods but, unlike homosexuality, I did not view religion as something to be cured but rather as a cog in a vetting process of dominance. If one is determined to be a sheep, let them. Natural selection will find them soon enough. (Or rather, whatever god they picked will put them where they are meant to be.) The distinction between the resurrectionist and myself lay partly in that idea: natural selection. Whereas he genuinely believed in the absurdities that are the manifest destinies, drapetomanias, and innate racial superiority, I simply viewed them as influential narratives, teeth sharpened to be more effective than the dull ones of other animals. Those other animals, whether dead or soon to die, would and will continue to pile, forming the ground, the stairs, and the structure of the world the head leads. Such principles and biases that the resurrectionist and his kind boasts are nothing more than chains, bits, and pacifiers. There can be no principle, no mindset, no emotion, no physical factor, no fear, no person nor dependency, no boundary – whether one's own or another's – that keeps one from rising. Given that the world's resurrectionists define humanity by such factors, it is of no surprise that there can be no humanity either, the crippling foundational flaw of them all.

The shackles of the resurrectionists, the "us," faith, and honesty did not and will not apply to me. And, I have no idea what happened to the young homosexual following our conversation.

The resurrectionist was also interesting in that he provided a feeling of security for myself, even with the constant threat of the tower's sway. And I think it was because he was content overall; in his hole of limbs and intestines, I understood exactly who he was, and there was no reason to believe he would ever change. A predictable, stable rung, and a rung among many. But of course, if one's poor white man is fussy, give him a black man and call him a nigger, if the black man is fussy, give him a homosexual and call him a faggot, and of course, the women and whatever else will fall where they may, but every overseer is a slave and every slave an overseer. To use the resurrectionist's understanding: God is to white is to black, as enslaver is to overseer is to enslaved.

So another breeze of calmness swept over me when I heard him say, "We might be poor, but at least we ain't black,' that's what my grandfather would always say. And I listened to him too. Different times back then, brother. Had order."

And he continued, with the same foundational contentment, "Kids these days are getting bold, new niggers are getting too comfortable. And you know what I think? I think it's because we've gone too soft on them. Yes sir, too soft. See, it all starts when you choose mercy, sparing the rod, when you try to bless 'em with one fewer lash, God knows. Tell me Doc, let's see if you can diagnose the problem here: how did we go from whipping niggers for reading at night to teaching niggers to read at night school?"

Although I found him amusingly average, this was a valid question, and I was genuinely curious as to what his answer might be. "Any thoughts?" I asked.

"Brother, I could give a whole dissertation on it. As far as that whole night school thing, I got two words for ya, two: money and war," he said, shaking his head. "That's what my grandfather always said. Said there wasn't a problem in the world that couldn't be explained by money, war or both. See, we started listening to money and stopped listening to God. We all went off to war, right, and so the schools started losing customers basically, started losing money, but rather than exercise faith, schools turned to the next market: the darkies. We got scared. We got scared, I tell you. Slaveholding kept us close to God, but we got scared. A fucking shame. Teaching the servants of the so-called servants. Order…" he trailed off, shaking his head. "I miss my grandfather."

"He died?"

"Maybe. I have no idea how long I've been in here," he sat down, his back against the back of another, flakes trailing down his shoulders. He looked up at me, "Only got ourselves to blame really. Know what I read this one time? Happened up in New York. This nigger, young one – but damn sure old enough to know better – this nigger stole some candy and soda or something from a store, right, then – listen here – had the fucking nerve to whistle at a little white girl, comely, on his god damned way out. Can you believe that shit? It's scary, you know. Wha-just what happened?"

Another appropriate silence passed, and I was about to ask what the girl looked like, but the resurrectionist spoke first, "But Doc, as sure as I sound, I will admit, sometimes my faith wavers just as much as this tower. But with all the time I've spent thinking, I figure both are just God reminding us of His power, from the beginning to the end, lest we forget our place in the now, you know? Lest we forget His supremacy. His image isn't his power, and doubt keeps the heart humble, I guess.

But yeah, sometimes I worry I'm on the wrong floor, hell, sometimes I even worry I'm in the wrong tower. But, it's not my place to *know* –"

"There's one tower. What do you mean '*wrong tower*'? There's only one. Who told you there were more?"

"God."

Jesus fucking Christ, I thought. But I could feel the mere possibility of more towers, higher towers, unscrewing my certainty. Given all the research I had ever done on the sick-minded, I should have stayed wary of how contagious delusions could be. I entertained him for too long but needed reassurance.

Delusions could strengthen a man, I told myself; challenging the delusion is an exercise. Strengthening the mind. Even I had a delusion concerning the tower. With its every lean back and forth, the delusion that it could fall rolled around in my mind. It was something to overcome.

He continued, "That's in the Bible. Right there in Genesis. The *children of God*, remember," he said chuckling a bit, giving an annoying smirk. I was tempted to pick up the shovel shaft and beat him with it. I imagined myself swinging until he blended with the mass below him. "The children of God made the tower from tar – hence '*tar*' skin, babies – and whatnot," he explained, gesturing towards the blackening brown patches peeling off of his shovel head, "but you have to read carefully, brother, with no personal interpretations. No assumptions. Notice: God didn't destroy the tower. God didn't reprimand the children, the men, nor the growing name of the men. He let the tower stand. He let the men's name live on, right?" He paused, looking at me intently, and I grew even more agitated not knowing what he was looking for. I just stood still, as still as I could manage. The tower began leaning towards the other side, and the shovel shaft rolled into the ditch like it was hollow; it was too light.

"Ah, you don't believe me? Well brother, I've been wrong before, but where does it say God destroyed the tower? Where does it–"

"Oh, oh. No, yes, you're right. It doesn't say that. It's been a while since I've read it. I was thinking. Trying to remember. Carry on."

"Right...Right, well most miss those details anyway. Some say God changed up all the languages to keep man from building the tower, but again – Bible doesn't contradict. That same chapter says, 'the people *is* one,' and the language we use doesn't define what 'one' we're a part of. You see? English, German, Spanish, still one. No, no, God switched up all the languages because the words we'd use to build this tower together here, aren't the same ones we'd need to build a tower somewhere else. If there are flood risks here, for example, but earthquakes there, we need different language concepts, different words, to explain how to work around that, right?

155

He gives everything you need to be everything you're meant to be. Everything. And rest assured brother, that's in the Bible. Genesis 9:3."

I could feel myself shaking, a headache washing over. My eyes flickered and given the speed of my mind, he seemed to be speaking so fucking slowly. "Others – do others say there are more towers? Have you *seen* others."

"Other towers or other people?"

"Either, Mr. Resurrectionist. Either."

"Brother, everyone I've talked to says there are other towers. Haven't seen other towers, least from what I can remember. Maybe you and one other guy, a surgeon too actual-"

"There is no other surgeon."

"What do you mean?"

"Surgeons, there are no others. I am the surgeon. I was – I was sent."

"Again, why wouldn't there be more? You said there was an outbreak or something right? There was a whole team of them, a long, long time ago, before I stopped here even. But I think it was only one, actually, saying that there are more towers. The others laughed at him, went on their separate ways. But yeah Doc, there are definitely more."

"I need – I have to go. To collect my group. I um – goodbye."

"Okay brother, good, good. God bless. It's good to stay tog-"

"And God be with you. Too, I mean."

Dizzy, I bust through the first exit I had seen, a bead curtain of rope-like hair. Just trying to escape the resurrectionist, I ran down the cramped hall and kept running, my coat catching onto bones jutting out of the walls. Clearly, I thought, the man was insane. He hallucinated the surgeons. His god gave him those surgeons; why would someone so high up stop to even glance at some poor, god-fearing field hand? Some nigger's nigger? It was irrational. But the delusions continued spilling into my thoughts, and the silhouette – I could not help but think that the shadow of the man on the stairs must have been the surgeon. The silhouette that dropped the bill from above must have been the surgeon too, or one of them – if there were more – which I knew at the time but had since forgotten. As rationality would have it, I concluded in the cramped hall, I could continue my path of ascension, not letting the episodes of some escaped patient interrupt. I kept running.

Bones in the brightening deep-green and maroon mass weaved like roots before jutting out and turning back into the ground. I kept running. My chest burned, my throat too, a throbbing stabbed at my side. My boots pounding the ground, but completely silent. Even when I stepped on one of the bodies, snapping it, losing my footing, no sound came about. I tried to regain my balance, stomping once more, but that foot sank deeper into the mass. I was sweating, the only heat I could feel was that of my sunken leg, clawed by whatever buried bones I could not see. I remember yelling. For someone's assistance. But the high-pitched siren sound building in my ears was too heavy to lift, my voice crushed beneath it, silent. It bothered me that I could feel my quick breathing but could not hear it. "Come back! Please, please come back!" I remember yelling – though not to anyone in particular, but rather begging the sound of my own breath. "Where did you go?" I hollered. Someone was pouring the feeling of numbness inside of my arm, it felt, so that it started at my fingertips slowly filling up my forearm, my bicep, and then eventually crawling up my neck and jaw. I do not remember how long I was there, but my leg sank farther. So far that I could not see it below my knee but could feel fluttering lashes caressing a clawed part of my shin. Ahead of me, there was only more hallway. Just as cramped. On either side of me were sets of tanned hides hanging slightly parted like curtains against the wall. Presented in the middle of the right set was a "face," though it had no jaw, no lips, and few teeth. Its uvula hanging abnormally low, a frozen pendulum before the cavernous throat thing. The "mouth" boasted an icy appearance with the way the light shot off the coating saliva. In the middle of the left set was the leg of a man. The tar skin was pulled up like a sleeve, revealing an artery throbbing softly, but the sound of the pulse felt like it was whispering to me, trying to tell me something. It gradually grew louder, as if the walls were getting closer as to channel the pulse's echo towards me. I did not know what it was trying to tell me, and I think it knew this because it kept getting louder. I covered my ears, but then a body heat slowly circled them, and I kept reassuring, promising – to

157

whom I am not completely sure – that the heat was not mine, but with each flush of the foreign heat streaming in my ears, matching the bruit rhythm of the artery, it felt like it was screaming and the screams felt like they were burning, and I broke down, unsure of what to tell it. But rather than hearing myself, I heard the calls of another behind me, faint beneath the siren sound, and I turned.

Behind me there was the braid curtain, but it was in arm's reach. Confused, I grabbed one of the strands and pulled myself out.

It must have been the resurrectionist screaming, or more likely the surgeon taunting, I considered. I stumbled back through the curtain, but rather than entering the resurrectionist's hall, I nearly tripped down an empty stairway. Defeated, I hobbled down.

But even then, my ears popped, meaning I had to have been up very high. My ears had been popping during the whole episode, but I must not have realized on account of my bathing in the delusions of the mad. I showed an improved resistance, however, during my encounter with the second homosexual. This one's appearance was unsettling, as he lay aged and confined to where was, glued to the ground like gravity's pet.

And although his appearance was unsettling, I remember the extreme humidity of the room more than anything else; everywhere I looked everything was wavy, moving. The watery whites, maroons, and purples oozing from the ceiling wriggled as they fell. I remember wondering if I would go so far as to remove my coat if I were sweating as much as I thought I should be. I would not. But the ground against my soles was painfully dry, as though the ground itself was a callus.

The walls of the room also stood out, as the builders' construction of them proved frugal, efficient, and meticulous, so much so that I came to remember the room as "The File Cabinet." The walls of The File Cabinet consisted of neatly stacked repurposed bodies – first dismembered, then disemboweled – each serving as drawers for limbs and entrails, each like a womb of parts. Different drawer sizes housed different organs. For instance, the one I studied in particular was that of a very dark woman with bite marks on her neck, who likely entertained a whorish appetite before she died; rather than storing something like short bones inside of her, the builders saved her for deflated lungs and intestines. They even managed to prevent spillage; crowns of stitches and staples marked the heads of each, as well as glued eyelids and lips, and a plaque clogging all other orifices. However, for the opening of each torso, a patching of excess skin was utilized.

The only difference between the walls lay in that the one opposite of me had a gargoyle, a boy's head, mounted on whereas the others did not. Below it, the old homosexual lay on his back, confined to where he was, an emaciated waste of pale skin and bones that was truly uncomfortable to look at.

"There's a second doctor," I had told him, "a surgeon, a medical assistant of mine – that may have passed through here. We're headed upward but had gotten separated. Do you remember seeing him or speaking with him perhaps, sir? He's slightly shorter than me, and almost – but not quite – my build."

"Oh, are you not the surgeon?" The old man spoke with a low gravelly voice.

"I am, yes. He's my assistant."

"And he got ahead of you? Student becomes the teacher, aye?" he chuckled weakly before a slight coughing fit. "Mark of a good team."

"Well, not that far ahead. And, I had stopped to help a homeless child, you see."

"Really? That's good. That's good. But yes, I did see your guy, but, um, I don't want to waste time on directions so how familiar are you with the tower? Where've you been?"

"The bottom 6 floors, the flooded hall with the hole in the ceiling, a private entertainment room, and then some areas are too difficult to differentiate, as I'm sure you know."

"'Private entertainment room'?"

"No, an entertainment room that was private. It had a makeshift sofa inside; a man was watching the wall like a television. That type."

"Wait, wait, so you haven't been to The Privacy?"

The Privacy was a room, about twice as wide as the File Cabinet, with closets in which women's lower halves hung low enough from the ceiling.

159

Surprisingly well kept, all had their nails a pure red, and all were properly waxed, with the exception of those in need of another coat, hair removal, or cleaning. Those were detached from their cords and placed on the mound of tangled legs outside of The Privacy's door. The only people who had not visited were thought to be the Harrises and – as the resurrectionist called them – the "nigger lovers." Even then, however, it was still crude to ask someone if they had been. But I figured the old man was testing me to see if I was a homosexual, and I responded, suavely, "My assistant got ahead of me for a reason. What can I say?"

The old man paused, staring upward, his easiness gone and his face difficult to read. "You've gotten very high, Doctor."

I was not sure what he wanted from me, but I could not jeopardize my chances of getting directions to the surgeon, directions upward. I figured complimentary and dignified would suffice, "And you as well, of course."

"You sound impressed," he mumbled, as if speaking with himself rather than me. My patience burning away, I walked to the left wall and examined the drawers, slowing my breathing.

"Sir, I would hate to be rude, but I'm in a rush –"

"Right, right. Your virus outbreak to handle, of course." I turned, studying him as he continued, dispirited, "Your assistant wasn't going up, Doctor. He came and left, but he was going down, right out the door you came in. Going to the fifth floor, he said. In quite the hurry too."

I kept my composure, but the old man caused great anxiety; I did not understand where he had heard of some outbreak, could not know if he had actually seen the surgeon, and if he had seen him, why the surgeon would be going *down*. Even more so, I understood that I was relying on the memory of someone equivalent to a conscious corpse; bed sores, dementia, and isolation defined my guide.

He continued, "You haven't heard about a, um, Deoine, Deoine Moore, have you?"

Trying to keep him in the present, I replied, "I trust my assistant will be able to make it back here, so would you mind just giving me the directions upward? Might there be a particular drawer to open or perhaps, a ladder somewhere, sir?"

"You wouldn't have remembered Deoine anyway," his voice cracking, shaking like the walls and the fluids from the ceiling. His attempt to keep from crying was irritatingly pitiful; the grown man could not even wipe the few escaped tears. "You wouldn't have even known it was him. You wouldn't. None of you would. But I'll know. I promise I'll know." With perfectly still eyes, the gargoyle above him began gagging. The eyes reddening but never closing, even as bags swelled beneath them, its crow's feet deepening. The gagging strengthened to choking. The old homosexual stretched out his neck, shutting his eyes, slowly rubbing his cheek against the wall. The gargoyle coughed once more, and a woman's severed hand escaped, its fingers stiff, splayed, all bent in various places as if each finger had extra joints above the knuckle and then above the regular joints. It too was unsightly. The hand fell – or lowered rather – like a spider descending with a strand of web, or as a scalp might with a thick cloud of breath beneath it, onto the old one's hand. "Thank you," he mouthed, before breaking into a cycle of intelligible speech and hysterical whispery laughs. "Deoine was – is my husband, best friend."

It was frustrating trying to understand him, but I caught enough of what he said to see what he was after and how it could help. "My condolences –"

"Don't – ju – don't say anything else. Please, please just stop talking."

"I know this must be hard for you, but I can help you look for him on the upper floors. If I find him, I can bring him back. Deoine, right?"

He whipped his head around glaring at me, gnashing the few teeth he had in his mouth. He whispered something, and the mass beneath his back, neck, and head rose and turned him so that he was sitting up, facing me.

Although I was caught off guard that he could control the tower, it was my sheer lack of understanding that won over me, and I glared back. But I managed a strained smile as I spoke, "I can help you, help you look. But is there any particular reason that you haven't already used – used *this* to carry you throughout the tower? If I don't need to go ahead up looking for you, and I can just go ahead up, I need you to articulate that."

"What makes you think," he said slowly, "that just because I'm okay in this room, means I'm okay in every room?" A wave of exhaustion swept across his face. He closed his eyes, lying his head back on the mound. "We listened to your whole conversation with the resurrectionist, and, to me, you were just so strange. You just listened, you didn't agree, and it was almost like you didn't even exist in the conversation at all. You were just there. You were strange to read." He opened his eyes, looking up at the gargoyle above, "I really didn't want to see you."

He paused and started crying, again, his breathing shaky, and he whispered, "I just, I want my best friend back. I really, really do…"

The gargoyle's eyes shifted toward me, and it spoke with a child's voice, though quiet and calm, that seemed to flood the entire room, "Go. When you walk out of the door you came in, a stairway upward will be waiting for you."

Cautiously, I walked backwards to the door, and as I opened it, I could hear the old homosexual's voice, "I'm sorry, I just – I don't want to go without him, and everyone's a reminder of what could have happened to him. I just want –"

I stepped out, and the door closed behind me. But rather than a stairway at all, it was another cramped hallway, with neither an incline nor a decline, the same cramped hall that I had been in before, though I could not be sure. Ahead of me there was only more hallway, and then behind me, there was only more hallway.

Evergreen Pastures: Upholding Jesuit White Supremacy on Loyola's Stages

Lucy Marous

How an institution entertains people is indicative of its values, and Loyola University Maryland's theater department is no exception. Looking at performances of *Othello* and *The Green Pastures* put on by the drama society, this essay traces the history and evolution of racist theatrical performances at Loyola. Loyola students performed minstrel shows throughout the late nineteenth and early twentieth centuries. With these shows, Loyola's theater department used performance as a tool to teach a long-held Jesuit value: white supremacy. In 1908, Loyola performed Shakespeare's *Othello*, erasing the titular character's Blackness. In the 1950s, Loyola's theater department put on shows with racist depictions such as *The Green Pastures* and *The Emperor's Doll*. The latter, a play done in yellowface, won the department an award in a Jesuit collegiate play competition. Loyola's various drama clubs, with support from both outside institutions and their own students, have historically prioritized upholding the Jesuit value of white supremacy over the harm caused by racist practices, including blackface.

From the beginning, racism has been a large part of Loyola's theatrical history. Though most of their early productions were the works of Shakespeare, Loyola students performed minstrel shows throughout the late nineteenth and early twentieth centuries. A primary form of entertainment at the time, minstrelsy's presence at Loyola was not as shocking as the motivations behind it.

Loyola's theater organizations have a history of performing minstrel shows dating back to the mid-nineteenth century, but the practice's continuation into the twentieth century, especially after the admission of Black students, proves just how ingrained racism was in Loyola's culture. In 1908, Loyola performed Shakespeare's *Othello* while erasing the main character's Blackness. The omission of Othello's racial identity is a prime example of Loyola's theater department using performance as a tool to teach a long-held Jesuit value, white supremacy. More broadly, white supremacy at Loyola was the idea that white Catholic students were the only ones who belonged there and deserved to learn. Being a part of the college's larger community meant adhering to their values, and the offerings of the school were curated to foster that. For extracurriculars, this can be seen in Loyola limiting the experiences of their students so that their worldview remained small and centered on the white and Catholic population.

In the case of Loyola and its theatrical history, white supremacy takes on the meaning of prioritizing white stories or using stories and depictions of people of color to uphold the dominance of white Catholics at Loyola. The theater department continued this tradition into the 1950s by performing shows with racist depictions. Students supported this horrific action by featuring photographs of the blackface done in *The Green Pastures* in their yearbook, and writing newspaper articles about the performance of *The Emperor's Doll*, a play done in yellowface. Loyola's various drama clubs have historically prioritized upholding the Jesuit value of white supremacy over the harm caused by racist practices, including blackface.

Minstrelsy was arguably the most popular form of entertainment in the nineteenth and early twentieth centuries. In "Deconstructing the Blackface Minstrel Show," Juyan Zhang and Wei Lu write "the popular blackface minstrel show started from a white's intentional borrowing from a black."[1] Beginning in the mid-nineteenth century, these shows developed and

---

1 Juyan Zhang and Wei Lu, "Deconstructing the Blackface Minstrel Show, (Re)constructing African American Identity: the Case of Olio by Tyehimba Jess" *Critical Sociology*, Vol. 48 (2022): 833, https://journals.sagepub.com/doi/pdf/10.1177/08969205211052616

featured white actors blackening their faces with burnt cork and performing mocking songs and skits.[2] This style of performance resulted in caricatures that perpetuated harmful stereotypes about Black people and led to the development of the vaudeville industry. Although it has its roots in British theatrical tradition, the blackface minstrel show is native and unique to the United States. The commonality of this practice exemplifies the racist foundation that our country sits on. With its widespread presence, it comes as no surprise that those values seep into our educational systems as well. Writers Emma Pettit and Zipporah Osei discuss the commonality of blackface's presence on college campuses and how it highlights racism in those spaces: "racism doesn't manifest itself in hatred alone. It's reflected in the pleasure that white people, including college students, take in mimicking and mocking other races."[3] Racism as seen in performance art was a general facet of collegiate theater departments, so Loyola's participation does not come as a surprise. These expressions of racism in performance are important to examine, because the art one creates and consumes reflects their culture. Loyola openly practicing racism in its extracurriculars made the college's historic stances on issues of race very clear to its students and to the world at large.

Looking back at blackface before its American roots, Zhang and Lu assert that "It can be certain that it is Shakespeare who popularized [blackface] in his play *Othello* in 1604."[4] Loyola's 1908 production of *Othello* is a perfect demonstration of the ties between racism and theater at the institution. *The Loyola Annual* from 1908 describes the production, particularly taking time to praise the actor playing the titular role. The piece notes that Mr. Mantell played Othello "not as an Ethiopian, but as a Moor, not as black, but as tawny."[5] Despite the overwhelming whiteness of the Shakespeare canon matching their demographics, Loyola chose to put on a play about

2 Juyan Zhang and Wei Lu, "Deconstructing the Blackface Minstrel Show, (Re)constructing African American Identity: the Case of Olio by Tyehimba Jess" *Critical Sociology*, Vol. 48 (2022): 826, https://journals.sagepub.com/doi/pdf/10.1177/08969205211052616

3 Pettit, Emma, Osei, Zipporah, "The 'Great College-Yearbook Reckoning': Why Scholars Say Blackface Images Aren't Outliers," The Chronicle of Higher Education, February 7, 2019. https://www.chronicle.com/article/the-great-college-yearbook-reckoning-why-scholars-say-blackface-images-arent-outliers/ (accessed October 19, 2022).

4 Zhang and Lu, "Deconstructing the Blackface Minstrel Show" 826.

5 Loyola University Maryland, *The Loyola Annual* (Baltimore, Maryland: 1908), Page 5, Loyola Notre Dame Library (LNDL) Archives, https://archive.org/details/loyolaannual00loyo/page/n5/mode/2up?view=theater, accessed on October 19, 2022.

a Black man and remove his Blackness. The author's review of the show praises Mantell for having the right deep voice and "stalwart" demeanor to play the role, calling his performance "wonderful" and "far superior to that of the Ancient."[6] In their praise for his performance as Othello, the author attributes Mantell with two traits that are thought to make him a good fit to play a Black man: his deep voice and his willingness to serve. Neither trait is necessary to play the character of Othello, but the aspect of servitude aligns with historical views of how a Black man should act towards white counterparts and the voice perpetuates the stereotype of the Black brute.[7] This perspective showcases how the Loyola theater department prioritized perceived Blackness over physical Blackness, a viewpoint that perpetuated the racism present in Loyola's culture.

The other point of contention in this portrayal is how the performance treats the religious background of the character. Examining Othello's religion, the yearbook cites the production of *Othello* as focusing on the titular character's place in society as a Moor. Erin Blakemore's "Who were the Moors?" examines the label in Elizabethan times, stating that the term Moor refers to "Muslims living in Europe. Beginning in the Renaissance, 'Moor' and 'blackamoor' were also used to describe any person with dark skin."[8] In the play, Othello is defined by his status as a Moor, both ethnically and religiously. When examining his race, he is repeatedly referred to as Black, even being called "the blacker devil" by his wife's maid Emilia in the fifth act.[9]

Religiously, Othello is born Muslim and has converted to Christianity. Although he identifies as a Christian, this is not accepted by wider society and Othello is repeatedly referred to as simply "the Moor," making it clear that his differences in race and religion are his defining features. The play emphasizes this by frequently using animalistic imagery when describing Othello, equating his Blackness and being non-Christian with being non-human. Loyola's choice to cast a white actor as Othello is prioritizing

6 Ibid.

7 Billy Hawkins, "The White Supremacy Continuum of Images for Black Men." *Journal of African American Men* 3, no. 3 (1998): 7–18. http://www.jstor.org/stable/41819337

8 Erin Blakemore, "Who were the Moors?," *National Geographic* (December 12, 2019). https://www.nationalgeographic.com/history/article/who-were-moors. Accessed on November 8, 2022..

9 William Shakespeare, *Othello*. Barbara Mowat, Paul Werstine, eds. Folger Shakespeare Library. Accessed on October 19, 2022. Washington, DC: Folger Shakespeare Library. https://shakespeare.folger.edu/downloads/pdf/othello_PDF_FolgerShakespeare.pdf

Jesuit values both by upholding white supremacy with the erasure of the character's Blackness and championing Catholicism. By focusing on the alienation and discrimination Othello faces as a non-Christian, Loyola's production presents a white Catholic view of the world as the only way one can live happily.

Loyola's racist theatrical practices persisted through the mid-twentieth century. While the production of Othello chose to erase Blackness, the midcentury brought productions that featured Blackness, but a misrepresentation steeped in stereotypes born from racism. The most horrifying example of these distortions of Black stories is Loyola's 1956 production of Marc Connelly's *The Green Pastures*. This play retells stories of the Bible in the setting of the Deep South with a cast of all-Black characters. The author's note in the 1929 edition of the script states that the play is "an attempt to present certain aspects of a living religion... that of thousands of Negroes in the deep South."[10] While the story seemingly centers Black experiences and spiritualism, it was written by a white man and has the perspective of American white supremacy. Curtis J. Evans writes in "The Religious and Racial Meanings of *The Green Pastures*," that while "*The Green Pastures* addressed certain psychological and spiritual needs of whites, it also masked deep fears about the movement of blacks into the urban North."[11] *The Green Pastures* was written for a white audience and caters to their desires and worries. The play focuses on the religious background of its storytelling more so than accurately portraying the lives of Black people, giving context to Loyola's reason for performing it. Despite the original Broadway production of *The Green Pastures* having an all-Black cast, Loyola's 1956 production used an all-white cast performing in blackface.[12] The write-up of that theatrical season titled "Dramatics" details that year's performances and focuses on the production. Bordered by photographs of students onstage in blackface, the piece discusses how *The Green*

---

10 Marc Connelly, *The Green Pastures*. New York: Farrar and Rinehart, 1929. https://archive.org/details/green-pastures0000marc_m3m2/page/4/mode/2up

11 Evans, Curtis J. "The Religious and Racial Meanings of The Green Pastures," *Religion and American Culture: A Journal of Interpretation*. 18 (2009): 60. https://eds.p.ebscohost.com/eds/pdfviewer/pdfviewer?vid=15& sid=aa0952a2-2f6a-4507-9181-6a4ad5d5e219%40redis

12 Ibid 61.

Pastures was a big hit with students, having "a wealth of audience appeal."[13] Although it was a selection of scenes rather than a full length performance, the yearbook notes that the production still had a cast of twenty eight, a choir, and a band. The scale of the production proves just how much Loyola was willing to put in the effort to make this a show that would impress the student body. The section ends with the note that the play was entered into a competition and lost. The loss at the Jesuit One Act Play Contest may be a footnote, but the play's being thought highly of enough to enter the contest at all displays white supremacy's reign over theatrical entertainment at Loyola.

Looking more broadly, Loyola's theater department participating in racism was rewarded within the Loyola culture at large. Racism was a practice deeply rooted in the organization, and students were incentivized to take part. The theater group clearly preferred the students who participated in artistic demonstrations of white supremacy. After playing Othello, Mantell was rewarded with being cast as many of Shakespeare's other leading men. Mantell was not the only student put in this position: all actors' past performances were considered in the casting process. The theater department's institutionalized white supremacy was present within the student body, but was even more on display at the top of the group's hierarchy. The *Loyola Annual* yearbook of 1908 notes that the first production of that year was a minstrel show directed by Edward P. Duffy, S. J., and that he gave students who participated in the show priority when it came to casting future productions.[14] As the faculty member in charge of many of the theater department's productions, Duffy was the adult in the room. The model for these students, Duffy should have demonstrated more desirable values, but instead embodied the racism that prevailed in Loyola's culture. Perhaps more important than his being a faculty member, Duffy was a Jesuit. Representing the Catholic church, the expectation is that he would have had good morals, but his racism was more in line with the values Loyola taught. The visual of a member of the Society of Jesus not only encouraging, but also rewarding

13 Loyola University Maryland, *Evergreen* (Baltimore, Maryland: 1956): 40-41. LNDL Archives, https://archive.org/details/evergreen00loyo_14/page/40/mode/2up?view=theater, accessed on October 19, 2022.
14 Loyola University Maryland, *The Loyola Annual* (Baltimore, Maryland: 1908), Pages 84-85, LNDL Archives, https://archive.org/details/loyolaannual00loyo/page/n5/mode/2up?view=theater, accessed on October 19, 2022.

participation in this institutional racism is a striking one that maintains the idea of Jesuits championing white supremacy.

The most notable example of Jesuit collegiate theater's white supremacy was in 1955. That year, the Mask and Rapier Society won the "Provincial One Act Play Contest" with a performance of *The Emperor's Doll*, a play set in Japan and performed in yellowface.[15] This competition was held every year in the mid-twentieth century between a group of Jesuit colleges. Trading off who hosted each year, the colleges each performed a one-act play. To be chosen the winner was a great honor that garnered much praise. Although Loyola entered many times before, it was *The Emperor's Doll* that earned them first place. The intention of this competition was to uphold Jesuit excellence through art, but it often upheld racism in the same way. Loyola's choice to enter the play and the competition's choice to award it first prize is just one way that these colleges praised their students for engaging in racist behavior. Winning for a play that utilized yellowface, Loyola was brought to the forefront of this community, even if only for a year. This reward for its racism proves just how deep-rooted the ideals of white supremacy were in Jesuit collegiate culture.

From erasing Blackness altogether to performing depictions of race in a harmful way, Loyola's choices regarding how race is portrayed on stage are very telling of how they felt as an institution. Taking little care for the feelings of Black people and other minority groups on campus, Loyola continued to prioritize their Jesuit values and uphold their history of white supremacy even into the late twentieth century. Looking at the theater at Loyola today, it is not perfect, but progress has been made. One fall 2022 production was a play written by an Indigenous woman and the other is the first Loyola production to be student-directed by a person of color. Telling stories from diverse perspectives allows Loyola's theater department to be a better reflection of our current student population and the world. While one cannot change the past, there is always the power to create a better future. Hopefully as Loyola learns more about this history and others like it,

---

15 The Students of Loyola College, "The Mask and Rapier Society," *The Greyhound*, March 9, 1955. LNDL Archives, https://archive.org/details/greyhound28loyo_7/mode/2up?q=play+contest&view=theater, accessed on October 19, 2022.

their theater department and the institution as a whole can take steps to be more inclusive and tell stories for and about everyone.

The Desegregation of Loyola College

Ikia Robinson

In 1949, Loyola College admitted its first Black student, Charles H. Dorsey, Jr. Dorsey applied a year earlier and was denied because the schools that he attended were unaccredited in the region. Loyola believed Dorsey was able to participate in all academic and extracurricular activities freely, but that was not the case. Dorsey was the only African American on campus, which many at Loyola College frowned upon. He was surrounded by peers and staff who not only did not look like him, but they also did not have his best interests at heart. For instance, some students carried Confederate flags on campus. Confederate flags are not very welcoming and are a hate symbol. While Loyola claimed to be an inclusive environment, the environment that Dorsey was in reflected the opposite.

Although Loyola's campus became desegregated due to Charles Dorsey's presence, it did not integrate Black students into the campus environment. There is a significant difference between desegregation and integration. Desegregation is the ending or eliminating of the practice of excluding a race or group from another race or group. Integration is diversity, equity, and inclusion of all races into a group or environment in a way that affords the same level of access to all opportunities. Dorsey was not welcomed by everyone on campus. Due to racial differences, some parents felt that they should disenroll their children from Loyola because of Dorsey's presence on campus. Despite the hostility and uncomfortable environment, Dorsey overcame stereotypes and proved every opponent wrong. This discouraging environment did not extinguish his fire but fueled it to become brighter and stronger. Dorsey's journey as a student at Loyola and his life pursuits reflect this truth.

Dorsey's college journey paused briefly when he served in the United States Air Force from 1951 to 1956. Dorsey excelled and became a lieutenant in Korea. He returned and graduated from Loyola College with a bachelor's degree in 1958, and subsequently received a Juris Doctorate degree from the University of Maryland School of Law in 1961. Next, Dorsey worked at a law firm in Baltimore, worked in the city solicitor's office, was the first African American on the Maryland Board of Law Examiners, and changed the lives of disadvantaged people as the Executive Director of the Maryland Legal Aid Bureau. Dorsey's service touched the lives of many through his time in the military and at the Maryland Legal Aid Bureau.

Loyola promoting inclusion did not mean a welcoming environment was guaranteed. The campus environment was in fact not inclusive and excluded Dorsey. As the first African American to be admitted to Loyola, Charles H. Dorsey Jr.'s experience was not easy. Dorsey was not integrated in Loyola's environment. Instead, he experienced racism.

Racism is defined as "a belief that race is a fundamental determinant of human traits and capacities and that racial differences produce an inherent superiority of a particular race."[1] Inequality and injustice have robbed African American people of the opportunity for better lives. Unfortunately, both are still present today. Some African Americans reside in areas that do not have the same resources that other areas enjoy. This disparity impacts access to services and opportunities and, ultimately, limits potential success. Inequality and injustice are like social malnutrition.

The story of Charles Dorsey is one of struggle against that. Dorsey was undeterred by the trials he faced at Loyola. He fought for his education, made the best of his opportunities, and was committed to a life of service. He exemplified this truth by joining the military as a means to give back to

---

1 "Racism Definition & Meaning," Merriam-Webster (Merriam-Webster), accessed February 10, 2023, https://www.merriam-webster.com/dictionary/racism.

his community. As a Black male at Loyola College, Dorsey had to constantly advocate and create opportunities for himself. Dorsey's experience at Loyola College sheds light on the difference between desegregation and integration.

In spite of these obstacles, Dorsey still answered the call to service throughout his career. He answered this call selflessly. With hard work and determination, Dorsey made a positive impact on the world. He became a member of the Maryland State Board of Law Examiners and was the first African American male to become a law examiner. As a law examiner, he wrote and graded essay questions for the state bar exam.[2] Dorsey clearly did not give up nor was he distracted by the narratives that other people painted of him. His journey is a testament of all his accomplishments. Dorsey worked hard to become a well-respected individual. In recognition of his impact, the National Legal Aid and Defender Association named an award after him to commemorate the time he poured into others. The Charles Dorsey Award "is given biennially to an individual who has provided extraordinary and dedicated service to the equal justice community and to organizations that promote expanding and improving access to justice for low-income people."[3]

Throughout his life, Dorsey encountered people who did not believe in his ability to succeed, but he did. Dorsey's journey is a result of his perseverance. His story serves as an inspiration for students of color like me to keep working towards their goals despite their environment. This essay will explore the life of Charles H. Dorsey Jr., the racist environment of his time, and how his story directly connects to the present.

The Life of Charles H. Dorsey Jr.

Charles Dorsey was born in Baltimore, Maryland in 1930. Dorsey went to St. Catherine's Academy for his elementary education and received his secondary education at Epiphany Apostolic College in New York.[4] He then applied to Loyola College in 1948 and was denied. The schools that he attended prior to Loyola were considered unaccredited schools in the

2 "Judiciary panel lists 12 for Supreme Bench, Discrict Court," *Baltimore Sun*, August 21, 1974. Loyola University Maryland Vertical File Collection, Loyola Notre Dame Library.
3 "Awards," NLADA, accessed December 6, 2022, https://www.nlada.org/about-nlada/awards#dorsey.
4 "11 appointed to Charities' advisoty board," *The Catholic Review*, March 22, 1968. Loyola University Maryland Vertical File Collection, Loyola Notre Dame Library.

region. Dorsey reapplied in 1949, and with personal endorsement from his Josephite instructors, was granted admission.[5] Dorsey's academic career at Loyola had officially begun.

A year before Dorsey arrived at Loyola, the *Greyhound* reported that "Martial law was declared last week in Gettysburg, Penna., to quell the near-riot which occurred when a car driven by Loyola's student honked through the streets with Confederate flags flapping playfully from the bumpers in untainted Yankee ether."[6] Dorsey was surrounded by Confederate flags. Confederate flags are racist and exemplify a strong distaste for non-white people. It is disheartening that those who so proudly flew Confederate flags were among Dorsey during his time at Loyola. Years later, Donald Vincent, a member of the Hip-Hop Society at Loyola, reflected on the power of those Confederate flags, and the language associated with them, writing "Blacks were reduced to nothing. They were property and chattel. Because of this, when I hear someone say the N-word or any variant of it, I automatically think of swastikas, Confederate flags, stereotypes and bigotry and hate."[7] Confederate flags were documented, but you can only imagine all of the other racist things Dorsey encountered that were not documented.

As a student at Loyola College, Dorsey was surrounded by people who did not have his best interests at heart. Dorsey faced the struggle of being excluded from a campus that now promotes inclusivity and diversity. When a former white member of the first desegregated class was asked about Charles Dorsey, he replied,

Oh, yeah, yeah, there was no fuss whatsoever about admitting one Black fellow, Charlie Dorsey. He was quite nice, but some people were disturbed, some of the guys. Thomas was an awful snob and said, "I'll never speak to him."[8]

5 Nicholas Varga, *Baltimore's Loyola, Loyola's Baltimore* (Baltimore: The Maryland Historical Society, 1990), 358.

6 Loyola University Maryland. *The Greyhound*, May 21, 1948, 4. https://archive.org/details/greyhound-21loyo_17/mode/2up?q=Confederate+Flags

7 Loyola University Maryland. *The Greyhound*, February 23, 2010, 12. https://archive.org/details/greyhound-83loyo_10/page/12/mode/2up?q=Confederate+Flags

8 John McGrain oral history interview transcript, 2021. LUMD.002.007, Loyola University Maryland oral history collection, Loyola Notre Dame Library.

Photograph of Charles H. Dorsey, who became the first full-time Black undergraduate student at Loyola College in 1949. Courtesy of Loyola Notre Dame Library, Loyola University Maryland photograph collection.

The phrase "quite nice" is intensely racialized. People did not have high expectations for Dorsey because he was Black. Black people were seen as inferior individuals. Clearly, some students had anticipated how they were going to deal with Dorsey's presence on campus based on his race. Loyola's *Greyhound* described how "an old taboo was quietly torn down to make room for the quiet friendliness of Charles Dorsey, the first negro student."[9]

9 Loyola University Maryland. *The Greyhound*, 1950, p. 14. https://archive.org/details/loyolaofeast00loyo/page/ n13/mode/2up?q=Charles+Dorsey

The language used in the newspaper encoded the racism of the campus, using the derogatory term "negro" to refer to Dorsey. To make matters worse, blackface minstrel shows still took place at the time and many students were influenced by the shows. Through the lens of oral history, newspaper accounts, and analysis of blackface minstrel shows, it is possible to glimpse the environment that Dorsey encountered. For a more in-depth explanation of the different minstrel shows during the time and their impact on Loyola's environment, see Lucy Marous' essay in this volume.

Dorsey's time at Loyola was interrupted when he enlisted in the Korean War in 1951. Dorsey served in the United States Air Force for a total of five years and was discharged with the rank of Lieutenant, evidence of his commitment to service. He then returned to Loyola College and worked hard to make a difference both outside of Loyola and on Loyola's campus. He completed his education at Loyola in 1958. He was a recipient of the Alumni Laureate Award in 1957. After he graduated from Loyola, he attended The University of Maryland School of Law to earn a Juris Doctorate degree in 1961.[10]

Dorsey's success as a lawyer was by no means easy. Five Black law school graduates alleged that the rate of Black candidates who passed the bar examination was very low. They filed a Federal Court suit because they felt that Black people failed the exam due to racial discrimination. The graduates felt that the law examiners were unjustly grading the exams.[11] The *Baltimore Sun* reported that, "the examination is culturally biased against Black persons and excludes Black persons from the bar at a much higher rate than whites, the suit alleged."[12] Dorsey was appointed to the State Board of Law Examiners the same year the suit was filed. His journey to answer the call of service did not stop there, however. Dorsey practiced law at a private firm in Baltimore for seven years and worked in the city solicitor's office as an assistant.[13] He continued his career at the Maryland Legal Aid Bureau in 1969.

---

10 Frank D. Roylance, "Charles H. Dorsey Jr., 64, Legal Aid Director," *Baltimore Sun*, September 29, 2021, https://www.baltimoresun.com/news/bs-xpm-1995-04-24-1995114060-story.html.

11 "Black put on law unit," *Baltimore Sun*, November 11, 1972. Loyola University Maryland Vertical File Collection, Loyola Notre Dame Library.

12 Ibid.

13 Frank D. Roylance, "Charles H. Dorsey Jr., 64, Legal Aid Director," *Baltimore Sun*, September 29, 2021, https://www.baltimoresun.com/news/bs-xpm-1995-04-24-1995114060-story.html.

The Maryland Legal Aid Bureau is described as a "private non-profit law firm that provides free civil legal services to low-income people statewide." Essentially, the Maryland Legal Aid Bureau defended the legal rights of the low-income community. Dorsey was credited with "propelling the Bureau into the front rank of legal service providers nationally and expanding its reach to serve the rural and urban poor."[14]

Initially, Dorsey worked as Deputy Director. He later was named the Executive Director in 1974. Dorsey dedicated his life to the role of Executive Director for a total of 21 years. As Executive Director, Dorsey helped people in Maryland who were unable to obtain legal services, fought for justice, and made a positive impact in the lives of those who were classified as low income by winning cases at the Bureau.

It is important to note that Dorsey faced obstacles while at the Bureau. One struggle that Dorsey encountered was the state government considering cutting the money allocated to the Maryland Legal Aid Bureau and giving it to other programs in 1976. That would mean that the service Dorsey provided to low-income Marylanders would be halted. As a result, the low-income people of the state would not have access to proper legal services nor be able to defend their legal rights because of their financial situation. Dorsey asked for support to change the governor's mind, but a lot of offices of other organizations closed because of the lack of funding. Funding from the state government was important because it "provided attorneys for Marylanders who cannot afford legal fees."[15] Nevertheless, Dorsey prevailed, leading a campaign that raised both public and private funding for a new building to accommodate the Bureau's growing staff, expanding his work across the state into a network of offices, and triumphing in the courtroom. One case he won was the overcrowding of state prisons. This was a disturbing problem for many in prisons. The case forced the state to address the problem.[16] Despite all the obstacles that Dorsey faced, he still managed to be successful.

14 "Charles Dorsey's 'Zest for Justice'," *Baltimore Sun*, September 29, 2021, https://www.baltimoresun.com/news/bs-xpm-1995-04-27-1995117208-story.html.

15 "Three Legal Aid Bureau Office To Remain Open," *Baltimore News-American*, July 1, 1976. Loyola University Maryland Vertical File Collection, Loyola Notre Dame Library.

16 "Charles Dorsey's 'Zest for Justice'," *Baltimore Sun*, September 29, 2021, https://www.baltimoresun.com/news/bs-xpm-1995-04-27-1995117208-story.html.

In recognition of these accomplishments, Loyola College awarded Dorsey with an Andrew White Medal honoring him as an exemplary member of the Catholic Church. Although Dorsey went through many challenges throughout his journey, he did not quit, but still helped others on his way to success. His journey inspires others to push through adversity and help others who may need support.

Racism Still Exists

Loyola remains a racist environment for those who do not look like the majority. It is unfortunate that Charles Dorsey had to encounter racist individuals at Loyola. Furthermore, it is sad that some of the same hateful images still surround Black students well after Dorsey graduated from Loyola.

The evidence of this persistent racism emerges powerfully from student letters from the 1994 *Greyhound*. Among the most compelling are Jill Hill, who wrote that "racism exists in several forms at Loyola. Among students, there is individual racism which is simply evident in the lack of support white students have shown in Black Student Association sponsored events."[17] Another compelling remark by Miriam Fader stated "at this forum it finally became so obvious to me that Loyola has far to go in its battle against racism. In the past four years, Loyola has become increasingly multiracial and multicultural. However, the school has failed to appropriately and adequately accommodate the students of color and of different cultures who have chosen to come here."[18] Finally, Elizabeth McKeever remarked, "It depressed me to think that institutionalized racism has become this big of a monster, but in no way did it surprise me. While my institution isn't as extreme, I could identify with the anger and disillusionment that the African American students were displaying. It is very hard to be anything that is different here, and this extends to many levels."[19] While Loyola claims to provide an inclusive environment for all students, the experiences of the students that attend say otherwise.

---

17 Loyola University Maryland. *The Greyhound*, November 22, 1994, 4, https://archive.org/details/greyhound-68loyo_7/page/4/mode/2up?q=racism
18 Ibid.
19 Loyola University Maryland. *The Greyhound*, November 22, 1994, 4, https://archive.org/details/greyhound-68loyo_7/page/4/mode/2up?q=racism

Today, there are still Confederate flags hanging in student dorm rooms. There are still people, both students and faculty, who are racist towards people of color and people with different cultural backgrounds. Maya du Plessis conducted interviews that provide a more in-depth account of students' experiences with racism at Loyola (see her essay in this volume).

To mitigate this struggle, Loyola University Maryland should publicly speak out against racism. Racism should always be addressed and never condoned. Loyola should set an expectation for all current and future students and faculty to follow. This expectation should disavow racism on and off campus. Loyola's community should come together as one and support one another despite race. This will pave the way and open the door for more Black students and people of different cultural backgrounds to integrate in Loyola's environment and get involved.

Why is Dorsey's Journey Significant?

Charles Dorsey's journey enlightens people about the hardships African Americans face at Predominantly White Institutions (PWI). It is not easy to be in an environment that does not look like you nor welcome you. Dorsey's story also inspires African American students at PWIs to display grit, persevere and be successful despite controversy. He encountered several obstacles on his road to success because of his race. Dorsey's example empowers black students to self-advocate, exceed expectations, and never settle for less because they know their worth.

Conclusion

In 1953, Dorsey married Agnes A. Smith, and they remained together for 40 years. They had nine children. Kathleen Dorsey, his eldest daughter, graduated from Loyola in 1975.[20] Dorsey's legacy and contributions to Loyola's community will never be forgotten by his family and many others. There is still work to be done to achieve an environment that is truly integrated, however.

---

20 "Charles H. Dorsey Jr., '57, Loyola's first student of color, led Maryland's Legal Aid." Loyola University Maryland, accessed December 6, 2022, loyola.edu/magazine.

Loyola University Maryland says it promotes inclusion and equal rights. Ironically, the campus environment says the opposite. Several students of color feel alone. Some do not receive opportunities that are directly for them, nor are they offered support from staff and faculty who resemble them. Loyola should provide more resources, opportunities, and activities for the minority community. Having a choice and being offered opportunities is the true meaning of integrating students of color. Without this support, Loyola University Maryland will remain a desegregated, rather than an integrated institution.

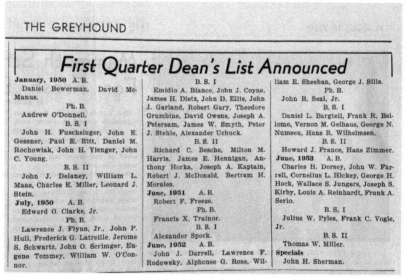

Charles Dorsey made the Dean's List in fall 1949, suggesting he worked hard to leave a mark on Loyola's campus. *The Greyhound*, November 18, 1949, page 8. Image courtesy of Loyola Notre Dame Library.

Facing the Archives

Brandon Nefferdorf

In December of 2021, I opened an email from the Office of the President, alerting me about Loyola University's connection to the long history of slavery. Jesuits in 1838 sold 272 African Americans to help finance Georgetown University, another Jesuit school closely connected to Loyola's founding. Recent findings suggested that Loyola had also benefited from the sale. This discovery prompted the University to explore and deconstruct its own history.

During the following summer, Dr. Lisa Zimmerelli asked a handful of students, including me, to dive into archival research to explore connections between Loyola University and the 1838 sale. We worked together along with Dr. David Carey, a history professor at Loyola, and his small group of students, who were just as eager as us to uncover Loyola's neglected history.

In addition to working with our professors over the summer, we also worked with Jennifer Kinniff. Jenny is the Head of Archives and Special Collections at the library. She is exceptionally well-versed in our archival findings and supported us as we delved further into our research. She was the glue that held us all together.

We returned to the university just a few weeks after finals and began our research. We were each tasked with investigating different areas of the school's archive. In the beginning of our initial research, I was responsible for rummaging through the first few decades of Loyola's yearbook.

I sat down at my desk to sift through Loyola's digitized yearbooks. The university's earliest yearbook, then titled "The Loyola Annual," dated back to 1908. In addition to providing pictures of classes, employees, and extra-curriculars, the yearbook was also a source for student publications and rhetoric. It was by the students, for the students. I began to scroll through the almost 150-page collection of writings and pictures, looking for implicit and explicit indications of racism, misogyny, and other instances of bigotry and white supremacy. My eyes darted from line to line, soaking in every instance of vindictiveness: References to women as members of the "fairer sex." Missionary work in the "wilds of Africa." Mentions of "the army of the South" during the Civil War. The newly instituted "Minstrel Show."

I froze. The team had discussed mentions of a minstrel show held on campus, but this was the first I had seen of it mentioned on paper.

Minstrel shows were comedy and entertainment routines that grossly stereotypically depicted Black people, with origins dating back to slavery in the United States. White people typically donned blackface, sang African American spirituals, spoke in exaggerated voices that mimicked Black dialects, and utilized a host of other abhorrent appropriations to mock and demean Black Americans. Minstrel shows were a fairly common and popular sight in the U.S. at the turn of the century, especially in Baltimore. It shouldn't have been surprising to see these "shows" on a college campus, but I never expected to see them on *my* campus.

"Minstrel Show"

I kept staring at those two words, saying them over in my head. Loyola contributed to one of the most vile and disgusting ways of demeaning and dehumanizing Black people. Students and faculty gathered together to promote racism and discrimination. This was *my* school community. I was afraid to keep reading; I didn't want to see what came next.

I braced myself and kept moving along through the text. Students, led by Mr. E.P. Duffy, a member of the Society of Jesus, worked effortlessly to put on a proper show for the community. The event, filled with songs and comedy, was met with laughter and praise from all in attendance. The spectacle was best summed up by this line: "We only wish to know that we have done credit to the name of Loyola and our generous supporters." Loyola had hoped to honor itself and its local community through the appropriation and vilification of Black people. The minstrel show wasn't a direct connection to the 1838 sale, but it was an explicit continuation of racist themes and ideas that permitted it in the first place.

I sat there in my chair for a while in silence, stunned as I reread every word. It felt awful to know that a minstrel show had occurred on campus. It felt even worse to know that it had been celebrated and immortalized in the yearbook.

After another few minutes, I started onto the next yearbook. I hoped the show was a one-off thing for the school. I came across a similar slew of white supremacist rhetoric: racist language, anti-women's suffrage suggestions, the "second annual Minstrel Show."

I froze again but quickly heated up with anger. The show was now one of Loyola's most popular attractions; it had become an *annual* spectacle. It was a recurring, yearly cycle of appropriation and racism. I grew more and more frustrated as I read on, learning that the show was performed to sold-out audiences for charity organizations in Baltimore! Not only was the minstrel show becoming an integral part of Loyola's early history, but the school's neighboring community benefited from it as well.

I sat there again just rereading every line of text as if seeing it again would make it go away. Nothing changed. Another minstrel show memorialized by the Loyola yearbook.

In that moment, I wanted to stop. *I really wanted to stop.* Maybe if I had just turned off my laptop, I could have slept more soundly that night, but not reading about the minstrel show wouldn't prevent it from happening in the first place.

I begrudgingly scrolled through the remaining pages of the yearbook and was welcomed by a plethora of pictures from school-sponsored activities, ranging from athletic team photos to photos of candid student life. My heart sank as I examined a picture of the Dramatic Society. "THE COLLEGE MINSTRELS" was the subtext plastered underneath a picture of Loyola's winter of 1908 minstrel show. A packed audience appeared in front of Loyola students on stage, several of whom wore blackface. The performers appeared to be in front of a backdrop of a plantation.

THE COLLEGE MINSTRELS

The yearly college minstrel show, Winter 1908. The Loyola College Annual, 1909; Archives and Special Collections, Loyola Notre Dame Library.

I was speechless. Reading about the show was one thing but seeing it was completely different. To be able to visualize and imagine the minstrel show as a real part of campus life was terrifying. I sat there for a couple of minutes, staring at the picture.

Then I felt dizzy. I had to step away from my computer, so I rushed outside to get some air.

I was lost and confused.

Why was there a picture of this in the yearbook?!

This wasn't supposed to be Loyola's past.

Loyola claims to be a safe haven for education and growth, grounded in respect for the human person. The school's core values even state how it "emphasize[s] openness and enthusiasm toward the whole of God's richly diverse creation and for the human person as its crowning glory." Loyola advertises itself as a paragon for inclusivity and integrity dating back to the initial organization of the Jesuits. These minstrel shows couldn't be further from these supposed truths; they were founded in hate, emphasizing dehumanization. I'd been lured in with promises of equality and fairness. Uncovering the minstrel shows felt like a cruel joke.

I felt betrayed.

There were too many secrets, too many things buried away. My trust in the school began to wither when Loyola revealed its potential connection with Georgetown and the 1838 sale last year. Learning that my school was another institution that benefited from legalized human trafficking was incredibly disturbing; it rocked my trust. Reviewing the content of the yearbook completely severed it.

Loyola was supposed to be a home, *my* home. In that moment, it felt like the furthest thing from it. My ideal vision of the university came tumbling down.

Why was I here?

I needed something to reassure me and pick me back up, so I called my actual home.

I talked with my parents for a while about what I had seen. I told them about the yearbook. I told them about the minstrel shows and the picture I'd seen, and they were just as disgusted as I was. I told them how it felt to see it and what I was feeling as I was on the phone with them. I told them that I was confused and didn't know what to do.

There was a brief silence, then my mom spoke up.

She told me it was okay to feel upset and confused. She would have been really concerned if I hadn't felt the way I did. She said that Loyola was not the first school to have a past like this uncovered and will certainly not be the last. She told me that I deserved to be here and that the work we were all doing was necessary work. She spoke with this eerie calmness, like she already knew everything. Her tone was defined by her own experiences, which she hoped I'd never need to encounter but knew I would.

Then she said something that stuck with me: "Those people that put on those shows all those years ago? They're gone. They're not there anymore. You're here now, and they're not."

I heard the words she told me, but at the time they meant nothing. I couldn't concentrate on anything other than that picture. Everywhere I looked, I saw that photo. I kept seeing a Loyola that appropriated people like me, a Loyola that didn't respect me. And I didn't think there was anything I could do to erase that image.

Something clicked after seeing the picture: Loyola was not a school designed to enroll people that looked like me. It never had been, and upon reviewing the yearbook, I wasn't sure it could ever be.

I thanked my parents for helping me talk through everything and hung up. I went back inside my apartment and was immediately greeted by the minstrel show still on my computer. I angrily exited my browser, turned off my computer, and started to cook dinner. I had done enough work for the time being. I went to bed that night with the image of the minstrel show stuck in my head.

A couple of days later, the archival team reconvened at the school library to go over our findings, with the minstrel show still fresh in my mind. During our discussion, someone mentioned the first Black student to enroll in the university, Charles Dorsey, as a part of their findings, prompting a conversation about the early role of Black people on campus. To provide more context, Jenny, the library archivist, spoke up and told us about Loyola's 1921 purchase of the Evergreen property, its current location in Baltimore. Specifically, she told us about the racist language and rhetoric that was only recently updated in 2020. The deed instructed "[t]hat at no time shall the land included in said tract or any part thereof or any building erected thereon be occupied by any negro or person of negro extraction. This prohibition however is not intended to include occupancy by a negro domestic servant or other person while employed on or about the premises by the owner or occupant of any land included in said tract."

The land deed barred Black people from being present on campus unless they were a servant or worker. It took over 100 years for Loyola to change the language on the official land deed.

I should have felt upset or angry after hearing that, but it didn't faze me. It only emphasized the point made by the minstrel shows just over a decade before the purchase: Loyola really was never meant for me. The land deed, just like the show, only continued to highlight the racism that the 1838 sale was based on.

Loyola had hypnotized me with its charm. Seeing the minstrel show brought me back to reality. Hearing about the land deed confirmed the legacy of this historic racism.

After that discussion, I went back to my apartment, feeling hollow. The Loyola I thought I knew had been completely ripped out of me. I began to pick apart my past at Loyola, looking at how the residue of the minstrel show and racism is still present today. How Loyola really lacked in diversity across campus. How I was often one of the few students of color in my classes. How I had only had one professor of color going into my sophomore year. How news of the sale first broke in 2016, and Loyola didn't dive deep enough into its history to uncover its past until research from Georgetown came to light.

I think the most jarring issue was just how long it took to get this research done. These online yearbooks and files were digitized *years* before. Someone else had to have seen these writings and images in the yearbook when the files were first uploaded online. Furthermore, yearbooks were openly distributed and available from the library. I found it hard to believe that nobody else had come across these materials in the same way I had. Were we really the first people to question and analyze these publications? Thinking about all the ways Loyola had perpetuated discrimination, especially the minstrel show's overt racism, infuriated me. It also made me deeply sad. I hoped Loyola would be different. I was wrong.

We live with a Loyola struggling with its past.

Acknowledging the past and uncovering the past is certainly a step in the right direction, but it seems almost too little too late. Why did it take the school *this* long to explore its past? And why was it thrust upon its students? Should it really have been the responsibility of an eighteen-year-old starting his second year at the school to be one of the first to experience this heavy history?

We shouldn't have to learn our history like this, stumbling across old yearbooks to connect the dots left behind. We shouldn't have to question our own identities as students because of our school's hidden past.

I don't think it's possible to ever reconcile with this history fully. No work we do moving forward can ever offset the university's past. Loyola's land deed for the Evergreen property may have changed, but it doesn't remove the original text. Even though Loyola accepted Black students, technically and legally according to the recently updated land grant, we weren't allowed to be here.

Loyola's yearbooks will always have inappropriate and bigoted jokes, filled with racist and sexist undertones and ideas. Loyola's 1909 edition of the *Annual* will always have its picture of the minstrel show. There's nothing I can do to remove that picture from my head. Loyola benefited from racism and it can't be entirely absolved. I've grappled with these issues, and I still feel uneasy. I know that's never going to change.

There's this sense of permanence that racism leaves behind in history. It's a carpet stain that won't ever come up, no matter how much you scrub or wash it. Every time you walk past it, you remember exactly how it got there. And I walk past that stain almost every single day.

Unfortunately, it's the history we have and the history we need to learn. It is unbelievably painful to learn that your school has acted so revoltingly in the past. To learn that your school has not only condoned but actively participated in racist behavior. To learn that your school attempted to deconstruct your identity time and time again.

I keep thinking back to that phone call with my mom. "You're here now, and they're not." While we still need to acknowledge the remnants of the minstrel show and racism we see today, the people responsible for the show aren't here anymore. They're not at the school anymore. They're long gone.

But we're still here.

We're here now, and they aren't.

Every time I repeat those words, I think about Mélisande Short-Colomb and her relationship with the Jesuits and their enforcement of slavery. Meli is a descendant of the 272 African Americans sold by Georgetown University in 1838. The research group met with her a couple of times over the summer to listen to her expertise and advice for understanding our own research.

She has this almost infallible way of speaking, like every word is perfectly plotted out before she talks. She told us about her experiences since uncovering the truth about her family and the horror she felt about her history being turned completely on its head. But through it all, she never wavered. Every day she challenged the systems and ideas that were built upon the racism that fueled the 1838 sale. She was living in the present, planning for the future. The Jesuits who permanently altered her family's trajectory were long gone.

It took me almost a year into my time at Loyola to really question the university and my experience here. There were so many warning signs that I just seemed to gloss over and ignore. I think I always noticed these things; I just didn't want to acknowledge them. It would have meant deconstructing my ideal Loyola, a Loyola that ultimately, never existed and honestly never can.

My ideal Loyola was shattered. The university needs to salvage its history in whatever way it can moving forward.

It's not our job to make decisions for what Loyola does next. It shouldn't be our responsibility to pick up the pieces that were continuously broken decade after decade. However, it is our responsibility to know and learn about this history. In order to hold Loyola accountable for the past, we need to face it, no matter how vile it is. We can't let the minstrel show become just another page in the yearbook.

Seeing the minstrel shows in the yearbook destroyed me. It hurt me in ways that I didn't even think were possible. It took me a long time to really process and deal with it. I still don't think I've completely done that, and I doubt I ever will.

But every time I think like that, I have something to fall back on.

"You're here now, and they're not.

Thinking back to my mom helps keep me strong,

We need to be willing to become vulnerable to the past, so it won't ever happen again. Sometimes we must let ourselves get hurt today if it means becoming tougher tomorrow.

Uncovering the minstrel shows has helped me become more comfortable with being uncomfortable. It made me strong enough to face the rest of my summer research and brave enough to tell my experience now.

Most importantly, exploring Loyola's history helped me understand that it's okay to feel confused and angry about these findings. If we're not upset or puzzled by these findings in the first place, how can we expect anything to change?

We're here now, they're not.

Each one of us is a unique piece in Loyola's long history; we deserve to be here. While Loyola's past has been polluted by racism conducted by the students and staff of the past, we have new and better stories to tell in their place. We keep working so that people 60 years in the future won't have to look back at the minstrel show in the same way I did. They'll see the pain and suffering it caused, but they'll see our response to it too. They'll be able to look back at the work we did to make sure it can never happen again. They'll see that we could never be content with standing by and allowing our past to control our identities.

Every day we get up and go to class is another day we confront this history and carry on in spite of it. It's another day to make a new history for our campus, a history that in all is far from ideal, but one that we don't have to be completely ashamed of.

We are here now, they aren't.

Every day I get to say that is a good day.

We are here now, they aren't.

Era Three:

Contemporary Challenges (1971 – 2023)

Loyola Student Researchers

Anna Young and Brandon Nefferdorf using microfilm at the Maryland Center for History and Culture. Photograph courtesy of David Carey Jr. Baltimore, July 15, 2022.

Deidra Jackson scanning biography card files in the Enoch Pratt Free Library's Maryland Department. Photograph courtesy of Jenny Kinniff. Baltimore, July 15, 2022.

Loyola undergraduates examining archival material at the Georgetown University Library's Booth Family Center for Special Collections. Photograph courtesy of Jenny Kinniff. Washington D.C., June 18, 2022.

Evy Ryan presenting research findings to President Terrence Sawyer. Photograph courtesy of Jenny Kinniff. Loyola Notre Dame Library, July 8, 2022.

Student Essays

Stuck in the Grey

Noah Hileman

I'd like to share with you my appreciation for Loyola; to do that properly, you will need to understand a few things about me. For the majority of my life, I have struggled with accepting my sexuality. This struggle was largely caused by internalized homophobia and self-hatred, and I used Christianity to force myself to be straight: praying to God to let me be normal. As you might imagine, this led to depression. So, as a closeted, depressed teenager, I began my first year at Loyola.

Change is never easy, but changing your self-identity feels impossible. Coming to Loyola, I was fully prepared to live life as a straight man. Yet, as I began and continued to interact with the Loyola community, the identity I had forced upon myself began to fracture. I took a theology course during my first year, and it was there where, through long conversations with my teacher both in and out of class, I began to create a comfortable and healthy relationship between myself and my religious beliefs. Throughout my first and second years at Loyola I utilized the Counseling Center, and an eventual full-time therapist; therapy helped me begin the process of working through my depression. Additionally, through the encouragement of my counseling sessions, I began to integrate myself into a group of queer students which helped me normalize and grow comfortable with my own sexuality. Then, during my third year at Loyola, I came out as gay.

I lack the words to express how much Loyola has helped me grow along my own personal journey, but I can say this: Loyola has shaped me into who I am today. When I think of Loyola, I think of the teachers who have helped me in my educational and personal growth. I think of the variety of on-campus resources that helped me in one of the most difficult periods of my life. I think of Loyola's dedication to inclusivity and how that has created a space that let me grow beyond what I thought was possible. When I think of Loyola, I think of how proud I am to be a Greyhound.

We are Greyhounds. We are representatives of a community that focuses on helping those in need, on showing what the education of the mind, body, and soul means, on creating a world that is inclusive and communal. We represent the Green and Grey, and the Green and Grey represents us. When I see our school colors, I know what they should symbolize. That's why I was dismayed to discover our grey does not stand for what we believe. Our grey is tied to a message of ignorance and hatred and oppression and racism. A message of the Confederacy.

The Choice of Grey

In the early 1920s Loyola changed its location to our current Evergreen campus. In addition to the change in location, Loyola students decided to change the school colors from the original Blue and Gold to our current Green and Grey.[1] Because of Loyola's new location on the Evergreen campus, as well as many of the students being of Irish descent, green was an obvious choice.[2]

Grey was also an obvious choice. In 1922, fifty-seven years after the Confederate army was defeated, the Loyola community was still immersed in that southern ideology. Former Confederate sympathizers and soldiers would often give speeches to Loyola students celebrating the Confederacy. In one example, in 1899, a prominent Confederate general gave a talk titled "Story of a confederate soldier."[3] This connection led the students of

---

1 Letter to Fr. Gerald McKevitt, 1986, SC.049, box 1, folder 40, Nicholas Varga papers, Loyola University Archives, Loyola University Maryland, Baltimore, MD (hereafter cited as Letter, Nicholas Varga papers).

2 Description of Loyola College's seal, color, mascot, and motto, 1929-1986, SC.049, box 1, folder 40, Nicholas Varga papers, Loyola University Archives, Loyola University Maryland, Baltimore, MD (hereafter cited as Description, Nicholas Varga papers).

3 Newspaper clipping, 1899, in Prefect's Diary, 1890-1900. LUMD.012.011, Dean of the College of Arts and Sciences records, Loyola University Archives, Loyola Notre Dame Library.

Loyola to choose grey as a new school color, as a way to memorialize the Confederacy.[4]

The Narrative of Grey

In the hundred years since, Loyola has continuously tried to change the narrative surrounding the grey's connection with the Confederacy. For example, instead of directly claiming that grey was a memorialization of the Confederacy in 1922, Loyola claimed that the grey was "a memento of the 'Lost Cause.'"[5] The narrative of the "Lost Cause" depicted the Confederacy as something heroic and decentered it from slavery. But the Confederacy was defined *by* slavery, and Loyola aligned itself with the Confederacy.

As recently as 1968, near the end of the Civil Rights movement, Loyola *re-invented* the narrative behind the grey. The school claimed that "(T)he passage of time permits us now to see in the grey the prudent tempering of the vivid hope embodied in the green."[6] It would be a misconception to believe that this new meaningless narrative was meant to represent the school's shame or regret of its connection to the Confederacy. In fact, no apology for the original meaning of the grey has yet been found within Loyola's records. The only discussion on the topic of the school colors came from a member of Loyola's faculty, who admitted, in a 1986 letter to a Jesuit priest, that the school adopted "green and grey – green for Irish, and grey for the Confederacy (although we don't mention that much any more[sic])."[7] We were a school that downplayed the truth. We were a school that didn't mention it. We are still that school.

As of December 2022, if you search for Loyola's History and Traditions webpage, you will find a small blurb on the Green & Grey. It states that,

In the early 1920s, as Loyola was developing its athletic teams, uniforms varied from green, red, blue, and white. The student body decided Loyola should have official colors to represent all sport teams and to build Loyola's identity. Grey has long been a traditional color among Jesuit colleges

4 Description, Nicholas Varga papers.
5 Ibid.
6 "The Green, Grey, and Greyhound of It." SC.049, box 1, folder 40, Nicholas Varga papers, Loyola Notre Dame Library (hereafter cited as The Green, Nicholas Varga papers).
7 Letter, Nicholas Varga papers.

(Georgetown University's colors are navy and grey; Saint Joseph's University's colors are crimson and grey)...[8]

Clearly, the narratives surrounding the grey have morphed over the past hundred years. At first, Loyola created a narrative to rebrand the Confederacy. It then created a narrative to hide its connection to the Confederacy. Currently, Loyola is using a narrative of tradition to defend the importance of the grey. But the argument of tradition is merely a façade.

The Anomaly of Grey

There are, within the United States, twenty-seven Jesuit colleges. Below is a visual representation of each Jesuit college and where it's located within the United States:

Jesuit Universities and Colleges in the United States. Courtesy of Marquette University.

Of the eight Jesuit Colleges built before Loyola, only three have grey as a primary color. These three colleges are: Georgetown University, Saint Louis University, and Saint Joseph's University. All three have publicly admitted that they, like Loyola, are connected in various ways to historical racism and Jesuit slaveholding within Maryland. It is then apparent that the claim

8 "History and Traditions – Loyola University Maryland." Accessed December 14, 2023. https://www.loyola.edu/about/history-traditions#colors.

of Jesuit universities having grey as a traditional color is only true for Jesuit colleges who engaged in slave trading within Maryland and surrounding states. Additionally, it is likely that the grey in these institutions all are purposeful reminders of the Confederacy. While Saint Louis and St. Joseph's haven't yet produced any material behind the origins of their school colors, Georgetown has publicly admitted that their own grey was a way to recognize the Georgetown students who fought for the south in the civil war.[9] So, like all other narratives surrounding the grey, the narrative of tradition is a lie. All of us currently living and working on the Evergreen campus have believed that the green and grey have represented something good; however, as a community, we have been continuously constrained by constructed narratives that have either downplayed or hidden our connection to the Confederacy. We are stuck in the grey, and it is time to change.

Changing the Grey

Change is never easy but changing our identity has never been so important. In recent years, the list of enrolled undergraduate students has become increasingly diverse. In fact, our current first-year class, the class of 2026, is one of Loyola's most racially diverse classes in history. Now, I'd like you to imagine something. Imagine you are a new student. You are excited because not only does your school have a good academic program, but it also promotes messages of inclusion and acceptance and love. Then, as your time at school progresses, you eventually find out that one of the school's colors is representative of a hate group who hates *you*. You also discover that your school knows about this and did nothing to fix it. Does that mean your school doesn't promote inclusion or acceptance or love? By keeping that message, doesn't it feel like your school is being oppressive? I believe that if Loyola keeps our current school colors, then we are being oppressive. We would not be the school we claim to be, the school I know we are. We need to change.

I propose that we change our identity from the Green and Grey to the Green and Gold. The green would remain as a representation of our

9 "When and Why Were Blue and Grey Adopted as Georgetown's Colors? | Georgetown University Library." Accessed January 14, 2023. https://library.georgetown.edu/infrequently-asked-questions/when-and-why-were-blue-and-gray-adopted-georgetowns-colors.

longevity. It stands to serve as a reminder of our past, but much like the Evergreen itself, it shows us that we have the capability to grow. Gold will be a representation of what is in our future. Loyola of the past, before the Evergreen campus, had the blue and gold.[10] We will reclaim that traditional gold as a representation of our Jesuit values. And with a return to our true tradition, a tradition of inclusion and love, we can begin to look forward to what comes next.

Loyola will begin again, new but familiar. Our school colors will be different, but our campus, spirit, and mission will stand strong, along with our mascot. While the greyhound is reminiscent of the Green and Grey, its only connection to the Grey is its color. The greyhound was chosen because "It too had a historic association with Ireland and was then (this was before the cheetah had been timed) believed to be the fastest animal."[11] So, together with the Green and Gold, and the Greyhound, Loyola will be ready to enter its new golden era. An era where we will no longer ignore the injustices that we've committed throughout our history. An era where our identity matches our values. An era where every student can be proud to be a part of the Green and Gold. We are Greyhounds. Let's run into Loyola's new golden age, together.

---

10 Letter, Nicholas Varga Papers.
11 The Green, Nicholas Varga papers

Black Notes in a Bottle

Jacolby Lacy

As I stand here, basking in the white and black glory of this book signing, I look at my hands, and then at the line of creased joyous faces, awaiting
my signature. In this local bookstore in Baltimore, I can see a poster on the
window flipped backward for the people on the street to see, saying, "Mae
Jones signs *Black Notes In A Bottle* last day!" I never wanted to be back in
Maryland, I never wanted to be back in Baltimore. It's green against red,
against red against green. The same dream, the same disillusionment, the
same uncertainty of what's black and what's white. The faces creep up on
me, and my hands feel nearly possessed. I can feel the anticipation seething
from the mouths of these curious disciples. They want to know about the
green patch, the island surrounded by seas of rolling red sap. They want to
know about Deb. They want to know about that evergreen campus built
upon 272 ghosts.

A man asks towards the back shelves of the bookstore all low with hesitation beneath his voice, "Where does this refuge reside?" "How far does this
thick sap spread?" His eyes hold me in this moment of eternity. I can feel
the questions behind the lips of every Black body in this room. "How can I
get out Miss Jones when I was born smack dab in the center of its ceaseless
embrace?"

"Can't answer that," I say with certainty in my tone. "I can only tell you
that I was stuck too, from the soles of my feet to the black blood that runs

within these veins." I never was able to shake that dream of green, harassed by nightmarish red.

"Maybe to get out, we have to get helplessly stuck in our past, our present, and our future. Those are the stories we can not erase and the red lines we can not wipe from our faces."

Mama never thought much of my writing or me as a writer. All the loose papers and broken scrawls from even more broken penmanship always left mama squinting asking, "Girl, what does this say." The answer is, most of the time I didn't know. I just wrote what I dreamed and feared and loved altogether on paper, and if people like it then that's that. "I want to be a writer, mama."

When I was a girl my mama would say, "Let's fall in love with the dream," eyes big and arms open wide–awaiting my embrace. I could almost feel the warmth of her words, but the instant chill of the lies that danced humbly behind them. Mama did not want me to be a writer. Those thin lying lips, those thin red lips, those thin red-lined lips–graffitied on her face from caked red lipstick. She'd apply that same cakey red lipstick before going to the department store for days and days of smiling as if all the white women shopping there saw her as any different from the mannequins wearing beautiful green scarfs and lovely-loose green gowns, paying with their beautiful bounty of greedy-green bills. Mama told me she wanted me to fly so high that I could buy her that whole store one day.

She and Miss D both worked at the department store out in Gwynn Oak. Miss D lived above us in our little blue house, with a bright red front door. The paint was chipping, and the door didn't close right, but they both made enough to take a bus to work, take a bus back, and scrounge enough money for some bread and spam. Miss D moved in with us once pop died because the silence started making mama as stiff as the mannequins in that store. Sometimes I think she sat still praying and wishing for pop's key to slide into that dingy old lock, but it never did. Miss D said she was from Tuskegee. She was a sweet older woman with this look on her tired face like her eyes were one blink away from pouring out a sea of piping hot negro tears. Mama said it was that depression that got Miss D all twisted up from the moment police showed up at her door in Tuskegee with no son, a dog tag, and those same warm words with chills waiting behind them.

My mama–cracked and eternally pursed from all of the words never said–always talked of this dream with Miss D, and they both seemed clouded by its promise regardless of its obscurity. "What dream, mama?" She would tell me it was the dream of my future, some future that all the Black folk around here saw in their kids. That glint of something great in the eyes, something beautiful, something green. All I saw in the mirror were my deep dark eyes staring back at me. I still see those same deep dark eyes, even as the skin around them has retreated and fallen with age.

One thing mama taught me about dreams is when you're young, dreams fall like glitter and confetti all around you. In the preface, I talk about mama. It's her tribute, her own story, her own soul immortalized on pages and pages of love I have for her.

"Tell us about your mama," a young negro boy asks me with the same holding gaze. I say, "Well, mama said everything seems chanceless, colorless, and cold without love, Mae." I continue, "I will never forget when mama's lips pursed harder than the fists of Hercules when I asked about what it meant to be a nigger." Silence fell quicker than rain and stuck around for some encore to my precise language like the heads I see all around me.

"I did not know then the measure of the hate, the deepness of those lines. Like a viperous bite to the heart. It hurt mama to hear my nonchalant voice spill such a hate-filled word at such a young age. I never spoke that hateful word again. Our parents are the windows into a past we must look into and face."

Being back in Baltimore, I remember how years passed, and my girl-hood faded like sand in an hourglass. I never left for school, I never bore a child from my loins, I just took care of mama when she was too sick to work and too stubborn to die. I liked to cook for mama. I made grits with honey for sweetness, some bread with butter for warmth, and those sweet ox tails for some soul. "You going to cook at that school as I told you?" she'd ask. I always told her I would. Some school named Loyola, an evergreen campus full of white folks and thin piety. I couldn't imagine cooking at the same

206

place that had no Black people in the open—but banished to the shadows of forgotten history. Though mama insisted, and when she did all you could say was yes and nothing else.

People ask me if *Black Notes In A Bottle* was about that evergreen campus. The answer's yes. I was in the eye of the storm, I had one foot in the green soil, and unstuck—or so I thought. I felt unfamiliar and out of the body like I was "passing and unseen," like I was a "speck of dust thrashed and thrown around the roaring wind of people's passing," I was "an unheard holler in these hallways."

When a white man in the audience asks about how I was paid I say, "If pennies could buy castles, I'd be a queen with a scepter of gold and a crown of jewels. But do you see my scepter or my crown?" His face grew pale and flat, and he left through the doors like a tornado rampaging.

Thinking back to my days in that kitchen I remember a large white man giving me clothes to wear, and gloves to get to work. He took off like lightning and left me with a few other Black folks in the kitchen. I told them my name was Murray, even though it was Mae. I could never tell you why I lied. It felt easier to be someone else. Being someone else didn't change the fact that I had failed to live a great life, it only changed the name I went by while I was doing it.

I worked with some other women in the kitchen. Some young, and some old. The better half of them spoke and said their names were Dotty, May, and Deborah. Words were scarce in that kitchen unless we threw something quick out into the silence like a game of catch and throw, and Deborah and I could play all day. People don't care for conversation with help, so we made up for it by talking to each other.

Still, I was in the eye of the storm, I thought. Some safe haven that would save me from the red lines that brutalized mama's face. But here, the Black folk are the help, called "staff," and tucked away like brooms in the closet to clean when nobody was looking.

Deborah was the oldest out of Dotty and May, and she and I were similar in age. She would tell me about her being a girl, the same story as mine.

Just two living corpses buried on top of the same bodies in the same casket as our ancestors.

She told me "You know my ancestors were slaves, sold so you could work right where you stand. Them pennies in your pocket, theirs. Them stones on the campus grounds, theirs. Them beautiful colored windows in the church, they put that there."

"They built this campus?" She nodded and said, "Stealing people and selling their name, body, and soul came at a pretty price around here." She'd tell me how it felt being a ghost come back to life when she started working for the same people that took her name, her pride, and her dream. All that history, stuck in a glass bottle and lost at sea.

"Now, we just scoop and serve, scoop and serve and forget, scoop and serve and forgive."

Those students sauntered through the halls like God's best children. Strong truths well-lived, huh? Deb pointed out which students were the kin of city big shots—as southern as they are proud, and it was those same students who would order us "staff" around like dogs.

"All that time on that green island, and I roll back out into the red sea like a note in a bottle—with nothing good written on the inside."

When holidays would roll around the kitchen felt less thick and suffocating. There was a time before the kitchen closed for Christmas when Deborah and I sat in on the Christmas mass. I scraped up something nice that I would wear on Sunday mornings and I went right on in and sat in the back right with Deborah. The two black sheep in a herd of wolves hiding under wool facades. While recounting, I tell the lot in the bookstore, "It was not my idea of a merry Christmas."

We listened, we smiled, we sank into our seats and I forgot for at least a moment that the people in that room were different than me. All that preaching, all that holiness, all that Christmas cheer and they still kicked us out on our behinds when Deborah let that "negro holy spirit" take her up out of her seat and sent her right out the door with me humbly following behind. A girl asks, "What did you do?"

As much as I love a good lie to cover the wounds of the past I say, "We left the church, and then I left that school."

I used to think God could bring us all together, the same way we all bleed red. But I know now that this white hate shows "no mercy for my community, no refuge on the green island, and no escape in the church—not even for the holy man himself."

Deb went all back to normal, smoothed her ruffled feathers, and let it go. She started cooking again with that same absent expression, the occasional look like she goes somewhere that isn't present in that kitchen. Like she was dreaming "a dream away from that kitchen steam, crawling so far up our clothes, our nose, and our spirit that our bodies would surrender bullets of sweat like little white flags all across our faces." A dream away from the same place that had people of color sold like faceless assets. A dream away from those deep dark eyes staring back at me, wondering where all the confetti went.

I read from the last chapter, "The dream set me at a distance. I thought it could be my refuge, but now it just seems like another prison. Like that Wizard of Oz behind the green curtain. It was all just a big red lie, draped in emerald green, and I was the mere chef in the story that served with that same cracked smile as mama. Just scooping and serving, scooping and serving and forgetting, scooping and serving and forgiving." The feeling of becoming a mere gear in the same system one can spend their whole life trying to escape can be the true moment you fall crestfallen upon the precipice of escape. I read more, "It is no longer that tingly carpal tunnel like those dreams where feelings are just fuzz that will pass, I was fully awake in a living nightmare—surrounded by God-fearing supremacists, capturing us Black victims in the amber of their wake like history's wash and repeat."

All silence fell in the crowd, and for its moment it felt familiar. That silence was the "thank you" unsaid. That silence was the eye contact unreceived. That silence was there when that church fell quiet the second we sat down to join in on a Christmas mass. That silence was mama's lips of unspoken truths—twisted and tied up—seething from the red cracked mouths of the folk just like her and me. Yet still, nothing stung more than the red cracks left on my face, running bloody and bruised–scarred and scabbed, and never the same. The eyes in the bookstore cascade glints of sadness meaning "I am sorry" or "poor thing."

In a moment of endearment I say, "Loyola reminded me of the Wizard of Oz. The streets of Baltimore were Kansas, and Loyola was the emerald city. I walked the yellow brick road of that campus that leads you to the grand Wizard of Oz. But as I chipped away at that emerald city it showed its true colors beneath that yellow chipping road, I could see the rich crimson. No heel clicks to take me back home, that sap got me good. There was no great Wizard. Just smoke and lies behind a great green curtain in this dream I don't love you one bit, but you do not have to be sorry. Sorry doesn't fix it."

I leave that signing, and I think back to sipping sweet tea, hearing small chat, going downstairs, and hearing mama and Miss D. talking about Miss D's lost boy and mama's lost love. Seeing them talk as age and exhaustion became more prominent across their faces. I wish mama's dream for me could have come true, and evergreen.

"When I roll onto shore and make my way to the sand I want them to know. I want them to break me open, graze their fingers over my scars, and decipher the truths from my Black body."

The signing came and went, and Baltimore fell like a backdrop gone small in my rearview mirror. I returned to Chicago, hoping people read that black message in the bottle.

Each message is so different, yet so ineffaceably graffitied with the same red lines that lay across our and our children's faces. The red is all you see, not the green gowns and green bills, but the red cracks in mama's lips, the red around Miss D's eyes when she lost her boy, the red all over Deb's name and body, and the thick red around the 272 bodies. The 272 bodies that no one wants to speak of on that island of green in a sea of red. But that is fine because I am the note in the bottle–lost at sea, and now I am found.

The Half of Loyola Buried in 1971

Natasha Saar

You'd be forgiven if you didn't know that Loyola only became a co-educational institution in 1971. It was one of the last few stragglers in the United States. The first American coeducational institution, Oberlin College, opened its doors to women in 1835; by the start of the twentieth century, over fifty percent of universities were admitting students regardless of sex.[1]

Unlike other Catholic institutions, Loyola opening its doors to female students was the product of merging with Mount Saint Agnes College, a neighboring female-only Catholic institution facing financial difficulties. A student exchange program had existed in the early 1960s, but it was short-lived, as the merger Mount Saint Agnes had expected – the Catholic College of Baltimore – did not come to fruition. The College of Notre Dame in Maryland didn't want to merge either. Presumably, the agreement with Loyola University (then Loyola College) was the next best option available.

But there was a reason this was their second-best option. Because Mount Saint Agnes College is not in Loyola's name and its campus has passed into the hands of Johns Hopkins University, it has the potential to become lost to time. Its name lives on solely through Mount Saint Agnes Alumnae Association, which was created to connect Mount Saint Agnes alumni. It's

1 Claudia Goldin and Lawrence Katz. "Putting the CO in Education: Timing, Reasons, and Consequences of College Coeducation from 1835 to the Present." *Journal of Human Capital*, vol. 5, no. 4, 2011, p. 379.

still active, but primarily serves as a vehicle to fund a scholarship for incoming students descended from Mount Saint Agnes alumnae.

Yet there is a more indelible mark, because by merging its female-only student body with Loyola's male-only student body, a co-educational institution came into being.

We shouldn't just examine Loyola's history of slavery. That's only half of the story. We need to look at Mount Saint Agnes, whose campus was on land bought and resold during the Civil War. We need to look at the yearbooks and newspapers that provide snapshots of Loyola's history. And, most importantly, we need to look at how exactly the integration of white female students differed from the integration of students of color.

Not only was Oberlin College the first collegiate institution to accept women into its student body, but it was also the first institution to accept people of color in 1840. George B. Vashon, the first person of color admitted, walked at his graduation four years later.[2] Loyola accepted Charles H. Dorsey Jr. a century later in 1949.[3] A late start, and not a good one.

It's unclear when Mount Saint Agnes College began to admit people of color. In the final 1971 yearbook, we can spot two people who phenotypically appear to be African American, but previous yearbooks have such a small graduating population that it's unclear if anyone enrolled before them, or if four years prior (1967) was their first concession.

Mount Saint Agnes opened in 1890 and was run by the Sisters of Mercy. They supported the poor, started educational facilities, gave medical assistance, and engaged in other acts of charity that prevented the name from being overly stained by history. While there's no evidence that the congregation owned enslaved people, "in Missouri the Jesuits assigned [the Sisters] to supervise and catechize the women they enslaved."[4] They were thus very involved in the institution of slavery.

Prior to being dissolved in 1972, Mount Saint Agnes never acknowledged this fact nor made any apologies regarding their institution's history. It was at the time that such declarations were considered unnecessary. Loyola

---

2 Roland M. Baumann, *Constructing Black Education at Oberlin College* (Athens: Ohio University Press, 2010).

3 "Charles H. Dorsey, Jr., '57, Led Maryland's Legal Aid Bureau to National Prominence." Loyola University Maryland, 2016.

4 Kelly L. Schmidt, "The pervasive institution: Slavery and its legacies in U.S. Catholicism." Cushwa Center for the Study of American Catholicism. https://cushwa.nd.edu/news/the-pervasive-institution/.

only started issuing them in the twenty-first century. There is a chance that the Sisters of Mercy at Mount Saint Agnes had a relatively sinless past, but there is a greater chance that they have a history that parallels Loyola's – one that we simply will never hear about.

If the remnants of Mount Saint Agnes will stay silent, we must not.

Let us then examine those remnants: specifically, how they manifested in their first year at Loyola, and specifically within the pages of the *Evergreen* and *The Greyhound*. Respectively, those are Loyola's annual yearbook and biweekly newspaper, and all of them are written and edited by students, supervised by teachers. They are the closest things to time capsules we have.

The 1971 annual edition of the *Evergreen* features Loyola's first co-educational class, with the graduates comprised of a mix of Loyola-only students and Mount Saint Agnes refugees. There are not many people of color. There are *some*, both men and women, but are so few and far between that you would need to look for them. You do not need to look for women. Mount Saint Agnes was not a large school, so the gender division isn't equal, but it's present, and is even highlighted in the publication.

Pages 11 and 12 are unique in that they feature exactly three photos, and all three of them are single shots of Black men. Notably, none of the three seem to be the typical age of students at the time Even more notably, there were no Black men who had a professorship or an administrative role. The easy conclusion is that they were workers on campus – one of the men is seen with garden shears and overalls, so it's an even easier conclusion. It's a seemingly nice gesture to include this photo.

In an era where Loyola put all of its energy into integrating women, where was a smidgen of that pomp and circumstance for Dorsey during his era? Where was it when Mount Saint Agnes College admitted their first student of color?

The easy answer is that the merger was a big event that affected the life of every student, and the dynamics of mixing two different, large groups for the first time generated tremendous energy. One or two students of a different skin color being admitted to a university was not a problem for the majority. Their low presence in yearbooks could easily be attributed to their low presence in the college population.

Standards might have looked very different in the 1970s, but that doesn't change the racially charged pasts that are endemic to higher education. It's not that Loyola was unaware, but the institution simply didn't make challenging these discriminatory standards a priority because they didn't have to. They took the easy way out. It's perhaps understandable, considering the circumstances and time period, but is it truly *admissible*? Is it admissible now, when Loyola cleans up their past for incoming students and alumni, to avoid the consequences of those easy, insensitive decisions?

Beyond that, is it admissible that, if nothing is done, the backs of the people on which the education of these students was built will go unnamed, unacknowledged, and unpersoned?

Women were also prominently featured in *The Greyhound* newspaper in 1970, the year before the merger. Students from Mount Saint Agnes, while not officially on *The Greyhound* staff, authored articles and were the subject of many essays discussing the imminent merger. On the front page of the November 1970 edition, *The Greyhound*'s staff goes to great lengths to maintain neutrality when reporting on Loyola's decision to allow Hammerman to house women, describing petitions, meetings, and speeches.[5] In a later edition, it was reported that student life elected to allow Mount Saint Agnes representation on their housing commission.[6]

Interestingly, at this point, *The Greyhound* is no longer presenting itself as a newspaper solely for its male student body: there are multiple advertisements warning against illegal abortions.[7] The college wasn't even co-educational yet.

This attempt at inclusion was certainly a greater attempt than any acknowledgement of students of color (of which there was absolutely none), but it was not a perfect one. Loyola hardly treated its female population fairly. But despite *The Greyhound*'s efforts, the coverage was not entirely neutral. In the aforementioned article, there was the comment "the [Mount Saint Agnes] campus will hold nothing for the Loyola student after the

5 "Hammerman to House Girls," *The Greyhound*, November 23, 1970.
6 "Mount in SLC," *The Greyhound*, December 11, 1970.
7 *The Greyhound*, November 1970.

merger" and with all women moving onto the Loyola campus. They also say that the campus is now empty, and Loyola is preparing for room shortages and other "inconveniences." Could there have been some level of unrest among male Loyolans? It's certainly possible.

The 1971 yearbook offers several insights into the mindset of Loyolans, particularly in some revealing quotes in the first section. On page four, the *Evergreen* staff pulls from songwriter Phil Ochs: "Sit by my side, come as close as the air, Share in a memory of gray; Wander in my words, dream about the pictures that I play of changes."[8]

Ochs uses words like memory, wander, words, dream, pictures, changes. The song it's from is literally called "Changes." It's everything you'd want people to associate with the college experience, but that notion of transformation and progress is upended two pages later. On page six, juxtaposed with an image of three women milling around a roped fence, we see the quote:

And the woman saw that the tree was good to eat, and fair to the eye, and delightful to behold; and she took of the fruit thereof, and did eat, and gave to her husband who did eat. And the eyes of them both were opened.[9]

This is the only quote from the Book of Genesis in the yearbook, and it's about Eve committing the first sin of mankind next to the first picture of women a reader comes across. The optimistic interpretation of the quote is that it's supposed to symbolize intellectual enlightenment, another interpretation is that it's a tasteless attempt at humor, but the pessimistic reality is that Loyola's Jesuit education would hardly let them gloss over the quote's Biblical context, which is perhaps the *most* well-known Bible story.

The use of that Biblical quotation in the yearbook seems potentially inflammatory and at the very least is a bizarre decision. Were the editors divorcing it from the context? The image of eyes opening has always been associated with enlightenment, but the image of eating an apple from a tree has always been associated with sin. The Bible is not lacking for quotes related to the concept of enlightenment—nor is it a stranger to the concept

8 Phil Ochs, "Changes." Track 4 on Phil Ochs in Concert, 1996.
9 Genesis 3:6-7.

of enlightenment, period—so this choice feels deliberate. So what does *that* say about the college experience? That coeducation was like a woman committing the first sin of mankind? It's difficult to ascertain the *Evergreen* staff's *actual* reasoning, but they must have had one.

These Loyola publications speak to a greater truth about the school. Loyola attempted a perfect neutrality towards controversial debates regarding the merger, but was perceptibly passive-aggressive when the topic of women asserting themselves was brought up, be it by speaking up about having on-campus housing or having a place in a yearbook next to all of the men.

But notice that Loyola did not respond to changing times: it remained neutral.

At this point, there were so few students of color at Loyola that the school could pay them no attention and be fine. Loyola certainly mocked, trod on, and disrespected its students of color by ignoring its history of slavery and racism, and the institution itself did not go out of its way to antagonize anyone or involve itself with racial politics until it became more of a talking point decades later. You might wonder what the solution was for Loyola here – should they have encouraged more students of color to enroll? Should they have disproportionately spotlighted the ones that were there? What does all of this have to do with Loyola's history of slaveowning?

This is true of most higher-level institutions, but it bites when you remember that Loyola is supposed to be a Jesuit institution.

It's now 2023, and Loyola would like for you—and especially incoming students—to think that things have changed in the past fifty years. They dole out statements such as "we are committed to creating a community that recognizes the inherent value and dignity of each person," but say nothing about who that community will encompass.[10] From my own experience, I was surrounded in all of my classes by people that looked very much like me: pasty, white, and incapable of getting so much as a tan. Many other students, however, will not have the experience of looking like their classmates.

---

10 "Get to know your village." Counseling Center, Loyola University Maryland, www.loyola.edu/department/counseling-center/public-health-initiatives/belonging/community-resources.html.

Let's examine gender ratio next. In 2022, Loyola's undergraduate registration was 43% male and 57% female, a complete reversal from the male-dominated days of 1971.[11] So things have changed, and indeed this reflects a national trend with women enrolling in college more than men.[12]

But haven't there also been changes in college enrollment for people of color? In 1981, enrollment by people who identified as Black had doubled since 1970, when Mount Saint Agnes shut down.[13] In more recent years, between 2000 and 2018, the enrollment from those who identified as Black increased by 30%, but enrollment from those who identified as Caucasian did not decrease in any notable way.[14] Where's the drastic proportional shift in Loyola's population? How can we have a student body that changed with the times and yet didn't change at all?

You can't blame this one on America. Stanford University, ranked #3 nationally in 2022, is only comprised of about 25% students who identify as white. The rest identify as Asian, Hispanic, Latino, or African American. If we look at universities in closer proximity to Loyola, such as Johns Hopkins, we'll find that their undergraduate enrollment was 42% white in 2020.[15] As for Loyola, 71% of undergraduate students were white.[16] Alone, this doesn't say much, but it does ask something: why does Loyola not reflect the changing world of its students?

This is not to say that all of Loyola's claims of diversity are fictions. Each incoming class is touted as the most diverse, and the Accepted Student Profile page on their website currently boasts 43% of accepted students identifying as people of color.[17] This is an improvement from 2021, which was also touted as the most diverse year. As were 2020 and 2019, and statistics back it up. In a few years, if this pace continues, Loyola will probably have a much improved, much more diverse student body.

---

11 Accepted Undergraduate Student Profile, Loyola University Maryland. www.loyola.edu/admission/undergraduate/application-process/accepted-student-profile, Aug. 2022.
12 Oksana Leukhina and Amy Smaldone. "Why Do Women Outnumber Men in College Enrollment?" Saint Louis Fed Eagle, Federal Reserve Bank of St. Louis, 3 Jan. 2023.
13 "Black College Enrollment Has Doubled Since 1970," *New York Times*, May 18, 1981.
14 "Data USA." *Data USA*, datausa.io, 2020.
15 Data USA, "Johns Hopkins University," 2020.
16 Data USA, "Loyola University Maryland," 2020.
17 Accepted Undergraduate Student Profile, Loyola University Maryland. www.loyola.edu/admission/undergraduate/application-process/accepted-student-profile, Aug. 2022

But why? Loyola hasn't suddenly started making amends for its history. This project was approved by Loyola, but the brunt of the work is coming from undergraduate workers and professors. It also came as a result of Loyola coming under fire for racism, the most notable episode of which was the naming of a building after Flannery O'Connor, only to rename the structure after Thea Bowman when a petition exposed O'Connor's racist remarks. Again, this was reactionary. It was the easy way.

Reactionary change is still change, and it should be appreciated. But appreciated does not mean we should be content. And reactionary change should not be treated as if it is equal to change done because Loyola considered it the right thing to do.

Catholicism has a dark history that isn't confined to the Crusades. The burning of Joan of Arc. Selling of indulgences. The Joust of Whores. Dozens of corrupt popes. Thousands of sexual misconduct cases. Not all of these are connected to the Jesuits directly, but they are indirectly connected by virtue of the Jesuits forming part of the Church institution.

Jesuit slave owning is founded on contradictions and excuses that originate from the idea that while slavery was explicitly frowned upon, Jesuits also weren't eager to stick their neck out more than they already were in Maryland.[18] Not stirring up the pot was easier. (Sound familiar?) More than that, they rationalized it to themselves by saying that compared to other masters, their slaves were getting a great deal: Jesuits were merciful and kind, and wasn't that so much better than the other options?

This wasn't true of all Jesuits, obviously, but there is a disturbing facet of this—namely that many of them turned to Saint Ignatius's book of spiritual exercises to interpret biblical passages related to slavery.[19] While never explicitly mentioned, as it was a day-to-day spiritual guidebook rather than a book of scripture.

Other aspects of Christianity showed up in slave owning – such as converting slaves to the order– but one aspect I think is often overlooked is how the enslaved are artistically depicted. Italian Baroque master Caravaggio depicted John, Judas, and Jesus all as Caucasian males in his work *The Taking*

18 Murphy, *Jesuit Slaveholding*, 129.
19 Ibid 92.

of Christ, even though most of the Bible took place in the Middle East. This is true of most other artwork depicting Jesus in the Catholic church. It's as if Jesuits did not want to consider that the people in the Bible could not look like them, because that was not comfortable. That was not easy.

There are plenty of women in the Bible, and whitewashing aside, Jesuits did not see any problem making them look like women. That's because that *was* easy.

There are exceptions. Women were integrated cleanly, efficiently, and are now a majority group at the college. That is quick for a college that only became co-educational fifty years ago. They clearly broke with the status quo there. The issue here is that Loyola only breaks the status quo when it wants to: it doesn't when Loyola attempts to preserve something that it thinks Loyola stands for. Mount Saint Agnes was just Loyola with a different coat of paint: student publications may have subtly griped about the changes, but that change to the population raised no major objections, especially since the majority of the new arrivals were pious and Caucasian.

But then we get to race. Loyola's history of race is troubled, and unspoken, marked by invisible people who made minimal yearbook appearances and received minimal attention, and who were forced to endure invisibility in an institution created with their ancestors' blood and tears.

In 1971, racial tensions reached new highs. In 2023, that same statement is true, but now the problem is bigger than ever before. When you look at Loyola's yearbooks, you'll see a lot of white people, but you'll also see people of color in numbers enough to not be ignored. But their demands are complex – not only do they ask that Loyola acknowledge them, they ask that Loyola take action, and this action is difficult. They ask that Loyola admit that it was at fault – and this fault is something rooted in the school's very foundations, its very history, and the very image it has as an institution. Loyola must bear a cross of its own making.

But make no mistake: Loyola can do it. That is what this essay is about. Women still have many things they're discontented about on campus, enough that we've been protesting and waving our flags, but our history with Loyola is perhaps less troubled. Our presence wasn't ignored because it was easier. When pressured, Loyola can make great strides – and our hope is, that when pressured, they will make greater strides, no matter how bitter the taste of it may be.

In fifty more years, 2023 will also be history. Only Loyola can decide how it will be received.

Two Different Campuses, Two Different Experiences

Maya du Plessis

Loyola's website announces that "our Jesuit tradition of scholarship is based on the concept of cura personalis, or care for the whole person."[1] But, we, as an institution, are not living up to this ideal. Loyola University Maryland was created during a time where the societal norm in the United States was extreme and outright racism and slavery. We know that because of this history in the U.S., traces of racism, ignorance and bias exist today. This essay will focus on the racial environment for Black students on Loyola's campus and how their college experience at Loyola University Maryland is 'less than' in terms of enjoyment, comfort, safety and the ability to thrive academically. By analyzing several sources including the school's newspaper, *The Greyhound*, and interviewing six Black students about their experience on Loyola's campus, the history of racism and ignorance on campus comes to the fore. Research has established that predominantly white institutions can be damaging to Black students, yet there are strategies to change and provide care for students of color. It is time for our great institution to become a campus that is enjoyable, comfortable, safe and dedicated to the academic excellence of all students. It is time for us to learn and understand our history so that we can build a better future for students of color.

---

1 Loyola University Maryland Admission and Aid. www.loyola.edu/admission.

Too often, when Black students at Loyola are victims of racism and discrimination, they are ridiculed and ignored when they stand up for themselves. Racism is a set of beliefs—it is not an action—and it takes many different forms, including but not limited to conscious beliefs, preconscious beliefs, and institutional biases. All of these can change the trajectory of a person's life. I find that the majority of white people at Loyola hold unintentional or preconscious beliefs. They grow up in predominantly white, privileged communities in which they do not often see or interact with people of color. They then form implicit or known biases against people of color and carry those biases with them to Loyola and throughout their lives. Dr. Lisa Wade, a sociologist who studies implicit bias in the media, explains that it is nearly impossible (even as a Black individual) to not have an implicit bias against Black people due to their dehumanization in U.S. history, education, and media. She says that, "these associations, unfortunately, are pre-conscious. Those neurons fire faster than we can suppress them with our conscious mind. So, even if we believe in our heart-of-hearts that these connections are unfair or untrue, our unconscious is busy making the associations anyway. Biased reporting, in other words, changes the minds of viewers, literally."[2] Biases are not something to necessarily be ashamed of: everybody has them. I had them. It is solely a manner of doing the work to dismantle it. So, yes, I have found that Loyola is and has been racist as an institution, with both unintentional and conscious biases among faculty and the student body towards Black students. This should not be interpreted as necessarily intentional racism or that Loyola is a bad school. Loyola is a great institution, but we, as a great institution, need to do the work necessary in order to dismantle the racism within our beloved school.

Today, the campus is changing, with each incoming class of first years being the most diverse in Loyola's history. Despite this, I will present several instances of ignorance and blatant acts of ignoring Black individuals on Loyola's campus throughout this essay. I will also present information from interviews with six different Black students about their time as students and experiences living in the dorms at Loyola. Black students compromise

2 Lisa Wade, "Racial Bias and Media Coverage of Violent Crime." 2015. Sociological Images. Retrieved February 3, 2023, from https://thesocietypages.org/socimages/2015/04/09/racial-bias-and-media-coverage-of-violent-crime/.

their happiness, safety, comfortability, and ability to thrive academically at Loyola. It is time to confront the harmful and toxic racial environment that exists on the Evergreen campus. The burden is great: Black students at Loyola need more counseling and services due to the racism they face; they do not always feel safe on campus; they feel left out as students; and they must expend a great amount of mental, emotional, and physical effort everyday to function as a Loyola student and, more recently, participate anti-racist activism.

The Greyhound contains several examples of racism at the school, which is not surprising considering the Jesuit's actions in the 1838 sale and U.S. history more generally. It is evident that over the years Loyola College has conformed to societal norms of racism. The December 18, 1964 issue of *The Greyhound* reported on the visit to campus by a member of the right-wing John Birch Society, who addressed students at an event.[3] The Birch Society is known to have opposed the Civil Rights Movement, claiming the movement had communists in important positions and that people of color were attempting to divide the country.[4] The 1964 Civil Rights Act, which had been passed earlier that year, outlawed discrimination based on race, color, religion, sex, and national origin, but was opposed by the Birch Society members, who encouraged congressional representatives to vote against it.

These views clearly resonated on campus, as the *Greyhound* described the Birch Society as "taking over the college," suggesting that many were against equity, equality, and saw people of color as less than or other. It is also telling that Loyola College as an institution thought that it would be beneficial for their students to learn about the racially harmful views of this organization.[5] Keep in mind, the first Black student was admitted to Loyola in 1949, which means that by 1964, it was becoming somewhat normalized for a small number of Black students to attend Loyola. Openly inviting an organization that was against the equality of Black Americans to speak to the Loyola student body was extremely unfair to the Black students at Loyola. Imagine Black students at Loyola sitting in a room full of white

---

3 *The Greyhound*, December 18, 1964.
4 "Racism and the John Birch Society, Part 3". Internet Archive. 20 August, 2021. Retrieved 3 February, 2023. https://archive.org/details/racismandthejohnbirchsociety3.
5 *The Greyhound*, December 18, 1964.

peers, teachers and faculty, and an extremely conservative group is speaking about why they do not support a law that would make you equal. This organization masked their ignorance and racism behind 'anti-communism' and Loyola College at the time proved that their own beliefs and standpoints aligned with this racist organization. It is not surprising that this takeover occurred in 1964, when racism permeated society. However, the episode allows readers to understand the harmful racial climate on campus even fifteen years after integration.

Decades later, the first page of *The Greyhound*'s February 21, 1995 issue announced a "Multicultural House Approved for '95-'96." The section begins by explaining that as a part of "Loyola's five-year 'Plan for Diversity', a new special interest Multicultural House has been established and approved by the Resident Affairs Council for the 1995-96 academic year." The intent of the house was to provide a space for students who were interested in learning about each other's cultural differences. Although no official leadership or support from the university was provided, "residents of the house will be expected to act as a support group/family to the other members of the house."[6] Instead of creating a system of diversity education or training for students, the school created a space for students to hash out their bias and ignorance on their own. By believing the solution to racism on campus was cohabitating students of different cultures, Loyola ultimately silenced Black students when so much more education and action was needed. Dr. Jasmine L. Harris, a professor at the University of Texas, San Antonio, explains that "Black students in [predominantly white universities] develop a distinctive consciousness rooted in their disempowerment on campus. This alternative consciousness includes all behavioral adjustments necessary to maintain access, if not belonging, at PWIs for Black students."[7] Those students needed licensed professionals to help them through an environment that literally altered their behavior and consciousness, not other students who did not have the resources, education or mental capacity to support each other.

Although American institutions have a history of not providing Black people resources, instead tasking Black people with serving as therapists to

6 *The Greyhound.* 68:14 (1995). Retrieved 3 February, 2023. https://archive.org/details/greyhound68loyo_12.
7 Jasmine Harris, "Inheriting Educational Capital: Black College Students, Nonbelonging, and Ignored Legacies at Predominantly White Institutions," *Women's Studies Quarterly* 48 (2020): 95.

their fellow Black people, doing so shirks institutional responsibilities. On top of managing one's own racial stress, conflict, identity and growth, to take care of another person's needs adds so much more additional stress. The first Black student was admitted in 1949 and the first Multicultural House, a space where students of color could come together to feel comfortable on a majority white campus, was not approved or even considered until 1995. It is evident that Loyola has a history of ignoring the needs of Black students on campus. Today, in 2022, we have more resources for Black students, whether it is the Black Student Union, the African Student Association, the Caribbean Student Union or ALANA (African, Latinx, Asian, and Native American) Services. However, these organizations are mostly student-led, once again leaving students to care for and listen to other students. It is unfair that we do not have counselors specifically for racial stress and it is unfair that Black students are the only group on campus lobbying for their needs, wants, and equity.

Professor Thomas DiLorenzo was a professor of economics at Loyola University Maryland's Sellinger School of Business from 1992 to 2020. DiLorenzo is known for writing several books, including but not limited to *How Capitalism Saved America: The Untold History of our Country, from the Pilgrims to the Present*; *The Politically Incorrect Guide to Economics*; and *The Real Lincoln: A New Look at Abraham Lincoln, His Agenda, and an Unnecessary War*. DiLorenzo's views are libertarian and aligned with the Confederacy.

The economist affiliated "himself with the neo-Confederate League of the South, which shares his view that slavery had little to do with the Civil War and that big government is the root of all evil."[8] The League of the South self identifies as a:

"Southern nationalist organization…whose ultimate goal is 'a free and independent Southern republic.' The League defines the Southern United States as the states that make up the Confederate States of America. While political independence ranks highly among our goals, we are also a religious

---

8 Carl R. Weinberg, "Does Lincoln Still Matter?" *OAH Magazine of History*, 23:1, January (2009): 64.

and social movement, advocating a return to a more traditional, conservative Christian-oriented Southern culture.[9]

This organization holds extreme pro-Confederate beliefs, and the website contains photos and videos of the Confederate flag, anti-Islam and anti-immigration signs. Confederate flags and anti-Muslim language are not allowed on Loyola's campus; if seen in a dorm room or heard on campus, students are asked to remove it from their room and/or submit a bias report. The League of the South's website asserts that Southern "culture is being sacked by an unholy crusade of leftist agitators and foreign religions and our very physical survival depends on us" to "stand together and secure a future in which OUR culture can survive, dominate and thrive."[10] The League of the South wishes for white domination over other races and Thomas DiLorenzo allied himself with these beliefs.

Loyola University Maryland is a Jesuit institution that is supposedly welcoming to all people of different religions, ethnicities, races, cultures and languages. If this were true and enforced when DiLorenzo affiliated himself with the League of the South, which is clearly a hateful, white, Christian supremacist organization, Loyola should have removed him as a professor. Affiliating with such an organization would have been enough explanation to remove DiLorenzo from Loyola, but the professor also made his defense of the Confederacy known to his students. Student reviews on the Rate My Professor website, both positive and negative include, "he's a libertarian and its [sic] definitely evident in his lectures"; "you'll enjoy his lectures and wild tangents about liberals in the humanities building"; "clearly Libertarian- just tell him what he wants to hear on tests and you'll do well. Don't bother debating- he's smarter than you"; and "his anarcho-capitalist ideas are a bit to stomach [sic] for any but the most devoted Libertarians. And his defense of the Confederacy is embarrassing and intellectually irresponsible."[11] From these reviews, it is clear that DiLorenzo made students feel that he was academically superior to them that they should not even try to

---

9 The League of the South. Retrieved 3 February, 2023. https://leagueofthesouth.com/.
10 Ibid.
11 Rate my Professor. Thomas DiLorenzo- Professor in the Economics department at Loyola University Maryland. Retrieved 3 February, 2023. https://www.ratemyprofessors.com/professor?tid=72974.

challenge his beliefs. It is also inappropriate for college students to listen to an educated and experienced professor's pro-Confederate beliefs every class; there is always the chance the students may be influenced by this language in the future. In addition, allowing students of color and of different religions to study under a man who makes it known that he is pro-Confederacy and affiliated with an organization that is against their very existence in the United States is not fair. Similarly, his strong libertarian beliefs discard a role for the state in ensuring the rights, liberties, and protection of people of color in the United States, and in doing so comes close to invalidating those very rights and liberties. There is a lot of work to be done in the U.S. to protect people of color from hate crimes, inequality, harmful legislation, and police violence. There is a need to build people of color up to a place in society that equals the advantages of white privilege. Libertarians are either indirectly or directly against this type of intervention and therefore indirectly or directly against the equity for people of color in the United States. DiLorenzo should not have stayed at Loyola for as long as he did. Loyola, again, denied students of color their comfort, safety, and ability to thrive academically by continuing to employ Thomas DiLorenzo.

Each of the three racial issues presented in Loyola's history show a general disregard for the wants, needs and success of students of color at Loyola. Because students still feel unseen and unheard today, interviews are one way to bridge the communication gap.

The first participant, who will be identified as Mary (not her real name) identifies as a light-skinned Black woman. When asked to describe her experience at Loyola, she said "in one word, 'wary'." She described how she is "constantly wondering if people are staring at me because of my hair or my clothes or judging me because they think I don't belong here. My friends and I have faced many instances of racism on campus since my freshman year, so I have become more judgmental and stereotypical when interacting with my white peers under the fear that they are secretly racist." Hearing this, I came to the conclusion that racism on campus has affected Black students' ability to be open-minded in making connections with other students. It is deeply upsetting that due to previous racist encounters, a student's mind may become mostly or completely closed off when meeting other Loyolans, and specifically white students. A large part of what is supposed to make the college experience so enjoyable is meeting new people and making connections. Black students are missing out on that experience because a percentage of the student body is racist. One study of Black experiences stated that "given the frequency with which Black students at PWIs encounter race-related stressors, students likely employ a number of coping responses across their time at the PWIs."[12] While white students typically avoid Black students due to implicit bias, Black students avoid white students due to fear, causing re-segregation on campus. This limits the experiences of both white and Black students and allows their biases to strengthen over time. Both parties will leave Loyola having the reinforced idea that they are able to and should confine themselves to people of their own race.

When asked to tell a story about an instance of racism she faced on campus, another student said "My freshman year, I was walking around Thea Bowman, which was my own building at the time. I was with four Black friends. We were laughing and walking back to my room when a white boy opened his door, looked us up and down and said 'the Blacks are being too loud'." Although there is an academic debate about whether the term "Blacks" is considered derogatory, it is dehumanizing. Calling someone a Black or Blacks reduces them to their race and dates all the way back to slavery. The use of 'blacks' and 'whites' has a distancing effect that divides and objectifies by design. Griffith et al describe how "isolated and cumulative discriminatory experiences can be cognitively and emotionally taxing and interfere with students' ability to achieve at their full potential."[13] It is not healthy for Black students to hear derogatory language in their living spaces, where students are supposed to feel safe, and at home. It undeniably reinforces the idea that they do not belong at Loyola and forces them to code switch or change the way they act to be perceived in the same way as white students. Only the interviewee heard this out of her four other friends, so she decided to ignore it and keep walking. She said that once they were

---

12 Isha N Griffith, Noelle M. Hurd, and Saida B. Hussain, "I Didn't Come to School for This": A Qualitative Examination of Experiences with Race-Related Stressors and Coping Responses among Black Students Attending a Predominantly White Institution," *Journal of Adolescent Research*, 34:2 (2019): 116.
13 Ibid.

safely back in her dorm room, she told her friends, who wanted to go back and knock on his door. They wanted to yell at him and make him realize what he said was wrong but she talked them down, explaining that they would be adding to whatever stereotype he already had about Black women. She thought it would perpetuate the same stereotype white Americans tend to hold: Black women are loud, aggressive, and angry. The girls decided to do nothing, tell nobody and carry that experience with them throughout their future years at Loyola.

When asked if it affected her perception of white students on campus, she said "Well, I wouldn't say affected. More like… added to." She said she had already heard so many stories of students being racist, that she held a negative perception of white students on campus and knew better than to go out of her way to interact with them. The self-segregation of white and Black students at Loyola occurs at other predominantly white institutions as well. One eagerly anticipated part of the college experience is the opportunity to leave your old self behind, create a new self, and meet new friends and different kinds of people from all over the state or country. But because of the everyday racism and ignorance that festers on the Evergreen campus, many Black students are robbed of this experience due to their fear.

Another interviewee described how she was one of three Black women in a French class in the fall semester of 2021. Despite the fact that her professor was able to remember all 27 of the white students' names in the class, he confused all three Black girls on a daily basis. As if this was not disparaging enough, he ended up saying something racist that he thought was a light-hearted joke. When teaching a new phrase in French, he pointed at the interviewee and in front of the entire class, said "I bet you she didn't know this when she got off the boat from Ghana." Every student in the class became silent and exchanged looks after staring at her, but aside from those five seconds of silence, class resumed. Although this was likely out of ignorance rather than intended racism, this professor made a racist joke. Jasmine Harris explains that "Black students learn their nonbelonging in school via interactions with white teachers and peers, as well as through witnessing interactions between white students and teachers. Experiences of racism in academic spaces are one way to remind Black students they do not belong."[14] Watching this professor recall the names of each and every white student in class every day while so clearly singling out the Black students and failing to remember their names was actively teaching this student that she did not belong in that class, in that building, or in this school. It brings up feelings of loneliness and questioning on whether she deserved to receive an acceptance into Loyola.

There are two other problems with this situation. One, this professor was clearly not trained to interact with people from different backgrounds, and two, it has become so normalized in multiracial environments for white people be bystanders in instances of racism. This professor was being racist out of ignorance in this situation and no action was taken by other students. This student expressed a fear of speaking up or reporting the incident to Loyola's board because she thought it might be turned against her. She feared the professor could have lowered her grades, or she could have been stared at for even longer by the rest of the class which would further single her out. University protocol for racist incidents should be shared university-wide to ensure every single student knows there will not be repercussions against them and that racist behavior is not tolerated at Loyola.

Another interviewee took the interview time to vent. When asked how she would describe her time at Loyola so far, she said "To be brutally honest, I would say it has been a constant let down in more ways than one. In high school I would be on social media watching the college freshman and sophomore from my home town hanging around in big, diverse friend groups and I feel like that doesn't exist at Loyola for Black women." She went on to explain that she tends to stick to her small friend group of three or four other Black women because of friend rejections. She said that in her three years here, she had watched the Black men that attend Loyola hang out with exclusively white people, post "Happy White girl Wednesday" on Instagram and Snapchat and even openly say they do not like Black people. I could tell this made her angry and confused because she was running her hands through her hair and talking with her hands to emphasize what she was saying.

---

14 Harris, "Inheriting Educational Capital," 95.

She began talking about one specific group of Black men at Loyola, which "is decently large." There were two specific dark-skin Black individuals who openly talk about how they don't like Black people in general and therefore avoid Black women on campus. One Black male student had said to the interviewee, "I don't like Black girls. I would only date [another Black student on campus] because she looks white with dark skin." By this, he meant this specific Black student had physical features that would fit Western beauty ideals. Within that quote is a deep-rooted hatred for Black skin and himself; it is internalized racism. Internalized racism "occurs when socially stigmatized groups accept and recycle negative messages regarding their aptitude, abilities, and societal place, which results in self-devaluation and the invalidation of others within the group."[15] Internalized racism is another disadvantage to being a Black person in a predominantly white area where racism is prevalent. When constantly surrounded by white individuals who undervalue you by making racist jokes, using derogatory language, hanging the Confederate flag in their dorm room, and using politics to camouflage their racism, it can be difficult to reject these ideas. If you have only ever lived in a predominantly white environment, you may start to absorb the same politics, derogatory language, racist jokes, and implicit bias against your own race. You may start to distinguish yourself as 'other than' your own race. But even if you carry this internalized racism throughout your early life, your collegiate institution should be committed to educating with the intent to dismantle it.

In addition to harming the individual, internalized racism also has negative effects on other members of the same group. The interviewee responded and said, "I mean, it's embarrassing that the Black men on campus don't want to be seen with Black girls." Feeling like you don't belong in such a way that members of your own race do not want to be seen with you as friends is a gut-wrenching, harmful feeling that can only lead to loneliness.

Black students did not gain access to prestigious predominantly white institutions until more recent years, meaning, as Harris writes,

---

15 Shaun R. Harper, "Peer Support for African American Male College Achievement: Beyond Internalized Racism and the Burden of Acting White," *The Journal of Men's Studies* 14:3 (2007): 338.

"generations of white men have benefited and continue to benefit from the capital derived from elite education, not just as a function of the education itself, but in the perceived value of the institution. Historical narratives of Black college students position them as anomalies, not as evidence of Black achievement but as a result of 'unusual' individual work ethic, an intended consequence of their typical exclusion from prestigious institutions. Black students cannot just gain higher education membership through attendance the way property ownership buys membership into the 'right' neighborhood, and they subsequently cannot pass down educational capital in the same way as white graduates. The structural and cultural foundations of educational inheritance limit how Black graduates are viewed, and subsequently suppress upward economic trajectories for Black people via educational achievement."[16]

Black students are already at a disadvantage in spaces like Loyola due to reasons they cannot change. Black students are disadvantaged in the U.S. and it is not Loyola's fault that these stereotypes exist. Loyola was built and has operated during times when slavery was accepted and racism was a social norm among upper-class white men. But, we, as an institution, are still functioning under that norm and while temporary solutions such as short-term counseling to support students of color have been offered, educating the student body about how these beliefs are harmful has not been done. The time is now to dismantle this system within our institution and build something new.

According to the ALANA website, "it is the intent of ALANA Services to support ALANA students and the entire Loyola community by enriching the minds of all in regards to the beauty of diversity."[17] We can see that Loyola is committed to increasing diversity as the class of 2026 is the most diverse class in our history, with 39% of students identifying as people of color. Although this is promising, increasing diversity alone has not and will not change the challenges Black students face on campus. Harris explains that "the admittance of Black students at PWIs improves institutional

16 Harris "Inheriting Educational Capital," 90-91.
17 ALANA Services, Loyola University Maryland. www.loyola.edu/department/alana.

appearances of increased diversity but is seldom evidence of engagement and perceived belonging within the institution."[18]

A new form of diversity training for staff and students must be implemented. Justina Osa states that the "best solution to racial prejudice would begin at the personal or individual level."[19] She notes that "everyone on campus needs to become more aware of how their individual behavior towards others contributes to the perpetuation of racial prejudice on campus and in society at large."[20] A curriculum that addresses these concerns and prepares students to embrace an unbiased life in a diverse world is needed. The Loyola diversity core requirement allows for substantial variation, with both a very in-depth sociological class on race and a business class that barely delves into gender, let alone race, meeting the requirement. Loyola students should all be learning the same curriculum for the diversity requirement. It should dive into prejudice and implicit bias, where students will take an online test to see if they have an implicit bias against Black people. It should focus on Loyola's racist history, including how the institution contributed to slavery and the dehumanization of Black people. It should give examples of bias, prejudice and internalized racism and provide insight on ways to break down bias and change. Our students, both Black and white, need a change in our education in order to prevent re-segregation on campus.

Lastly, Black students require more resources on campus. Research has made this clear, with one study arguing that:

"Given the clear relationship between level of stress, particularly psychological/interpersonal stress among Black students, it seems important to further efforts on PWI campuses to find ways to reduce levels of stress. Programs designed to address stress related to relationships, including male/ female relationships, as well as stress related to feelings of loneliness, isolation, and self-esteem would be particularly helpful. In the same vein, finding ways to encourage points of connection on campus for Black students may also assist

---

18 Harris, "Inheriting Educational Capital," 95.
19 Justina O. Osa, "The Pervasiveness of Racial Prejudice in Higher Education in the U.S: Raising Awareness and Solution," *Forum on Public Policy Online* No. 3 (2007): 3.
20 Ibid.

in decreasing levels of psychological and interpersonal stress. "[21]

Personally, throughout this project, I was made aware of several resources for Black students that I had never heard of before. If there are resources on campus, they need to be advertised across campus in a more effective way so that all students of color are knowledgeable about their options. Loyola should also provide counselors who specialize in helping students of color navigate their experience through a prestigious, predominantly white institution. Besides these calls for change, a panel should be formed for and with students of color on campus that is dedicated to making a real change that is beneficial to all. Professors, staff, students, alumni and future students deserve more. Loyola deserves more. We all deserve more.

Interview Information

I interviewed six Black students who currently live on Loyola's campus. I selected six questions to ask each individual:

1. What is your race/ethnicity?
2. How would you explain your experience at Loyola as a Black student?
3. How many times would you say you have experienced racism or discrimination on campus from students or professors?
4. Can you tell me a story of one experience of racism or discrimination you have faced on campus?
5. Do you think Loyola has enough resources on campus for students of color? Explain if possible.
6. In what ways do you think your college experience differs from White students on campus?

These questions allowed me to share some experiences Black students face every day on the Evergreen campus and what they think could be done to improve our experiences. Although I did ask more personal questions, like ethnicity, I will be keeping interviewees anonymous for their safety and protection.

---

21 Paul P. Heppner, Peter Ji, Helen A. Neville, and Russell Thye, "The Relations among General and Race-Related Stressors and Psychoeducational Adjustment in Black Students Attending Predominantly White Institutions," *Journal of Black Studies* 34(4) (2004): 612-613.

Scio Nihil

Camille Barrón

Hair relaxed into beautiful submission
Face acrylically defined and chemically composed
Adornments meticulously chosen
Scent tested and approved
Smile practiced and performed
I am a porcelain doll.
Sipping tea, at 6 am in the quiet of a sleepy-city apartment
Porcelain doll dainty wrists
Washing dishes, feeding cats
Folding linens, singing hymnals
Praying for peace and safety.
Porcelain doll knitting sweaters
And folding paper cranes
Reading poems, setting tables
Wearing cardigans and pearls.
Porcelain doll decorating cupcakes
Lighting scented candles
Watering potted plants and humming childhood lullabies
With my porcelain painted lips.

But lipstick can be dark.
Eyes lined black as city alleyways.
There is anger at injustice
The world outside the confines of a pastel doll house—
It's messy.

It's hard.
It's iron and concrete and coal.
And I am too.
Biking through the brick metropolis
Black berets and silk bonnets

Sunglasses and headphones
And anarchist literature.
Evenings spent sprinting through the smog
Heartbeats synchronized to the crude drumming of the city—
So hard to impress.
I'm on the metro
Eyebrows structured and defined
And adorned with a calculated air of apathy.
See me social justice march
Down highways with fervently entitled youths.
See me armed against misogyny
Until my peers learn to better conceal it.
See me smoking cigarillos,
Drinking black coffee,
Breathing the tainted air of the city that birthed me,
And chanting manifestoes.

But my manifesto can be love.
And love can conquer anger and fear
And hatred.
Love can reconcile, it can erase timidity
And it can abolish resentment.
Let it wash my face and take the need for vengeance from my spirit.
Let it replace the thirst for power with thirst for truth.
I burn incense
And wear long skirts.
Naked face and natural hair

And braless lazy days
Reading pacifism in the park.
I walk far to find pure air to breathe.
I sit and deconstruct my dichotomy
Under a wise and ancient tree.
I trace myself backwards and forwards.

I meditate on the paths I have traveled.
I cry for the things I have seen
And for the things I have done.
I contemplate transcendence.
I drink wine and listen to folk music
On the balcony of my home.
I bike barefoot to buy Indian takeout
And eat it in silence on the floor of an empty room.

I think about swords and pens.

About opposites and compliments
And how to progress in knowing how divergent pieces of myself can learn
to harmonize.
I think about minimalism and materialism
Sentimentalism.
I think about blackberries
And the complexity of their literary and symbolic significance.
I think about the number seven as I see it reoccurring in every possible
sequence and equation.
I think about God,
And Sylvia Plath,
And If I dare disturb the universe.
I think about porcelain dolls and activists and hippies
I think about being radical,
And how both sides of this ideological war are defined by fear.
And I think about love, as radical but defined by the absence of fear—
The absolution of fear
And how I am fairly certain it is the answer.
I think about the inevitability of art and war
how they create each other.
how they destroy each other—
inspire each other and annihilate each other
and how there is nothing that is innocent.
I think about pain and privilege
And stacked decks of cards.

I think about grace and all the things I don't understand
And toil and fate and destiny.
The shape of these things, their origins, and culminations

And what this black box of secrets contains.
I think about dreams and nightmares
And prophesy.

I think *always* of death
And resurrection.
Of betrayal and redemption

And how this race I run was rigged from the start.

I think about war and peace and politics
About corruption and poverty and imperialism
About western ideals and conspiracy theories

About communism

And slavery and misogyny and antisemitism.
I think about the darkness within me—
Tendencies to lie and manipulate and steal.
The darkness that I know could make me very great but alone in the ashes
of the world.
I think of the curse of wealth and power
And I try to evaluate my motives
And the driving force of my ambition
But I don't know.

I think about so many things,
Until everything I was on the outside is gone.
My body is gone.
My painted face and sculpted hair
My pierced ears and tattooed skin
All my clothes and appendages and freckles are gone.
My blood evaporated
My brain an invisible energy in the wind
My home and street
And city
Are gone.
And even in such complete concentration
When it is only my essence and nothing else
And I transcend throughout my past and future,
When I am spread thin

And stretched into the corners,
When I fill the cracks and crevices
And melt into the pores of everything,
And my spirit is awakened to a dimensionless reality
Even then,
Scio Nihil

I know nothing.

Reflections and Recollections

Finding Answers in the Archives

Jenny Kinniff

I love helping people find answers to questions. As an archivist in an academic library, each week I work with students, faculty, staff, and others outside the university reaching out for guidance with their research. Unearthing information that solves a genealogical puzzle or clarifies a thorny dissertation question gives me deep satisfaction. *I have been useful. I am good at this. The archives are fulfilling their mission.* The inverse, of course, is the feeling of inadequacy when the trail goes cold. *Have I missed something? Or is this question unanswerable, given the materials available in the archives?* All too often, records that could answer important questions simply do not exist, in our archives or anywhere else. These "archival silences" can be frustrating and even painful for those who find their ancestors, their community, or their identity missing from the historical record. In this volume, Loyola University Maryland student contributors grapple with both these silences and with the important records they uncovered, shedding new light on Loyola's historic ties to slavery that reverberate through the present.

Archives are not neutral. They are not passive recipients of a complete record of the organization, group, or community they document. Decisions made over years, decades, and even centuries by archivists and those in power regarding which records are worthy of preservation shape archival collections. We can trace decision-making even further upstream, where those in positions of power determine which records are created in the first place. For instance, the 1860 United States Census Slave Schedule documents the number of enslaved individuals owned by a person, but not the names of the enslaved. This erasure of Black identity makes our quest to identify a sixty-year-old enslaved woman owned by Jesuits in Baltimore monumentally more difficult.[1] In Loyola University Maryland's archives, documentation of non-white students and employees from earlier decades is scarce, even more so records created by these individuals that would preserve their voices and perspectives. There are many significant gaps in Loyola's archives, and in archives around the country, where the records of marginalized communities should rightly reside and be cared for with the same loving attention historically given to the records of powerful white men.

Loyola's student researchers began their work knowing that they would likely find a frustrating lack of relevant records, and that the window offered by the archives into this particular history might be cloudy and dim. I am immensely proud of the archival research that these dedicated students conducted during the summer of 2021 and in their subsequent History and Writing courses. They sifted through a tremendous volume of documents with the patience and keen eyes of seasoned scholars, flagged new information for us to examine as a group, and created a shared research file of notes, images, and reports that will be an essential tool in continuing this research for years to come. They also created their own compelling works of scholarship and creativity that can be found in this volume.

As recently as 2016, Loyola University Maryland disavowed a connection to the Maryland Province of Jesuits' 1838 sale of 272 enslaved people.[2] Less than a decade later, the university's perspective has shifted. It no longer denies complicity in the Jesuits' slavery-fueled economy, but has tasked a group of faculty, staff, and students with digging into the historical record to learn more. Relevant records sit, as they have for decades, in Loyola's archives and elsewhere. Scholars writing histories of Loyola (until now, all white men) have consulted them before. What has changed over the years, however, is the lens through which we view these materials. Historians cite excerpts from documents as evidence, and sometimes the same documents

---

1 1860 U.S. Federal Census – Slave Schedules for Baltimore (Independent City) Maryland, Ward 11. Accessed via Ancestry.com.

2 "Georgetown University to give admissions preference to descendants of slaves sold by the college," *Baltimore Sun*, September 1, 2016, https://www.baltimoresun.com/education/bs-md-loyola-georgetown-slavery-20160901-story.html.

are used to support very different conclusions. A striking example encountered in our research relates to our team's discovery of an 1833 letter by Henry Barnard, a law student traveling through the South Atlantic states, describing his visit to Georgetown College. Barnard recalls being given a tour of Georgetown by its president, Father Thomas Mulledy, S.J., who showed him among other museum objects "a piece of a Negro's hide tanned—it was as thick as calves skin."[3] Historian Robert Emmett Curran omits this repugnant description in his 2010 history of Georgetown University, while nonetheless drawing from the same letter to describe Mulledy's energy and magnetism.[4] When our team shared this letter with Georgetown in 2022, the university attempted to corroborate the description with records in its archives and shared news of the horrific account with the community.[5] The Barnard letter demonstrates how interpretations of records can shift dramatically, even within the relatively short time span of a dozen years.

As with this example from Georgetown, the published histories of Loyola also invite closer scrutiny and re-evaluation of archival sources. The earliest is *Historical Sketch of Loyola College, Baltimore, 1852-1902*, by Father John J. Ryan, S.J. This important window into the first fifty years of Loyola includes students' reminiscences on their time at Loyola, the faculty they knew, and events both major and mundane at the college. *Historical Sketch* focuses on Jesuit faculty, Loyola alumni, commencements, and ceremonies, but fails to provide any details on the presence of domestic workers at the college or the presence (or lack thereof) of enslaved laborers.

Historical Sketch's celebratory and nostalgic tone extends to more than just Loyola's history. Published during a peak of Lost Cause rhetoric, the book describes how a guest lecturer, Robert E. Lee's former aide-de-camp Col. Charles Marshall, "carried his audience back in fancy to the period of the Civil War and the campaigns before Richmond" and shared his insider's perspective on "the great Southern commander."[6] The Union or Confederate

---

3 Bernard C. Steiner, ed., "The South Atlantic States in 1833, as Seen by a New Englander," *Maryland Historical Magazine* 13 (1918): 289-90.

4 Robert Emmett Curran, A History of Georgetown University, Volume I (Washington, DC: Georgetown University Press, 2010), 117-119.

5 "Library Archivists Investigate Troubling 1833 Account of Artifact at Georgetown," October 25, 2022, https://library.georgetown.edu/news/library-archivists-investigate-troubling-1833-account-artifact-georgetown.

6 John J. Ryan, *Historical Sketch of Loyola College, Baltimore, 1852-1902* (n.p., 1903), 136-37.

service of students receives an occasional, brief mention, with no indication of how opposing loyalties may have affected the college community. Father John Abell Morgan, a Loyola president, faculty member, and Confederate sympathizer from a Maryland slaveholding family, is described as having possessed "the old-time Maryland geniality and *bonhomie*." Charles C. Lancaster, a procurator in residence at Loyola who was involved in the Maryland Province of Jesuits' 1838 sale of enslaved people, is described as "a man of worthy character…[who] possessed the old-time Maryland courtesy."[7] In relying largely on alumni nostalgia to construct a history of Loyola, Ryan's work itself stands as historical evidence of the Lost Cause sympathies in abundance at Loyola at the turn of the 20th century.

Nearly 90 years later, Loyola history professor and archivist Nicholas Varga published the last major exploration of Loyola's history, his hefty 1990 volume *Baltimore's Loyola, Loyola's Baltimore*. It is no exaggeration to say that Varga worked for decades on this book; correspondence in his personal papers referring to a research project on Loyola history dates back to the late 1960s.[8] Varga's book brings the rigor of a professional historian to the examination of Loyola's past. It introduces a much greater degree of detail than *Historical Sketch* offers, along with many citations of archival materials at Loyola, St. Ignatius Church, Loyola Blakefield High School, Georgetown University, and other archival repositories. As an archivist, I find Varga's encyclopedic chronicling of events at Loyola helpful and consult it often when researching university history.

Varga uses Ryan as one of many sources for his history, so nostalgic alumni reminiscences are shared again in his work. When we compare Varga's description of Loyola's first fifty years with that of Ryan, though, we see a dramatically expanded picture. Varga incorporates topics such as financial wrangling, donor relations, the broader social and political situation in Baltimore, and the school's connections to the Maryland Province of Jesuits. The hazy, golden image of Loyola in *Historical Sketch* is brought into much sharper focus. And yet, Varga also ignores or glides over the surface of many difficult questions that students seek answers to in this volume's essays. Varga

---

7 Ibid.
8 Loyola Notre Dame Library Archives, Nicholas Varga papers (SC.049), Box 1, Folder 11.

notes that "the 1850 census found over 140,000 whites, about 25,000 free Black persons, and nearly 3,000 slaves within the bounds of Baltimore."[9] After defining the racial demographics of Baltimore through census data, the meticulous historian fails to follow up with information our research team uncovered: a 60-year-old enslaved Black woman is listed in the 1860 U.S. Census Slave Schedule as owned by the Jesuits in Baltimore City's Ward 11, where Loyola was located.[10] Varga cites the Maryland Province Archives held at Georgetown University many times in his work. However, he does not mention the ledger that student researcher Deidra Jackson found in that collection indicating that Loyola rented "servants" from a Baltimore slave-holding family, the Mannings, from 1855-1860.[11] *Baltimore's Loyola, Loyola's Baltimore* never broaches the topic of Loyola and slavery.

Varga does mention the longtime service of one Loyola employee, Madison Fenwick, described as "a Black man who worked in the kitchen," though he notes "He had less occasion to meet the students, so there are fewer references to him in publications and reminiscences."[12] According to a Jesuit house diary in Loyola's university archives, "Matty" Fenwick worked for more than 40 years in a Loyola refectory.[13] We still have much to learn about Madison Fenwick, but our research has identified some of his residences in Baltimore as well as the names of descendants and ancestors (including a possible link to Port Tobacco, the site of a Jesuit plantation). Had Varga applied his same intense attention to detail to the lives of Fenwick, Alexander Briscoe, Dominick Butler, George Short, and Thomas Short—other late 19th and early 20th century Black workers at Loyola we have identified in census records and city directories—we might already have a more complete understanding of the contributions of these men to the growth and stability of Loyola. We might also know of any ancestral links they have to those enslaved by Jesuits.[14] Thirty-three years after its pub-

9 Nicholas Varga, *Baltimore's Loyola, Loyola's Baltimore* (Baltimore: The Maryland Historical Society, 1990), 44.
10 1860 U.S. Federal Census – Slave Schedules for Baltimore (Independent City) Maryland, Ward 11. Accessed via Ancestry.com.
11 Maryland Province Archives (Georgetown University), Cash and Day Book, July 1855, March 1856, May 1857, and December 1860.
12 Varga, *Baltimore's Loyola, Loyola's Baltimore*, 129.
13 Loyola Notre Dame Library Archives, Loyola University Maryland Jesuit Community records (LUMD.008.001), Minister's Diary, 1904-1929, August 18-22, 1924 entries.
14 Anna Young's essay in this volume explores the history of enslaved and free Black workers at Loyola.

lication, *Baltimore's Loyola, Loyola's Baltimore* continues to serve as a useful chronicle of Loyola history. As these examples demonstrate, though, the lens through which its author viewed Loyola's past limits it as a tool for understanding the full, complex history of Loyola that we seek today.

It can be all too easy to pick apart the work of the past from our modern perspective, and I assume that future readers will find many shortcomings in our current efforts. As society develops new ways of seeing and understanding the past, and as our collective reckoning with centuries of racial injustice in the United States continues, our interpretation of the records available to us will continue to evolve. In addition, ongoing technological advances will allow us to examine archival records in new ways. Archives continue to make strides in providing online access to digitized and transcribed records, allowing researchers to review and search records remotely and pinpoint content that previously would have taken days of careful reading to find.

While recognizing our research findings and interpretations as a product of our specific moment in time, I believe that our collaborative research process is moving our understanding of Loyola's past in the right direction. Descendants of those enslaved by the Maryland Province of Jesuits serve on Loyola's Universities Studying Slavery presidential task force and work closely with student researchers. Their wisdom and guidance have been instrumental to our success so far, and their generous sharing of knowledge and family stories gives materials found in the archives deeper meaning and resonance. Loyola students continue to bring their passion, energy, and creativity to the project and to generate ideas for positive change at the university. Descendants and students provide inspiration and vision for using research on the darkest aspects of Loyola's past as a catalyst for reparative action and growth.

This volume should not be construed as an endpoint or even as the definitive telling of this aspect of Loyola's history. It is an update and a retelling, and I hope future researchers will continue to build on and improve what we share at this juncture. Like a family that avoids hard conversations, a university that fails to provide space and support for reckoning with legacies of racism and discrimination only deepens divisions and isolation.

Having the courage to continue this research, have these conversations, and uplift the work of students and the voices of descendants is what will bring the Loyola community closer together.

I still love helping people find answers in the archives. With this ongoing research, though, there is no binary of success or failure. Our research process has revealed important evidence about Loyola's past, but it has also uncovered a path that students, descendants, faculty, staff, alumni, and community can walk together as they build a stronger university committed to racial justice. It is through asking, discussing, sharing, and connecting—not just finding—that we are discovering deeper truths about Loyola.

Archaeology and Jesuit-enslaved Ancestors

Laura E. Masur

I'm always nervous on the first day of fieldwork. As we haul our equipment—screens, shovels, trowels, buckets, GPS—on site, I think, "I hope I planned this out right. I hope we're digging in the right place." This has been particularly important during our fieldwork in the summers of 2021 and 2022, since we've had so many guests and volunteers on site. Doing public archaeology projects is about research, but it's also a performance: I want to make sure we have something interesting to show everyone.

On our first day of digging at the former St. Inigoes plantation—now the Navy's Webster Field Annex—we started excavating a 5 by 5 foot square "test unit" in a location that should show building foundations, based on a recent ground-penetrating radar (GPR) survey. There was a lot of debris: bits of oyster shell, brick, mortar, and a few tiny artifacts. At the end of that day, I was still nervous. On day two, visitors arrived, including Angela Wilson. Angela's third great grandfather, John Bennet, and his family lived at St. Inigoes in 1870. The family had been previously enslaved by John Lilburn. Beyond this, her family's connection to St. Inigoes has been difficult to discern. Angela was a good sport and picked up a shovel to start digging. Within five minutes she said "I think I found something!" And sure enough, she had hit brick—part of an intact brick foundation that had mostly been removed.

Figure 1a-b. (a) Angela Wilson digging at St. Inigoes. (b) Angela's discovery, the robbed brick foundations—probably of an eighteenth-century chapel. Photos courtesy of (a) Angela Wilson and (b) Steve Lenik.

Angela's discovery was important because it revealed the remains of what we suspect was an early eighteenth-century Catholic chapel at St. Inigoes, the predecessor of the 1788 St. Ignatius Church, built less than a mile away. The field where it was found has long been called "Old Chapel Field" by locals, but the location of the chapel itself has been elusive. It's also important because it was *Angela's discovery*, and her contribution plays an important role in the continuing story of Old Chapel Field.

Bricks and Stories from St. Inigoes

We were digging at Old Chapel Field as part of a two-year project aimed at understanding the landscapes of three former Jesuit plantations in Maryland: St. Inigoes and Newtown in St. Mary's County, and Bohemia in Cecil County. These places are long remembered in local histories as the sites of the colony's earliest Catholic churches, and home to pioneering Jesuit missionaries. Their stories have focused on the challenge of achieving religious freedom for Maryland's Catholics, who faced persecution in England in the wake of the Protestant Reformation and the formation of the Church of England. These stories usually acknowledge the plantations' connections to slavery, but paint a picture of a benign institution managed by kindly paternalistic priests. In the words of America's first Catholic bishop: "the few to whom this management is committed, treat their negroes with great mildness and are attentive to guard them from the evils of hunger and nakedness; than [sic] they work less and are much better fed, lodged and clothed, than labouring men in almost any part of Europe."[1]

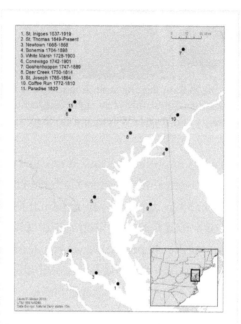

Figure 2. Jesuit plantation sites in the Middle Atlantic, with date ranges showing period of Jesuit ownership or occupation. Image courtesy of Laura Masur.

In recent years, because of research and activism related to the Jesuits' sale of 272 enslaved persons in 1838, the former plantation sites and their histories have received increased—and appropriately critical—attention.[2] The goal of our archaeological project is to reflect on archival silences, particularly as they relate to the lives of enslaved persons, and to recover places important within their everyday lives that have since been forgotten—places like homes, kitchens, and yard spaces.

1 John Carroll, "'The Present State of the Catholic Mission, Conducted by the Ex-Jesuits in North-America.' By Rev. Patrick Smyth: Unpublished Reply by Rev. John Carroll, 1788. Rev. John Carroll's Answer to Smyth," *The American Catholic Historical Researches* 1:3 (1905): 193-206.

2 Adam Rothman, "Georgetown University and the Business of Slavery," *Washington History* 29:2 (2017): 18–22; Adam Rothman and Elsa Barraza Mendoza, eds *Facing Georgetown's History: a Reader on Slavery, Memory, and Reconciliation* (Washington, DC: Georgetown University Press, 2021); "Georgetown Slavery Archive," Georgetown University, http://slaveryarchive.georgetown.edu/.

The possible chapel in Old Chapel Field—Angela's discovery—could be claimed as a place of religious freedom for the English Catholics who attended mass at St. Inigoes. Indeed, it was likely built shortly after the closure of a magnificent brick chapel at St. Mary's City, just a short sail up the St. Mary's River. Some of the bricks may even have been reused from the St. Mary's chapel. "Chapel bricks," bearing the same characteristic indentations made by a certain brick mold, and distinctive limestone pavers, which had covered the floor in the St. Mary's chapel, have been identified elsewhere in Old Chapel Field, confirming a long-standing oral tradition.[3] But if we veer away from narratives of English Catholics' religious freedom—if we focus on different characters—other stories emerge.

Angela was only able to discover a few bricks *in situ* (in their original location) because this chapel, like the one at St. Mary's, had been disassembled. We knew that brick foundations had been there, thanks to the impeccable memory of Christopher Butler. Christopher was born enslaved on a tenant farm at St. Inigoes around 1855 (one wonders if he knew Angela's great-great-great grandfather, John Bennet), and recounted to Jesuits that during the 1870s he had disassembled a brick wall, about 2-3 feet high and 25 feet long. At the time, he was told that these bricks had formed a part of the old Catholic chapel. The sub-surface foundations were uncovered about sixty years later by tenant farmer Lynwood Trossbach and Jesuit students vacationing at the St. Inigoes villa.[4] And either those excavators or members of the U.S. Navy further disassembled the brick foundations so that little intact foundation remains today—save the few bricks that Angela found.

3 Timothy B. Riordan, Henry M. Miller, and Silas D. Hurry, "Birth of an American Freedom, Religion in Early Maryland: Archaeology of the St. Mary's City Chapel Field (18ST1-103)," Report submitted to National Endowment for the Humanities Grants Office, Washington, D.C. 20506 Completion report for NEH grant RO-22102-90. St. Mary's City, MD: Historic St. Mary's City, 1994; Ruth Ann Armitage, Leah Minc, David V. Hill, and Silas D. Hurry, "Characterization of Bricks and Tiles from the 17th-Century Brick Chapel, St. Mary's City, Maryland," *Journal of Archaeological Science* 33:5 (2006): 615–27; Marcus Key, Leslie Milliman, Michael Smolek, and Silas Hurry, "Sourcing a Stone Paver from the Colonial St. Inigoes Manor, Maryland," *Northeast Historical Archaeology* 45:1 (2016): 132–55.
4 "Interesting Items from Saint Inigoes." *Woodstock Letters* 62: 3 (1933): 359–64.

Figure 3. Brick foundations identified by Butler, Trossbach, and the Jesuits in 1933. Image from Beitzell's *Jesuit Missions of St. Mary's County*, 1976.

Christopher Butler's story itself is remarkable. His father, Ignatius or "Nace" Butler was a member of a large family, all of whom were sold by the Jesuits to Louisiana enslavers in 1838. Nace evaded the sale (an 1838 census notes that he "ran away") and remained enslaved at neighboring Cross Manor until 1864. His son, Christopher Butler, also lived near St. Inigoes for his whole life. He was married twice and had at least eleven children. He owned a house on his own land, and census records indicate that although he could not read or write as a young adult, he learned later in life. He served as the sexton or caretaker of St. Ignatius Church and graveyard until his death in 1933.[5]

As yet we know little else about the chapel in "Old Chapel Field" whose walls Christopher Butler disassembled in the 1870s. During the eighteenth century, the chapel would have been located to the southeast of the major

5 Malissa Ruffner, "Ignatius "Nace" Butler Jr. (GMP-199)," *Georgetown Memory Project*. October 14, 2021. www.georgetownmemoryproject.org. Accessed December 23, 2021; Butler, Ignatius (Group 46). *GU272 Descendants, 1785-2000*. (Online database: *AmericanAncestors.org*, New England Historic Genealogical Society, 2019); https://www.americanancestors.org/DB2756/rd/56433/M0063/1425844039. Kirk E. Ranzetta, "Christopher Butler House," Maryland Historical Trust Maryland Inventory of Historic Properties Form SM-283. Leonardtown, MD, August 2000. Technical report, accessible here: https://mht.maryland.gov/mihp/MIHPCard.aspx?MIHPNo=SM-283.

domestic area of the plantation, which we also began to excavate in 2021-22. It is clear that the plantation expanded in the early eighteenth century, when enslaved Africans were first documented there. A map dating to around 1735 map shows two main structures in Old Chapel Field, and what appears to be a yard or garden area extending to the west. Several records circa 1730 mention the presence of a house, quarter, kitchen, cellar, barn, and tobacco house. The confirmed location of a house, cellar, and a smokehouse or dairy—replete with fragments of drinking mugs, milk pans, buttons and even small fragments of crab claw, eggshell, and maize—have been identified archaeologically. The names of those living at Old Chapel Field are few: Ben, Jenny, Betty, and Matthew—all enslaved; overseers John Pavat and John Jones, among others. While there are records as early as the 1730s, they are scattered at best.[6]

The plantation at Old Chapel Field was abandoned, probably during the construction of a new brick manor house at "Priest's Point," a promontory of land in clear view of passing ships along the St. Mary's River. Key details about this structure, once again, come from the recollections of a man enslaved at St. Inigoes. Through an elaborate 19th-century game of telephone, we learn that Matthew "carried the bricks" that were used to build the manor house at Priest's Point.[7] A perusal of archival records shows the provisioning of linen for a shirt for Matthew in 1734; in 1744 he was "added for a share" of crops, indicating that he was considered an adult laborer at that time. By 1760, he had married Betty, and by 1767, Matthew, Betty, and their daughter Betty were all members of the St. Ignatius congregation—based out of the chapel in Old Chapel Field. This is almost certainly where Matthew and Betty were married, and where they baptized their daughter and any other children. Matthew passed away at. St. Inigoes in 1812.[8] Although we do not know the origin of the bricks that Matthew

6 Map of St. Inigoes dating approximately 1735. Box OS1, folder 11, Maryland Province Archives of the Society of Jesus (hereafter MPA), Georgetown University Archives, Washington, D.C.; "St. Inigos Rents," St. Inigoes, Records Book (1 of 4), 1757 - 1763. Box 89, folder 4, MPA.

7 Edward I. Devitt, "History of the Maryland-New York Province, I. St. Inigoes, St. Mary's County, Maryland 1634-1915," *Woodstock Letters* 60: 2 (1931): 211.

8 "St. Inigos Rents," St. Inigoes, Records Book (1 of 4), 1757 - 1763. Box 89, folder 4, MPA; "St. Inigoes overseer contract, 1743," *Georgetown Slavery Archive*, accessed January 26, 2023, https://slaveryarchive.georgetown.edu/items/show/342; "St. Inigoes enslaved community, c. 1760," *Georgetown Slavery Archive*, accessed January 26, 2023, https://slaveryarchive.georgetown.edu/items/show/356; Edwin Warfield Beitzell, *The Jesuit Missions of St. Mary's County, Maryland*. Revised edition. (Leonardtown, MD: St. Mary's

moved—perhaps from St. Mary's City, Old Chapel Field, or a nearby brick clamp—like Christopher Butler, he played an intimate role in the formation of the archaeological record as we experience it today.

We see bricks not only in the ruins of the manor house at Priest's Point (it burned in 1872), but also in the chimney of a nearby house. During a survey in 1997, archaeologists excavated a test unit over the remains of this chimney, which most likely marked the residence of another enslaved individual: Louisa Mahoney Mason. We know, from Louisa's own incredible memory, that after emancipation in 1864 she lived in a small house, located near a pond on the St. Mary's River. She undertook domestic tasks for the Jesuits who lived in the large brick manor house at Priest's Point. While many other enslaved individuals still labored on the Jesuits' plantation, most of Louisa's extended family network—like Ignatius Butler's family—had been sent to Louisiana in the 1838 sale. Like Nace, she had evaded the sale—by running away into the woods when the ship came to carry her kin and community away. The majority of the plantation was rented to tenants who enslaved African American laborers, including Christopher Butler, his mother, and his siblings. Louisa married a free Black man, Robert Mason, who worked as a laborer for the Jesuits. The couple had six children before Robert was murdered in 1860, shortly after enlisting in the Union army.[9]

The archaeological survey from provides a clear location for Louisa's house at St. Inigoes, and it is also depicted in nautical charts, photographs, and early aerial photographs. The house also adds to Louisa's story, as remembered and written by her many descendants, some of whom I've had the privilege to meet and work with over the past few years. Yet the site of Louisa's home is difficult to access, behind the gate of a secure Naval installation. Conducting archaeology at St. Inigoes, and opening the site to volunteers and visitors, provides an opportunity for her descendants to visit this

County Historical Society, 1976): 70; "A "Multiplicity of Deaths": Fr. Mobberly to Fr. Grassi, on a series of deaths that occurred at St. Inigos, 1812.," *Georgetown Slavery Archive*, accessed January 26, 2023, https://slaveryarchive.georgetown.edu/items/show/113.

9 Georgetown University Library, "Paul Rochford, "Louisa Mahoney Mason and her family" (2020)," *Georgetown Slavery Archive*, accessed January 25, 2023, https://slaveryarchive.georgetown.edu/items/show/503; Laura J. Galke and Alyssa L. Loney, "Phase I Archaeological Investigations Aboard Webster Field Annex: NAS PAX, St. Mary's County, Maryland." Report presented to Natural Resources Branch Environmental and Natural Resources Division Department of Public Works Naval Air Station Patuxent River. (St. Leonard, MD: Jefferson Patterson Park and Museum Maryland Historic Trust, 2000): 128–45.

important place. We also seek to tell her story through a newly developed website and through school lessons that incorporate images, documents, and 3D scanned artifacts from her home.[10]

St. Inigoes and Newtown: Family Connections

Louisa Mahoney Mason was the daughter of Harry and Anna Mahoney. While they were enslaved at St. Inigoes, the Mahoneys had family connections to White Marsh—another Jesuit property—where some family members had successfully sued for their freedom, citing descent from a free woman named Ann Joice.[11] The Mahoneys were among many enslaved persons, uprooted from their family and community networks when they were moved from one plantation to another, according to the Jesuits' needs.

Louisa had an older sister, Nelly, who also evaded the sale in 1838. But unlike Louisa, she did not remain at St. Inigoes, where she had lived the first forty years of her life.[12] Instead, Nelly Mahoney was sent to St. Mary's Church in Alexandria, Virginia, where she served as the housekeeper to the Jesuit pastor. Just a few years later, in 1843, Nelly was sent back to southern Maryland—but this time, to Newtown—to work as a cook, housekeeper, and sacristan, making the bread used for the Eucharist during mass. At Newtown, Nelly lived in a small enslaved community; most of the large community had been sold in 1838. Alongside Len, Robert Thomas, a man, a woman, and a boy, she served a household of five Jesuits.[13]

---

10 Henrietta Pike, Jeremy Alexander, Melissa Kemp, Negest Rucker, and Lynn Nehemiah, "Louisa Mahoney," Still, We Speak, January 26, 2023. https://stillwespeak.org/louisa-mahoney/; Bernard K. Means, "Archaeology of Jesuit-Enslaved Ancestors," Virtual Curation Lab, January 26, 2023. https://skfb.ly/oD7SH.

11 "Paul Rochford, "Louisa Mahoney Mason" Georgetown Slavery Archive. [The citation I used was provided by the GSA here: https://slaveryarchive.georgetown.edu/items/show/503]

12 Nel, 6. Maryland State Archives, "St. Inigoes tax assessment, 1804," Georgetown Slavery Archive, accessed January 26, 2023, https://slaveryarchive.georgetown.edu/items/show/344; Nelly, 33. Maryland State Archives, "St. Inigoes Tax Assessment, 1831," Georgetown Slavery Archive, accessed January 26, 2023, https://slaveryarchive.georgetown.edu/items/show/78. [Maryland State Archives is different, but Maryland Province Collection/Archives are the same.]

13 Maryland Province Collection, "Bill of sale for Len, September 4, 1843," Georgetown Slavery Archive, accessed January 26, 2023, https://slaveryarchive.georgetown.edu/items/show/283; Maryland Province Collection, "Fr. Nicholas Steinbacher hires Robert Thomas, an enslaved man at Newtown, 1847," Georgetown Slavery Archive, accessed January 26, 2023, https://slaveryarchive.georgetown.edu/items/show/373; Maryland Province Archives, Society of Jesus, "On the management of Newtown: Fr. Vespre to Fr. Woodley, April 16, 1844," Georgetown Slavery Archive, accessed January 26, 2023, https://slaveryarchive.georgetown.edu/items/show/389.

Nelly's faith, intelligence, and strong will emerges from the letters written about her. As she served the Jesuits dinner in Alexandria, she listened to their discussions of the sale. Her enslaver described her as "a Black girl, full of religion and very intelligent."[14] She was described by another Jesuit enslaver as "an excellent cook and industrious servant and house keeper and sacristan...her only fault, is too long tongue [sic]; for the rest, the best servant."[15] Another Jesuit noted in 1848 that at Newtown, she "has ruled and partly rules this house."[16] One wonders how being separated from her family and moved frequently around the region influenced Nelly's opinions about the Jesuits and about enslavement.

Nelly and the other persons enslaved at Newtown in the 1840s probably lived in small wooden houses near the manor house and church, like the one pictured in an 1882 photo (see figure a on p. 24) and identified archaeologically in 2022. Like the home of Louisa Mahoney Mason, the structure was identified by the foundation of a chimney (see figure b on p. 24), although this chimney base was made of sandstone. Eighteenth- and nineteenth-century artifacts—bone button backs, tobacco pipes, fragments of a utilitarian stoneware vessel, and part of an eighteenth-century shoe buckle (see figure c on p. 24)—were unearthed from the possible site of her home, immediately adjacent to the extant St. Francis Xavier Church. This home site had clearly been forgotten, with soil layers churned up by plowing, the construction of a rectory, and the installation of a modern HVAC unit.[17] The archaeological identification of this domestic structure provides an opportunity to tell Nelly's story.

14 Archivum Romanum Societatis Iesu, ""I had for a cook, at Alexandria, a Black girl" Fr. Dubuisson to Fr. Roothaan, June 21 and July 2, 1839," *Georgetown Slavery Archive*, accessed January 26, 2023, https://slaveryarchive.georgetown.edu/items/show/462.

15 Maryland Province Archives, ""Belonging to us": Fr. Dzierozynski recommends Nelly as housekeeper for Fr. Lancaster, January 1843.," *Georgetown Slavery Archive*, accessed January 26, 2023, https://slaveryarchive.georgetown.edu/items/show/139.

16 Maryland Province Archives, ""She will not Rule Me": Fr. Steinbacher airs his grievances against the female slaves of Newtown, April, 1848.," *Georgetown Slavery Archive*, accessed January 26, 2023, https://slaveryarchive.georgetown.edu/items/show/144.

17 The photograph shows St. Francis Xavier Church, a fence line, and a small frame house with a brick chimney. The Newtown Manor House is pictured in the background. Beitzell, *The Jesuit Missions of St. Mary's County*, 1976; Dennis J. Pogue, "Archaeological Investigations at St. Francis Xavier Church in Newtown (18ST16), St. Mary's County, Maryland." Report prepared for the Archdiocese of Washington (1982), 8.

In 1850, the Jesuits planned to lease or sell Nelly. As a result, Nelly tried to claim her freedom, seeking assistance from a Jesuit priest. He wrote her a pass to escape, but Nelly's fate remains unknown.[18]

Archaeology: Evidence and Interpretation

As a discipline, archaeology relies on the systematic application of scientific methods. We use principles from geology, biology, and chemistry to interpret the layers of sediment and soil that we excavate. We adapt tools from geography to painstakingly map our finds on the landscape. We rely on carefully-constructed artifact typologies—and sometimes even chemical testing—to identify and interpret the thousands of artifacts that we unearth.

But the interpretation of these finds can be more open, relying on insight from genealogy, history, literature, and even philosophy. Interpretation is flexible—and it is also how archaeologists can use evidence to engage with narrative. What if—counter to every history that has yet been told about Catholicism in southern Maryland—the background, the stories, and even the names of the Jesuits are left unspoken? Instead of telling the story of a Jesuit who "built" a brick church in Old Chapel Field or "built" a brick manor house at Priest's Point, we use those bricks to tell the story of the people whose unfree labor paid for the buildings' construction, who made each brick by hand, who carried each brick across a landscape, and who painstakingly deconstructed that building when it went out of use?[19] What if, instead, we elevate the stories of Matthew and Betty, Louisa Mahoney Mason and Nelly Mahoney, Ignatius and Christopher Butler, and so many others, to tell a story about the *costs* of religious freedom in early America?

Over the past two years, I have had countless conversations with descendants of Jesuit-enslaved ancestors, many while we are on site—at St. Inigoes, Newtown, Bohemia, and most recently, at White Marsh in Prince George's County. I have always emphasized that their versions of narratives and their

---

18 Maryland Province Archives, ""I have parted from Nelly": Fr. Woodley to Fr. Brocard, September 25, 1850.," *Georgetown Slavery Archive*, accessed January 26, 2023, https://slaveryarchive.georgetown.edu/items/show/165.

19 The below entry likely describes the construction of the brick manor house at Priest's Point. Debit: "To building & furnishing a dwelling house 50 by 30 745:0:0" Credit: "By benefactions – Economy – Good times – & Industry – 862:13:4½" George Hunter, "The State of Accts of Maryland Factory with London Office &c from 1729 to 1766," BN/3/1, British Jesuit Archives, London, United Kingdom.

perspectives matter more than my own, "because it's your history, not mine." But, as one descendant, Guilford Queen, reminded me on the phone: "it is your history, too." We all share this history—as American history, Maryland history, Catholic history, Jesuit history, university history—however you want to frame it. By spending time doing archaeology at former plantation sites, by experiencing their landscapes and remembering their former inhabitants, we all become a part of this story—like Angela, and her discovery of the chapel in Old Chapel Field.

Being present in a place—particularly a sacred place, a place of memory—is powerful. Robin Proudie, whose ancestors were enslaved at White Marsh and forced by the Jesuits to Missouri to support the founding of St. Louis University, has spent time with us in the field and in the lab. She wrote, "When I picked up a rusty nail from the colonial period, or sifted through the soil with hopes of finding a one-of-a-kind artifact, I never let on that I could see shadowy figures illuminating out of the hallowed ground that was being dug up."[20] Ancestors remain present in these sacred places, and the careful process of doing archaeology helps to tell their untold stories, one artifact at a time.

But visiting sites also provokes anger. Anger that one may never recover a family history. Anger at limited access to historical sources. Anger that these stories are told only when a privileged white academic (like myself) decides they should be told. Anger at the lack of openness to dialogue and collaboration.[21] And for this reason, actions are powerful. Jesuits who came and labored with the field crew—while descendants were on site—showed a willingness to serve, an important gesture of apology and humility. The archaeological site itself becomes a place for dialogue and symbolic reparations, as we pull oyster after oyster from quarter-inch hardware cloth, as we wash bits of pottery, and share meals. And through those dialogues, I see archaeological sites differently. The process of excavation, washing, and cataloging changes little—but the interpretation is utterly transformed.

20 Kev Homan, Robin A. Proudie, Clarissa Ashton Stripling, and Greg Beaman, "What descendants felt during a dig at a Jesuit-owned plantation," *National Catholic Reporter*, August 19, 2021, https://www.ncronline.org/news/opinion/what-descendants-felt-during-dig-jesuit-owned-plantation.

21 Homan et al., "What descendants felt" *National Catholic Reporter*, August 19, 2021; Steve Hendrix, "A church that once enslaved people sees the light in a chapel cemetery," *Washington Post*, January 17, 2023, https://www.washingtonpost.com/history/2023/01/17/jesuit-slave-cemetery-maryland/.

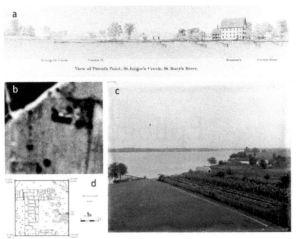

Figure 4a-d. Home of Louisa Mahoney Mason and her family at Priest's point as depicted (a) in the center of an 1876-91 coastal chart, (b) in the upper right corner of a 1930s aerial photograph, (c) in the right corner of a 1933 photograph, (d) in a 1996 archaeological test unit showing a hearth foundation. (a) Image courtesy of History St. Mary's City; (b) Image from Smolek et al. 1983, 65; (c) Photo by Rev. John Brosnan, S.J., 1933, image courtesy of DigitalGeorgetown and Woodstock Theological Library; (d) Image from Galke and Loney 2000, 136.

Epilogue

Terrence M. Sawyer

At its best, a Jesuit, liberal arts education gives students the skills they need to succeed—the ability to think and communicate clearly, the curiosity to ask and delve into difficult questions, the insight to take an innovative approach to problem solving, and the commitment to be engaged and thoughtful citizens. If Loyola University Maryland is living out our mission, we are graduating individuals who think beyond themselves, with minds centered on justice and hearts full of compassion.

During the Fall 2022 semester at Loyola, I attended presentations by eight students working under the direction of Dr. David Carey Jr. and Dr. Lisa Zimmerelli. I also visited these students while they were doing scholarly research in the Loyola Notre Dame Library Archives. This work was undertaken alongside a larger effort at Loyola to study and understand our past relationship with enslaved peoples. The report from the broader scholarly research undertaken by Loyola's Universities Studying Slavery Task Force over the past two years is still forthcoming. That analysis will offer additional insight into some of the materials shared in this book. As a university we must wrestle with our past, learn from it, and move forward with intentional actions. The efforts represented in this volume are crucial to this enterprise.

As President of Loyola and one who supports this work, I am conscious that it will affect many in our community in different ways. Studying and learning about elements of our past that are shameful and uncomfortable is hard. An ability to have difficult conversations about our past is something our society is struggling to figure out how to do well. And this is why I think it's so important for a Jesuit institution to lead the way in modeling how to have hard conversations about racial injustices in our past. The Jesuit values of *eloquentia perfecta* (eloquent expression for the common good) and *cura personalis* (respect and care for all that makes up an individual person) offer our community familiar frameworks for guiding our conversations. Importantly, both values are premised on the important skill of empathy – of seeking first to understand another person and then taking steps to speak and act for the common good. In our increasingly divided and polarized society, we need empathy to help us understand the impact of racism on those around us as well as to engage with those who may struggle to understand why a university would take on such an uncomfortable task as this one. As others engaged in similar efforts have noted, these actions "are meant to improve our capacity as communities and as a country to see ourselves in each other, so that we can shape a more equitable future."[1]

The information presented through this student-led project identifies a Loyola that, rather than standing apart from the culture of the time, engaged in common racist practices occurring across the United States in the nineteenth and twentieth centuries. These are hard and troubling realities. We aspire for Loyola to be a welcoming haven for all, a leader in fighting for justice, and a place known for honoring the dignity of all. These historical essays and creative works show that has not always been the case and that we have fallen short of our ideals. The student work presented here, challenges us to grapple with the historical truths in our past and to find ways to move forward together. If we hope to make true and lasting change, we must seek to understand our past, to reconfirm our commitment to living out our values, and to practice empathy as we begin the hard process of racial healing and transformation.

I am deeply grateful to Dr. David Carey Jr. and Dr. Lisa Zimmerelli for their research and for leading their classes through this project. They have opened the door to important conversations that we will continue to

---

1 Truth, Racial Healing & Transformation Implementation Guidebook, W.K. Kellogg Foundation, December 2016. Truth, Racial Healing & Transformation Implementation Guidebook (issuelab.org)

conduct as a university community. I am also deeply encouraged by the professionalism and dedication of the students who participated in the project. They remind us that our past is complicated. We cannot undo what has been done. We can work to take steps toward greater peace and justice. We can work to increase empathy for one another and work to find a common path forward that honors the dignity of all.

As we seek to understand our past, ourselves, and our institution, I invite all of us to follow Saint Ignatius in his call to show love through words *and* deeds and to work together in our ongoing pursuit of "strong truths, well lived."

Terrence M. Sawyer
President
Loyola University Maryland

Afterword(s): Descendant Voices

Although the histories and creative writing contained herein have played pivotal roles in uncovering and conveying the hidden legacies of slavery and racism at Loyola University Maryland, descendants of the 272 offer the ultimate testimonies. Melisande Short-Colomb, Dr. Lynn Locklear Nehemiah, and Kevin Porter represent the final word (or Afterwords) of this volume; their essays represent the centerpiece of the sacrifices made to make this research and scholarship a reality. While many individuals have contributed to piecing together these histories, the descendants embody what it means to embrace another chance to share untold truths.

Here I Am

Mélisande Short-Colomb

The excerpt that follows is from a play written and performed by Mélisande Short-Colomb, a descendant of families who were enslaved and trafficked by the Society of Jesus in the documented 1838 sale. Here I Am weaves narrative, music, and imagery, inviting the audience on an experiential journey exploring a complicated history and relationship with the institution that enslaved her ancestors. Her family's narrative forms the centerpiece of an expansive curricular effort to engage the complex histories around slavery as part of the Jesuit expansion of education in the United States of America. Colomb learned about her ancestral ties to Georgetown several months after the story of Georgetown's slave history broke in April 2016 in the *New York Times*. In 2017 Colomb enrolled as a freshman at Georgetown.

A native of New Orleans who began her studies at Georgetown in 2017, Mélisande Short-Colomb is a direct descendant of Abraham Mahoney and Mary Ellen Queen who were among the 314 members of the group known today as the GU272, enslaved people owned and sold by the Maryland Jesuits in 1838 to rescue Georgetown University from insolvency and bankruptcy.

MELI

Harriet Queen 43

Her children:
Elizabeth 23
Isais 21
Mary Ellen 17
Nancy 15
Martha 10
James Francis 1 year.

Robert Mahoney 43 His wife, Mary 38
Their children:
Abraham 16
Robert 14
James 12
Bridget 11
Mary Jane 10
Susan 8
Sally Anne 7
Nelly 6
Charles 5
One "unnamed child" 2 years.

I see them - these ancestors - all around me.

I am humbled by the moment - this is for me.

What a wonderful day to be here. In the here, and in the now. We are graced by small blessings and very tender mercies. On behalf of 11 generations of the women of my family,

Here I Am.

Paying homage to the incredible women who have come into me and who are part of me. I am here to tell their story.

Handed down over more than 300 years, 11 generations, of an American family story.
A colonial family story.
A not-the-Mayflower family story.

But here we are - descendants and builders of America in the most fundamental way.

I feel like my whole life, and all of the lives that have come before me, are all balled up inside of me.

Everything that we will be doing here – together – will be what I've always wanted to do.

Here we are.

———

The story goes like this.

On a glorious but very cold Saturday afternoon, somewhere in February of 2018,
we gather as priest, parishioners,
and descendants of enslaved persons,
to ceremoniously dedicate a marker to the unknown buried in the cemtery

at St. Mary's Church,
on the grounds of White Marsh Plantation in Bowie, Maryland.

Prayers are said,
holy water is sprinkled on the cold stone of the unknown, and the wind
comes up across the trees of the cemetery,
drowning out the sounds of the words of this man in his holy vestments,
proclaiming good news for all of us who are gathered.

I am glad for the wind,
and for the sounds of the leaves that catch the words from the lips of the
man in vestments, and scatter them.

I see them
—these ancestors—
all around me,
and I find myself transfixed by wisps of billowing clouds, flying by without
a backward glance.

We wander through the grounds with these women, all in their seventies
and eighties,
Marylanders through and through,
who are the bedrock of this community, with deep roots,
familial connections to this religion,
and to this land.

Their life's work has been about preserving the importance of this place -
where the document to establish Georgetown College was signed in 1789.

They are the last guard, and
they know they are the last guard. They are it.
There is nobody else,
no young people to pick up the banner of the work that they've done, for
all of their lives.

I respect these women and their feelings.
I feel things too.

We are their guests.

We walk,
we observe graves that are very old.
 Some are very well-kept.

The women in their well-rehearsed narratives,
speak lovingly of family names.

But as we continue to walk, they point out the fence-line and what lies on
the other side. Along the fenceline there are broken headstones,
vines and bramble-covered graves, all very old -
all
Completely
Unkept.

Uncared for.

Thrown away.
Enslaved people.

Enslaved people,

always on the edges.

On the other side is the rest of the story.
Because tunnel vision is impossible.
If you're gonna see some things, you've got to see them all.

And then there are the divots.

One doesn't know about divots until one is told what a divot is.
Those depressions in the ground happen because of decomposition.
And the ground just sinks a little bit right there.

So we know that those along the fenceline are graves, because there are
divots. There are no markers
There were no markers ever there to begin with

Every grave becomes a divot unless it is continuously built up.
Who was building up the graves on the fenceline?

Who will?
You?
Me.

_____

'Baby, we're all walking on somebody's grave, and breathing each other's
air. We're continuously walking on graves. The earth itself is everybody's
grave.'

My daddy used to tell me that all the time when I was young. The thought
- just - rang.

It just rang through my mind, just now.

_____

We are chatting
under the female osage orange trees,
brought back from the Lewis and Clark Expedition, laden with fruit

President Thomas Jefferson gave these trees to the Jesuits who planted
them here
at White Marsh.

So, the trees are hundreds of years old.

My first question to the group… "Can we eat this orange?'

The only answer comes from Margaret:

'Nobody eats these oranges, except maybe cows.'
Pause.

The ladies talk to us about the rich history of this place, but don't include the people on the fenceline

Margaret continues…

"Can I just say, thank you for coming today.
It means so much to us here at the church.
We're so proud to be part of all this wonderful work being done!

I met you last spring, when we came up to DC for that beautiful event.

I cried all the way through.

We love Georgetown so much. I read about you in the paper.

I admire you so much too!

The Jesuits have done so much for me, and for my family.

My husband graduated from there."

Husband is standing there, BEAMING!

"We were married on campus fifty years ago!

My two brothers both graduated from Jesuit high schools and finished at Georgetown! I just don't know what we would have done - without the Jesuits, in our lives."

What would we have done without the Jesuits in our lives?

————

My story starts simply enough.

I was born.

New Orleans, Louisiana.
April 10th 1954. 12:45pm on a Saturday afternoon.
I am Saturday's child.

In the West African tradition of naming children on the day of the week that they are born, and in the order of their birth, I am called Meli Ama, *(Vocals)*

first-born daughter on Saturday.

My name, Mélisande, a big name, with a big calling, for a little girl.
A few weeks after my birth. May 1954.

The Supreme Court hands down a decision that will come to be known as Brown vs. Board of Education.

My mother is holding me in her arms when she hears of the decision. My newly minted mother holds her newborn baby - me - very close, knowing in this moment, that my worldview and my life will be so much different from her own.

This decision by the Supreme Court effectively strikes down the Jim Crow laws that had been legislated after the abandonment of Reconstruction.

The Plessy vs. Ferguson decision of 1896 ushered in years of domestic terrorism, murder and disenfranchisement under the guise of law, order, and "white supremacy."

On that day in May, 1954, my mother says a prayer for me and all the babies like me; that things will be different.

I came through my mama, but I was my grandmother's child.
As a girl, I was always going somewhere
but the most important person in my life was my grandmother Geneva Ruby Taylor Lawless Smith.

Big Mama, big grandma, mother, my heart. She was my best friend.

––––––––

I was with my grandmother from the time I was born until she died in 1994. At the age of 97.

She was the one who told me who I am.
The begats, the story, the story telling, the food, the heart, the history.
And the names, the names, the names.

––––––––

My mother gave me something different.
As a little person I was very, very shy.
My favorite place was hiding behind my mama's leg.
 I would sort of peep out
and look at people
and go back behind her and peep out again.
I don't know when,
but my mama started taking me by my little head and pulling me from
behind her and putting me in front of her.

She set me on a path of openness, to not be afraid.
"If somebody asks you a question, don't look at ME," she said. "Have an
answer."

My mom was the first generation to go to college.

She went to Spelman College when she was 15, graduated at 19. She was
blazin' trails and breakin' ceilings.

Cooking wasn't her thing.

And growing up there were things that I wanted her to cook and she
would tell me,

"Oh baby, if you want to know how to cook that, you gotta go by your
grandmother's house, talk to your great grandmother. They do that. I don't
do that. You got to go get that from them.
"Because when they die, honey, it's gone."

As I was growing up, I loved cooking more and more, and my mom was
fine with it. "Baby, there's the stove. Just make sure you clean up when you
finish."

So I did that.

And there came a point where that was what I wanted to do with my life. I told my mom, I want to cook.
My mother was furious.

She told me, "That's not what I raised you for. Your grandmother and your great grandmother, everybody broke their backs in the kitchen. That's not what you're gonna do. You are going to college."

So I went to college.

I have lived my whole life with my mind open, my heart open,

and my two hands - open.

This is my life. Nobody is living it for me. But

I never stand in the back

And I never forget my begats.

I took my first breath which set me on an appointment with my last.
These are the two really big events of our lives.
We are born, I know, and we are going to die, I'm sure. Everything that we do between those two events, is life.

I decided a long time ago that I was going to live.
I would not be corralled by my fears, my insecurities or my inabilities.
It ain't easy.
So I am not an easy person, and I don't pretend to be.

My daughter says I'm confrontational.

She's like, "Mommy, you are the most confrontational person I know." I disagree.

I'm not confrontational.

AND I WASN'T INTENDING TO BE "CONFRONTATIONAL"
THAT DAY
AT THE SITE OF THE DIVOTS
AT THAT SITE OF THE ANCESTORS' GRAVES STANDING OP-
POSITE MARGARET
NO
But change can happen in a minute, can't it?

———

THE REASON WHY I'M HERE
 is because my heavenly grandmothers were here.
– Geneva, Stella, Eve, Mary Ellen, Harriet, Elizabeth, Susanna, Phillis,
Eleanor, Ann Joice, Queen Mary.
They are with me all the time.
The heavenly grandmothers are the beat of my heart, the bone of my bone,
the flesh of my flesh.
I can depend on them.

AND I TOLD THEM THEY CAN DEPEND ON ME

I REMEMBER CLEAR AS DAY

April 16, 2000

I pick up a copy of *The New York Times*.

A front-page article…It says -

…Fall, 1838…

…No ordinary Day…
…Human cargo ships
a bustling wharf in the nation's capital…

…destined for plantations. no one was spared:
not the 2-month-old baby and her mother…

…Forgotten for more than a century. No ordinary slave sale…

…The enslaved belonged to the nation's most prominent Jesuit priests…
…Sold to secure the future of Georgetown University. NOW
IN RESPONSE 177 YEARS LATER
racial protests roiling college campuses…
trying to find out what happened to those 272 men, women and children… Confronting a wrenching question:
What, if anything, is owed to the descendants of THE ENSLAVED who were sold to help ensure the college's survival?

As I reeeed it

my heart is filled with joy,
that there are people who can now directly connect to a seminal event in the lives of their families,
and say,
we know what happened. Good for them.

And then four months later,

I get a Facebook message from a genealogist named Judy Riffel.

She has been hired by Richard Cellini, a Georgetown alum who founded the Georgetown Memory Project in order to locate descendants of the families who were sold.

Oh my god.

My people were part of the 1838 JESUIT sale?
My people were part of the 1838 JESUIT sale.

I've read about the connection to families in Maringouin, Louisiana, and never associated those families with my own family from Terrebonne and Lafourche parishes.
So this is an "oh my god" moment. I had never connected my family,
OR the stories that I heard from my grandmother about the Queens and the Mahoneys,
TO THE JESUITS.

My grandmother always said that we were free people.

I've always known that they were Catholics, that my grandmother's great grandmother was a Catholic and born in Maryland.

But I had not connected it to the Jesuits until this Facebook message opened this Pandora's box.

———

The story of my family was given to me by my grandmother who got it from her grandmother,

who got it from her grandmother, who,

As it turns out,

was among more than 200 young people sold in the 1838 sale

-all under the age of 18.

This is the history of a family that went from heart and mouth and soul into each generation of us.

I am the descendant not of "slaves"

but of people Like you

Who were denied their right to freedom by law,

Whose labor was commercialized, capitalized, Exploited

For profit.

THEY WERE NOT SLAVES

NO PERSON UNDER GOD'S SKY IS A SLAVE THEY CAN ONLY BECOME ENSLAVED

by enslavers.

———

Reading Judy's Facebook message

I felt like I was imploding and exploding at the same time I became sad.

I felt hurt.

Then I got mad.

Which in truth

is something that I feel all the time

for all of my life

as a Black American child born in 1954.

I am a Black woman who has inherited this righteous anger.

―――――

In 1715, my ancestor of record, Queen Mary Papow,

arrived in the Maryland colony from England, as a free woman.

Her sponsor, Thomas Larkin,

sold her indenture contract to James Carroll.

Queen Mary served out the terms of her indenture. And when that was over,

rather than being freed, as her contract required, she was criminalized and enslaved for life.

That meant for Queen Mary

that all the future generations of her family would be kept enslaved.

When James Carroll died, his will dictated that All his property and holdings

Be donated to the Jesuits and the Catholic Church.

This gift would later serve as the foundation

for his nephew, John Carroll, to purchase the Hilltop, on which Georgetown now sits.

What kind of people craft laws that forever consign the children born from the bodies of Black women

to be slaves in perpetuity for all of their lives?

And so the children of my heavenly grandmother, Queen Mary, were all kept enslaved until her grandchildren and some of her great grandchildren sued the Jesuits for their freedom.

Edward Queen, Queen Mary's grandson, started his case in 1791. And won his freedom in 1794.

This was good.

But what of the other grandchildren?

In 1810, Priscilla Queen sued the president of Georgetown College for her freedom, but her petition was denied.

There is no definitive record of Priscilla Queen after that case, but there remain many records of her attorney: a man who wrote a poem that, for better or worse, we still exalt today.

Francis Scott Key, the attorney of record for Priscilla Queen. My family was here in the light of the rockets red glare.

———

I stopped standing or participating with the Star Spangled Banner when I was about 14 years old around the time of the assissination of Rev. Dr. Martin Luther King, Jr.

When the music would commence, I would just sit down. And I continued to sit down

I have embarrassed my family and my children. They'd say, you know,

"Stand up mama,"

"Hell no, you stand up if you must stand up, I'm not standing up."

Even when I learned that

Francis Scott Key had been Priscilla Queen's lawyer in her fight for freedom I couldn't stand up.

Despite his services, I know his song is a lie. This has not been the land of the free.

This is still not the land of the free.

Why should I put my hand over my heart? Over my heart?

No.

AFTER THE SALE, the Queens and the Mahoneys were among the first people who were shipped on the boat from Maryland to Louisiana.

The ship they were on was called the Uncas and 51 people were onboard. Seventeen of them were my family members. 16 year-old Abraham Mahoney and 17 year-old Mary Ellen Queen met on that boat.

They went straight to Terrebonne Parish.

I saved a newspaper article from 1980 of my grandmother talking about the sale, and telling how her grandmother told her that they were on a flatbed boat that went down the bayou and the alligators would come off the banks of the bayou and follow the boat.

They didn't know alligators - do they have alligators in Maryland?

So these people - these families - who had been in this place in Maryland, for many, many, many generations, are summarily packed up one day in 1838, put on a boat and sent down the river to cut sugar cane.

All of this because the Jesuits needed... money.

The cognitive dissonance between their religious beliefs and their capitalist needs had even the Jesuits looking for some worthy justification.

In a letter to the Jesuit Father General in Rome, they wrote, "Are our slaves not proverbially the most wicked in the whole country?"

"They are lazy and unclean."

"It is impossible to make them good Christians."

"The slaves' rule always is to work as little as possible."

"Perhaps they will abandon their sins under harsh Masters and be saved."

I imagine them saying,

"What we will do is gather them up and we will send them to the deepest, darkest, most desolate and dangerous new part of our country and convince ourselves that they're going to be happy there. Because...it's warm there. Y'all don't like snow, right?"

Who the hell likes snow?

———

On November 12 1838, Reverend Peter Havermans wrote a letter to the superior General of the Society of Jesus Reverend Jan Roothaan and these were his observations.

"How sad these days have passed, I am not able to say.

The slaves with heroic fortitude weren't giving themselves to fate. And with Christian resignation, relinquishing themselves to God.

One woman more pious than the others and at that time, very pregnant, demanded most of my compassion.

She was coming toward me so that for the last time she could greet me and seek benediction. She observed as she was genuflecting, if ever someone should have reason to despair do I not now have it?

282

I do not know on what day the birth will come whether on the road or at sea. What will become of me?

Why do I deserve this?

I was saying, trust in God, trust in God, trust in God and so it was. She agreed and I offered myself completely to her.

All were coming to me seeking rosaries, a medal, a cross so that they would remember me, and with how much obedience they went to the boat."

This bill of sale comprises a listing of the largest recorded human trafficking incident in the United States of America.

People often say, "well, there are slaves today." And, yes, there are.

That doesn't say anything about the people who are enslaved. But it still says a lot about the people who enslave.

————

WHEN I WAS A LITTLE GIRL, MY GRANDMOTHER

talked about the Leonids meteor shower and how her grandmother Mary Ellen Queen

as a young girl

went out into the tobacco fields of southern Maryland

with her grandmothers and great grandmothers and cousins, and they all watched for many nights as the stars fell.

Everybody across the eastern United States saw the meteor shower, and many wrote about it, including Abraham Lincoln.

And when I was growing up,

my grandmother told me it was Halley's comet.

But as I got older and was looking at encyclopedias, I'm like, it couldn't possibly have been Halley's Comet.

During my first semester at Georgetown,

an archivist at Nicholls State University in Thibodaux, Louisiana found this photograph of my uncle Frank Campbell.

And on the back of the photograph, someone had written, "Frank Campbell, who was 19 years old the night the stars fell."

That was in 1833.

Some five years before my family was sold.

So those falling stars,

That collective memory is a connecting thread across the generations.

From my grandmother's grandmother to her

to me,

and now to you.

Those are stories that I heard as a girl in New Orleans, Louisiana, about my ancestors

who came to the Maryland colony as free women, indentured servants, international travelers, in 1677, and 1715,

as did so many to this new world.

But laws were changing in the colonies at the time,

those women - Black women - at the end of their indenture,

They and their children were incarcerated and made slaves for life. For one reason only—the color of their skin.

It's as simple as that.

And here I am, Under the same sky, generations later,

returned to the places they lived and moved and had their being. Returned to restore them to the national narrative, to honor their lives for time immemorial.

[SEVERAL SCENES EXCERPTED OUT FOR THE PURPOSES OF THIS VOLUME]

Forgiveness is a very tricky thing.
When we talk about American-ness --

Whose stories we have told, whose stories we have been told, and whose we have not ….

The telling isn't by accident.

The work that we are doing now has to be as deliberate and intentional as the work that has been done to exclude.

This is the responsibility of institutions of higher learning. SO, YES, I AM ANGRY.
ANGER IS AS APPROPRIATE A RESPONSE TO ACTUAL INJUSTICE

AS PHYSICAL PAIN IS APPROPRIATE TO A GUNSHOT WOUND TO THE BACK.

ANGER LET'S US ALL KNOW SOMETHING IS WRONG IN THIS UNCIVIL SOCIETY IT LETS US KNOW THAT SOMETHING
MANY THINGS
NEED TO CHANGE FOR HEALTH AND WELL-BEING TO BE RESTORED SO DON'T ASK ME
"ARE YOU STILL ANGRY?"
TO NOT BE IS TO BE HARDENED, NUMB, OR OBLIVIOUS TO THE HARM BUT

My anger should not be misconstrued as hatred. I don't hate you because I'm angry.

I don't hate anybody.

Because I don't believe that hate is a constructive force, nothing good comes from hate, as we see.

So I'm not,

I cannot

hold that energy in me,

I can't cook beautiful food and warm your soul and make your belly and your heart feel good if I got hate in my heart.

That doesn't work.

So, because I cooked

because food was so important to me for so many years, I retreat into the kitchen,

as a place where I could be safe,

I could be expressive and emotive and emotional, focused and disciplined. And that was very positive.

And has put in me a respect for human beings that no matter what,

I am a caregiver. I will feed you.

If I am angry, it comes from a place of absolute love It is because I love you that I can demand accountability Through your behavior and your actions

———

'When the heart is touched by direct experience, the mind may be challenged to change.' Reverend Hans Klovenbach, Society of Jesus, 29th Superior General.

We spend so much of our time as human beings in our little viral way of survival.

The Earth is huge, and old, and we only have a little place to live on it. And all we do is fight, and make it hard for other people to live.

People, human beings, have made it hard for living things on this Earth. That's not right.

The Earth is not a promise. Our existence is not a promise. Here I am

Here you are.

Pause.

Here we are. In this moment. I am you.

You are me. We.

None more magnificently made. Suited to this time. To go out with your neighbors, strong and prepared. To speak hard truths.

Here I am. Here we are.

The Mahoney Mason Line: A Journey of Redemption

Dr. Lynn Locklear Nehemiah

Introduction

This is the story of Anne Joice and the Mahoney family line. The uncompensated labor which was extracted from Anne and her progeny for multiple generations was foundational to the creation of wealth which supported the Jesuits and ultimately led to the establishment of Georgetown University and Loyola University Maryland.

Anne Joice, my seventh great-grandmother, arrived in Maryland in 1675 as young woman likely between fifteen and twenty years of age from the port of Bristol, England. This would be at least the second transatlantic voyage she would make in her short lifetime. It is probable that Anne had been born in Barbados, perhaps of mixed Scottish, and African ancestry, given the make up of the enslaved population during that era. She was described as a "dark Mulatto woman," and had been contracted as a cook in the service of Charles Calvert, the third Lord Baltimore.

Anne's legal status was not unlike that of Mathias Sousa, a mulatto man also from Barbados who arrived on the shores of Maryland as an indentured servant approximately forty years earlier. Sousa, the first person of African descent recorded in the Maryland colonies, was part of a passenger list which included a convoy of Jesuit priests aboard the *Ark* and the *Dove* who were seeking religious freedom and the expansion of their missionary works. After completing his indenture, Sousa went on to serve in the Maryland state legislature and became a respected leader in the colonies. Anne, arriving forty years later also as an indentured servant, would have a far different experience.

Pasquier, M (2008). "Though their skin remains Brown, I hope their souls will soon be white." *Slavery, French Missionaries, and the Roman Catholic Priesthood in the American South*, 1865. Church History, 77 (337-370).

Anne may have served as a cook during a transatlantic journey between Barbados and England and then subsequently have been indentured for the same role for Lord Baltimore's voyage to the colonies as a result of her "work history." Anne likely spoke English as a second-generation Bajan, of mixed descent, and may even have been a practicing Catholic, which would have made her a well suited "companion" for the Catholic seafaring colonizers. We are not certain of the exact circumstances of her transport from Barbados to England and then to the British colonies. However, what is very clear is that Anne had agency and was fully aware of and willing to stand up for her status and rights as an indentured servant expectant of freedom and liberty at the end of her term.

Let Freedom Ring

In the late 1790s into the beginning of the next century the Mahoney family name was widely known, mainly because of the freedom suits launched by my uncles: Charles, Daniel, and Patrick Mahoney. These early freedom fighters petitioned the courts for manumission based on their descendancy from their great-grandmother Anne Joice, who had consistently and emphatically proclaimed that her freedom and that of her children had been unequivocally stolen by Colonel Henry Darnall. Darnall was a wealthy Roman Catholic colonizer who had arrived in the Maryland colony in 1664 and acquired over thirty thousand acres of land in the regions of today's Washington, DC, Prince George's County and Montgomery County by the time of his death in 1711.

Before the expiration of Anne's indenture, Lord Baltimore (Charles Calvert) sold Anne's contract to his cousin Henry, who was also the brother of his first wife. When Anne's bond term was fulfilled, Colonel Henry disregarded Anne's rights to begin her new life as a freewoman and reclassed her as "slave for life." This act set into motion a history of enslavement of my family by the Catholic gentry credited for the creation of Georgetown University that would last nearly two hundred years. Many of Anne Joice's children and grandchildren came to be owned by various branches of the Carroll family through channels of marriage and/or inheritance. By the last decade of the 18th century several resided at White Marsh under the management and ownership of Jesuit priest John Ashton, one of Georgetown's founding fathers.

In 1790 Anne Joice's great-great grandsons Charles, Daniel, and Patrick, aware of their lineage and fueled by a strident cry for justice and righteousness, launched a case for manumission against Rev. Ashton. The transcript of the Mahoney trials records the testimony of Anne through her grandson Peter Harbard, who was born in 1719 and had grown up hearing his grandmother's testimony. In the court record of May 25, 1792, Peter spoke of Anne's frequent and bold claims to freedom. Harbard confidently recounted how his grandmother persistently asserted that she and all of her children were owed their freedom by legal right. Anne had been well versed on the terms of her contract. She insisted that her service was for the term of four years which was consistent with the contract of other immigrants to the colonies during that time. After four years she was to have been a freewoman.

Before a jury Peter relayed a firsthand account of Anne's declaration that Lord Baltimore had sold Anne's indenture to Colonel Henry Darnall who then burned the legal contract and bound Anne as a "slave for life." Harbard further incited that Darnall, adding insult to injury, then locked Anne in the basement of a neighboring plantation for a period of 5-6 months, to punish her for speaking out. After her release Darnall assigned her the role of cook at his Woodyard Plantation, in today's Prince George's County, Maryland. Of note is the fact that this same Henry Darnall had been given the role of 'keeper of the seal' by Lord Baltimore, giving him the ability to issue grants of large parcels of land to his favored cronies. He is known to have issued the original land patent for the beginnings of Georgetown on November 18, 1703.[1] Thus, from the very beginning of this nation's history my family has been intertwined with the history of the Jesuit community and the foundation of the Jesuit institutions Georgetown University and Loyola University Maryland.

The Mahoney trial was a landmark case which sparked an onslaught of freedom suits that were sprinkled by names prominent in the textbooks of American history—for example, Francis Scott Key and Gabriel Duvall, who became one of the country's first Supreme Court justices. The Mahoney trials lasted for more than a decade with appeals and alternating verdicts. Finally, in 1804, John Ashton himself, perhaps by act of contrition, awarded the Mahoney brothers their freedom.

Many members of the Mahoney family were proactively freed by Charles Carroll of Carrollton, signer of the Declaration of Independence, due to the controversy stirred up by the suits. However, that was not the fate of my four times great-grandfather Harry Mahoney. Harry, alongside the three brothers Charles, Daniel, and Patrick, had been enslaved at White Marsh in Prince George's County, Maryland. Harry's birthplace is documented as White Marsh in the Zwinge documents, recorded by Jesuit Priest Joseph Zwinge.

The history of the White Marsh Plantation plays prominently in the building and transference of wealth and property to the founders of

---

1 Elizabeth Duhamel, "Col. Henry Darnall and His Family," *Records of the Columbia Historical Society, Washington, D.C.*, Vol. 26 (1924): 129-145

Georgetown University. The land that became known as White Marsh was initially owned by James Carroll, the nephew of Charles Carroll, the Irish settler of the Maryland colonies, and husband of Mary Darnall, Colonel Henry Darnall's daughter. Charles and Mary Darnall Carroll's inventory of enslaved people included Anne Joice's granddaughter Sukey Harbard. Sukey's daughter, Eleanor Mahoney, was the mother of Charles, Patrick, Daniel, and Harry, along with many other Mahoney children.

Charles Carroll the settler and his son, Charles Carroll of Annapolis, were intimately involved in assisting their relative James Carroll in establishing fortune and prominence in the Maryland colonies. James had immigrated from Ireland with nominal means following the family's loss of title and property during the Jacobite uprisings in Ireland. With the financial backing of his cousin, uncle, and other members of the Catholic gentry, James amassed a large estate. James was particularly helped by Henry Darnall II, Colonel Henry's son, who became James' business partner. Henry Darnall II was also heir to the Woodyard plantation where Anne Joice had been bound for life. A letter from 1718 documented in *A Reading of James Carroll's Daybook* highlights the involvement of Henry Darnall II in the transatlantic slave trading ventures of James Carroll: "Two letters from merchant Gilbert Higgonson show the involvement of Henry Darnall II and Edward Lloyd in the trade…James Carroll's 1718 shipment of slaves sailed to Maryland onboard the ship *Margaret* of London owned by London Merchant Samuel Bonham…"[2]

When James Carroll, who never married, died in 1729, he left his slave holdings and land that included White Marsh to Jesuit priests.[3] He strategically bequeathed the estate with a view toward establishing Jesuit prominence and influence in the new world in the area of education and culture. Three properties totaling over two thousand acres and all of the enslaved people became the property of Father George Thorold, S.J., and this exchange resulted in an exponential increase of Jesuit-owned slaves.[4] In 1741, after the construction of Sacred Heart Chapel, White Marsh became

2 Charles Flanagan, "The Sweets of Independence: A Reading of the 'James Carroll Daybook, 1714-21'" (Ph.D. Dissertation, University of Maryland, College Park, 2005).
3 Thomas Hughes, *History of the Society of Jesus in North America* (Longmans, Green, and Company, 1907).
4 Flanagan, "The Sweets of Independence."

a fully operational plantation benefiting from the labor pool of dozens of enslaved people which including my Mahoney relatives. The ongoing dehumanization and monetizing of Anne and her descendants and others like them resulted in the building and transference of generational wealth and legacy.

The Chapel at White Marsh, located in today's Bowie, Maryland, became a central meeting place for the Jesuit priests. At a meeting held there in Dec of 1792, Georgetown College's first president, Bishop John Carroll established the Corporation of Roman Catholic Clergy (CRCC). Under this newly chartered entity, property ownership and control—including of three hundred and twenty-three enslaved men, women, and children, and nine properties totaling thirteen thousand acres —was transferred from individual Jesuits to the newly incorporated and established CRCC.

The stakeholders involved in the creation of the CRCC were also those credited with the foundation of Georgetown and Loyola.[5] This exchange put the American Jesuit order and Georgetown and Loyola squarely in the middle of slave ownership and made them one of the largest owners of enslaved people in Maryland. Ironically, Georgetown's first president and the chief organizer of the CRCC, John Carroll, was the great-grandson of Colonel Henry Darnall. He had grown up at the Woodyard plantation, which his mother Eleanor Darnall had inherited, the very same plantation for which Anne Joice had labored as an enslaved cook three generations earlier.

The Calverts, Darnalls, and Carrolls were also intimately connected through several generations of marriage. Charles Carroll, the settler married Colonel Henry's daughter, Mary Darnall; it was their grandson, Charles Carroll of Carrollton, who emancipated the Mahoney descendants in response to the suits against Rev. John Ashton. Even Ashton's mother was a Carroll relative. The practice of selling, gifting, or trading enslaved people between members of these closely knit kinship connections and church clergy (who were more often than not also related) was normative. Thus, some members of the Mahoney family were held at the Jesuit-run plantation of White Marsh, others are found on the plantation of Charles Carroll,

5 Bernard Cook, "Maryland Jesuits and Slavery, Pt. I." *Cura Virtualis*, September 8, 2021.

while my four times great-grandfather Harry Mathias Mahoney became one of the few enslaved laborers at the St Inigoes Mission.

Unsung Heroes

Harry Mahoney was born at White Marsh, around 1763; at some point after his birth he was relocated from White Marsh to Saint Inigoes Mission immediately adjacent to St. Mary's City, the initial landing place of the first Jesuits in 1634.[6] It is not clear whether Harry was aware of the freedom suits of his brothers and the resulting emancipation of many of his family members. Harry was referred to as one of the "Jesuit Negroes," the cooks, domestics, stable boys, and coaches.[7] Rev. Zwinge wrote "they were slaves, but were called servants, and they had some standing in the community…"[8] Harry worked as a foreman at St Inigoes alongside a white overseer. His role was to assist in supervising the daily workings of the farm.

Harry was among a distinct group of the enslaved, and although still at the beck and call of his masters, he experienced a bit more autonomy and responsibility. His position afforded him a limited sense of liberty and leadership in the enslaved community, and he was known to provide spiritual guidance to the community of Black people at St Inigoes. His daughter Louisa, whose life is explored in the next section of this chapter, recounted how her father had purposefully married a "pure African woman," Ana. Ana was said to have been an orphan. The Zwinge manuscript reports specifically that Harry wanted "such a person as a wife."[9] It is of interest to note that Harry, who has been described in some accounts as "mulatto," thought it advantageous to augment the African DNA of his offspring and was intentional about doing so. His wife Ana may have been a descendant of one of the groups of African people from Sierra Leone that had been purchased by James Carroll from a London merchant in 1718.[10]

---

6 Edwin Warfield Beitzell, *The Jesuit Missions of St. Mary's County, Maryland*. Revised edition. (Leonardtown, MD: St. Mary's County Historical Society, 1976).
7 Joseph Zwinge, "The Jesuit Farms in Maryland. Facts and Anecdotes," *Woodstock Letters* XXXIX, no. 3 (1910): 374-82.
8 Zwinge, "The Jesuit Farms in Maryland."
9 John LaFarge, *The Manner is Ordinary* (New York: Harcourt, Brace and Company, 1954).
10 Flanagan, "The Sweets of Independence."

In the fall of 1814, during the war of 1812, we are given an additional window into Harry's character. St. Inigoes, located at the mouth of the Potomac, had witnessed many attacks on neighboring properties since the war had begun, but had enjoyed a measure of safety due to its religious status and posture of neutrality. As the war progressed and availability of supply sources diminished due to previous raids and destruction of property, St. Inigoes became a more vulnerable target. A news article dated August 7 described a near call encroachment by the British a couple of months before the attack, conveying the vulnerability of the farm: "On Tuesday morning, one frigate two tenders and several barges proceeded up St. Mary's and landed on the St. Inigoes side with a plundering party of about 1000 men…" The general tone of the community was fearful and precarious sensing that an attack was imminent.

On October 30, what had previously been limited to close calls became reality. Just a little over a month after the redcoats had set fire to the Capitol in Washington, D.C., this was the scene described in a letter by Rev. Moberly to Father De Grassi at Georgetown College: "I saw the chapel door was open and heard an alarming noise. I ran to the chapel, saw 4 or 5 ruffians at work, ran back and begged the captain to interfere. He ran with me and ordered them out. But oh! painful to relate! The sacred vessels thrown and dragged here and there…."[11] Rev. Moberly described how he himself barely avoided being shot. Father Horace McKenna, S.J. also recounts a story related to the incident involving Harry and Rev. Rantzau, the Superior at St. Inigoes. He relates how, when the priest who had been in hiding reemerged following the attack, he exclaimed to Harry in distress "They carried off my bag containing several thousand dollars." To which Harry laughed and replied, "When I saw the men coming, I took all the young girls from the Manor farms, and I took the money. I led them two miles away to the top of the hill in the woods. They are safe now, and there I buried the money." The priest out of gratitude promised not to send the family away.[12]

Some may question Harry's decision to serve and protect those who claimed him as property rather than to flee, as many others had done during

11 Woodstock Letters, Vol XLII, Number 3, October 1, 1913.
12 Woodstock Letters, Vol LXXIX, Number 1, February 1, 1950.

earlier raids. The British had broadcast the promise of freedom for those who joined their troops. It is recorded that over 700 enslaved people in southern Maryland fled and joined the British, including some members of the Mahoney family.[13] (While some obtained the promise, after the war ended, sadly many were resold into slavery to plantations in the south and the Caribbean.) Harry's noble actions offer insight into his values and character. At the time of the war Harry and Anna had at least five children between the ages of three and fourteen and it is certain that they would have been at the forefront of his heart and mind. Harry was the head of his household. He would have held close the value and protection of the family bond as sacred, especially given its tenuous nature in a society where families could be suddenly and permanently separated with no recourse. Harry's act of heroism and integrity was most certainly performed with a view of the long-term wellbeing and safety of his family. It is also likely that Harry had been exposed to and immersed in cornerstone virtues of the Catholic faith, given his close proximity to the Jesuit fathers. Qualities like self-sacrifice, truth, and righteousness were values which he took seriously, which had likely afforded him a coveted position in the community, and which he perhaps adhered to more dearly than some of his owners. Certainly, Harry would be familiar with the Biblical passage "For what does it profit a man to gain the whole world and lose his own soul."[14]

The Bad Times

In May of 1838 Henry Johnson, sixth governor of Louisiana, and Dr. Jesse Batey, both of whom owned large sugar plantations in the state "went down to St. Mary's by stagecoach to meet Father Mulledy and take a look at our negroes." On June 19, 1838, Father Mulledy signed agreements with Batey and Johnson, and the Jesuits agreed to deliver two hundred seventy-two enslaved people to Alexandria, D.C., fifty-one of them as soon as possible. The rest were to leave between October 15 and November 15, together with their clothes and bedding. In return Batey and Johnson agreed to pay $115,000.

13 Cook, "Maryland Jesuits and Slavery."
14 Mark 8:36, *King James Bible*.

Within days, fifty-one enslaved people filled with anger, desperation, fear, and uncertainty, with clothes and bedding in hand, were forcefully ripped away from a life and community that their families had been enmeshed in for generations. The first groups affected by the upheaval were from the communities of St. Inigoes and White Marsh, all were under forty-five, just under half were under the age of 18. The heaviness in the atmosphere was palpable as they boarded the ship en route to the Alexandria port. Father Peter Haverman provides a vivid description of the somber atmosphere in his letter describing the final installment of the remaining "Jesuit Negroes" to be delivered to Henry Johnson as they boarded the ship on November 12:

How these sad days passed I am not able to say. The slaves with heroic fortitude were giving themselves to fate and with Christian resignation relinquishing themselves to God. One woman more pious than the others, and at that time pregnant most demanded my compassion. She was coming toward me so that for the last time she could greet me and seek benediction, and she observed as she was genuflecting: "If ever someone should have reason for despair, do I not now have it? I do not know on what day the birth will come, whether on the road or sea. What will become of me? Why do I deserve this?" I was saying "Trust in God." So it was, she agreed... All were coming to me seeking rosaries, medals, a cross or something...."

This tragic episode clandestinely became known as "the bad times" for generations to come, as those affected were too traumatized to speak about it openly.

Harry and Anna Mahoney, now in their seventies, along with all seven of their children, and twenty-three grandchildren, were part of the Jesuit bailout plan, despite promises made to Harry for his loyalty and heroic acts twenty-four years later. When the final ship arrived to carry the last of the Jesuit enslaved, my third great-grandmother, twenty-three-year-old Louisa, the youngest of the Mahoney siblings, and her aging parents were strategically missing. They had been urgently warned to hide out in the woods until danger passed, perhaps as a result of the pledge of protection made to Harry fourteen years earlier.

After the ship left the vicinity, Harry's daughter Louisa and her mother emerged out of the woods with Father Carberry welcoming them back with gladness. Two years later Father Carberry would repurchase Louisa from Henry Johnson for $648 claiming her as a Jesuit "slave for life." After the last slave ship for the sale left for Louisiana, Harry's daughter Louisa remained at the manor alone. Where she had once been surrounded by family and community, she was left to fend for herself. The loneliness and grief of the chasm of separation must have been overwhelming, yet she persevered. She eventually began a family of her own, marrying a free Black man by the name of Alex Mason who fought in the Civil War but was brutally murdered while walking on a highway enroute to St. Mary's City in August of 1861, just four months after the onset of the Civil War.

Tradition tells us that Louisa maintained contact with her relatives in Louisiana and would send rosaries and other items of spiritual support through the Jesuit fathers. She was a respected and revered member of the St. Inigoes community and in her later years was known by all as "Aunt Louisa." She was said to have had an excellent memory, considered the resident historian by priest and lay alike. She was known to share memories of the bygone days, the days when the numbers of Black people on the farm exceeded the number of white people. In a 1977 *Baltimore Sun* article commemorating the one hundredth birthday of her great-grandson who ran the Jesuit kitchens at Woodstock Seminary for over sixty years, Gabriel Bennett reminisced on the "funny sing-song way" his grandmother Louisa spoke, "even though she had been born in America."[15]

When the Maryland slaves were emancipated in 1864, Louisa and her five children were enumerated under the ownership of the Corporation of Roman Catholic Clergy (CRCC), the organization that had been created by John Carroll and other founders of Georgetown College nearly a century earlier. As stated in her obituary, "She came into this world a slave and was the property of the Jesuits up to the time of the emancipation." When she died at the age of 97 her obituary appeared as an article in the St Mary's

---

15 "Looking Back, Woodstock Resident to mark 100 th Year," *Baltimore Sun*, August 4, 1972.

Beacon and her funeral was lauded as the largest procession the county had ever seen. A requiem mass, typically reserved for priest, was held in her honor. She was buried at St. Ignatius Church on the property of St. Inigoes among the Jesuit priests whom she had served the bulk of her long life. The priest who penned her obituary wrote of her "In that long lapse of time, he never heard a charge, hint or insinuation that she was not eminently honest, virtuous and obedient to her God, faithful to husband…" He went on to direct that "immediate steps be taken to build a monument in her name by the young and active" to extol her honor and perpetuate her virtues.[16]

No Longer Slaves But Sons And Daughters

Beginning with Anne Joice's arrival in the colonies in 1775, to Louisa Mahoney Mason and her children's emancipation in 1864, members of my family provided free labor that benefited the Jesuits and their enterprises. While the history is painful, it is also one from which to derive pride and meaning. It is a privilege to be able to tell the stories of my ancestors and to give them credit that is long overdue. The journey has been one that has been Divinely guided and inspired. There has been healing and restoration as family members descended from siblings torn apart by the 1838 sale find one another. We are reconnecting and regenerating the broken branches of our shared family tree and experience as those who have been subliminally shaped by generations of Jesuit subjugation and the trauma resulting from separation.

I am particularly struck by the memory of my daughter holding a copy of Will Thomas' book *A Question of Freedom* as she conducted her Zoom interview for Georgetown Law School; the book relates the story of Anne Joice and the trial of the Mahoney brothers versus John Ashton. When I asked her about it she said that she had it there "for inspiration." Many of Harry's progeny have benefitted from the seeds of integrity and self-sacrifice that he sowed and which I believe have resulted in spiritual blessings that I pray will continue to bear fruit. We who were once enslaved are arising and claiming our places as cherished sons and daughters of the Nation. As each of us resurrect, share, honor and even confess the stories of our ancestors and

16 Georgetown Slavery Archive, GSA83, St. Mary's Beacon, July 22, 1909, Louisa Mason obituary, 1909.

their contribution to the foundation of this nation we bring opportunities for atonemement, reconciliation and healing for both slave owners and the enslaved.

Holy Scripture tells us that all of creation is waiting in eager expectation for the sons and daughters of God to be revealed, for the vestiges of slavery to be broken, and for those who were formerly in bondage to take their place as honored sons and daughters. And so it is for our former Jesuit enslaved ancestors who cheer and guide from beyond the veil. Rejoice, for your redemption draws nigh. We honor them and the legacy of integrity, perseverance, loyalty, righteousness, and family they have left for us to carry forward.

In 2016 Georgetown made a public apology and committed to giving "special consideration" to the descendants of those who were part of the 1838 sale. Several of Harry and Ana Mahoney's multi-generational grandchildren have or will attend schools connected to the Georgetown sale in their honor, including Melisande and Chase, (Georgetown University); August and Jesse (Georgetown College Preparatory); and Kyla (Georgetown University College of Law). We are grateful and indebted to our ancestors for paving the way. I for one have found a profoundly absent piece of my identity restored through the recovery and telling of my family story. I have been empowered with a greater sense of purpose and commitment to see honored and extolled these lives upon whom Georgetown University and Loyola University Maryland owes their very existence.

Freedom on Trial

Kevin Porter

The Queen

When he sued the Jesuit Father John Ashton in 1791, Edward Queen initiated the family's claim to freedom arguing that he was the grandson of Mary Queen (1680–1759), a free woman of color whose terms of indenture were violated in the eighteenth century. His case, *Queen v. Ashton*, was litigated in the General Court of the Western Shore and took three years before the jury rendered the verdict on May 23, 1794, making Edward Queen a free man. That same year, Edward's mother, Phillis Queen, and over forty other people descended from Mary Queen also sued Ashton. Represented by future U.S. Supreme Court Justice Gabriel Duvall and Philip Barton Key (uncle of Priscilla Queen's attorney Francis Scott Key), the Queens recovered their freedom on April 15, 1796.[1]

Not all of the Queen freedom suits were successful. Other members of the Queen family challenged the legality of their bondage against their Jesuit slaveholders throughout the courts of Maryland. Nancy Queen, "being the Descendant of a free Woman named Mary Queen," brought the Reverend Charles Sewall to trial in Charles County. Then, on August 16, 1794, Sewall's closest protégé the Reverend Sylvester Boarman was summoned to

---

1 *Edward Queen v. John Ashton*, General Court of the Western Shore, Docket, May Term 1794, S492-22, Maryland State Archives (hereafter "MSA"); *Edward Queen v. John Ashton*, General Court of the Western Shore, Judgment Record, May Term 1794, Lib. JG 23, S497-22, MSA; *Phillis Queen v. John Ashton*, Prince George's County Court, Docket, April Term 1796, C1203-43, MSA.

the Harford County Court to defend the claims that he was "unjustly &
unlawfully [holding] in bondage" David Queen and his niece, Ann, "the
Daughter of Henny, who was the Daughter of Nanny who was the Daughter
of Mary Queen." David and Ann Queen would remain enslaved at the Deer
Creek mission until their case was settled in 1801. Nancy Queen's trial on
the other hand commenced two years later, the same year that the judgment
was ruled in her aunt Phillis's favor. However, unlike her counterparts up the
Patuxent River at the White Marsh plantation in Prince George's County,
Nancy Queen was not so fortunate.[2]

On August 15, 1796, a jury consisting of prominent Charles County
slaveholders rendered the verdict in favor of Father Sewall, ruling that:

> "the said Mary Queen the great-grandmother of the Petitioner from whom
> by descent the petitioner claims her freedom always was a slave as the said
> Charles Sewall by his plea aforesaid above hath alledged [sic]. Therefore it is
> adjudged by the Justices of the Court here that the said Nancy Queen is not
> entitled to her freedom, so as aforesaid by the Jurors aforesaid found and that
> the said Nancy Queen the petitioner return to the service of her master the
> aforesaid Charles Sewall and in the service of her said master to remain &c
> and that the said Charles Sewall of the Petition and premises aforesaid go
> thereof without day &c."[3]

The jury denied Nancy Queen's freedom based on the sketchy deposition of Benjamin Duvall claiming that Mary Queen was "from the Pappaw
Country there being as he understood several different Countries from which
negroes came such as the Golden Coast and others."[4] The implication and
perfunctory interpretation made by the Defendant was that Mary Queen
was born in Africa and therefore a slave. Unbeknownst to the court, several
months earlier Gabriel Duvall summoned the testimony of Fredus Ryland

---

2 *Nancy Queen v. Charles Sewall*, Charles County Circuit Court, Court Record, August 1796 - March 1797,
    IB, pp. 143-153, T3236-1, MSA; *Ann Queen and David Queen v. Sylvester Boarman*, Historical Society of
    Harford County, Maryland, County Court Records Collection, Bel Air, Maryland, Folder 32:14 - Court
    Records, via *OSCYS*, https://earlywashingtondc.org/doc/oscys.mdcase.0007.007.
3 *Nancy Queen v. Charles Sewall*, T3236-1, MSA.
4 Ibid.

of Cecil County. Had Nancy Queen's attorneys read Ryland's deposition out loud to the jury, they would have discovered that Mary Queen was "born free" in South America, possibly near the Popayán Providence between modern-day Colombia and Ecuador; that she sailed to London between 1709 and 1711, eventually entered a seven-year indenture, and was later transported to Maryland around 1715.[5]

Nancy Queen was born in a slave cabin on the White Marsh plantation. She was the great-granddaughter of Mary, the "Poppaw Queen," grand-daughter of Nanny Cooper, and the eldest daughter of Mary Queen, who was born on 28 February 1737 in Prince George's County. Nanny's daughter, Mary Queen, had four daughters: Nancy, born around 1755, Kate, born around 1758, Rachel, born around 1760, and Priscilla Queen, born around 1762. Mary and her four children were possibly removed from White Marsh sometime after 1764 and sent to the St. Thomas Manor plantation in Charles County near Port Tobacco. There is also the possibility that Nancy Queen was later sent to Harford County to labor at the Deer Creek mission with her younger uncle, David Queen, and first cousin, Ann Queen.[6]

After Pope Clement XIV suppressed the Jesuit Order in 1773, future Archbishop John Carroll—along with Fathers Charles Sewall and Sylvester Boarman—left Liège in Flanders (present-day Belgium) and returned to Maryland to perform missionary work. Sewall took over management of the Deer Creek mission until he was succeeded by Boarman in 1780. Father Sewall may have taken Nancy Queen back to Port Tobacco while David and Ann remained at Deer Creek with Boarman.[7]

Long before Bishop John Carroll and the Reverend Ashton hammered out the foundations of Georgetown College, the Jesuits operated the clandestine Bohemia Manor Academy on the Eastern Shore of Maryland in Cecil County. In 1728, planter James Carroll breached the terms of Mary

5 Deposition of Fredus Ryland, *Winifred Queen v. Soloman Sparrow and Charles Queen v. John Ashton*, Historical Society of Harford County, Maryland, County Court Records Collection, Bel Air, Maryland, Folder 32:14 - Court Records, via OSCYS, Depositions from Winifred Queen, Charles Queen, & Phillis Queen Petitions for Freedom, https://earlywashingtondc.org/doc/oscys.mdcase.0007.004.

6 John Lewis Small Book, Box 29, Folder 2, Maryland Province Archives, Society of Jesus, Georgetown University Manuscripts.

7 Clarence V. Joerndt, *St. Ignatius, Hickory, and Its Missions* (Baltimore, Printed by Publication Press, 1972), 362-70, 372; for an account of David Queen in Harford County, see J. Alphones Frederick, "Notebook IV: Notes from Medical Ledgers of John Archer 1772-ca. 1802," *John J. Tierney Collection*, 1767-1807, SC 1158-5-2, MSA.

Queen's indenture when he bequeathed her to his nephew, Anthony Carroll, who was receiving his "lower studys" at Bohemia. In 1730, Mary Queen was separated from her daughters at White Marsh and "sent across the [Chesapeake] Bay" to care for young Anthony Carroll. Many years later, John Carroll—then called "Jacky"—and his cousin "Charley" (later known as Charles Carroll of Carrollton) also attended Bohemia Manor Academy while Mary Queen was held there in bondage. They departed Cecil County together and sailed to the Colleges of St Omer's and Liège where they came under the tutelage of Anthony Carroll. There, they would also become acquainted with their Irish-borne distant cousin, John Ashton—the nephew of Anthony Carroll. It was Anthony Carroll that dispatched his nephew Ashton to Maryland to act as his legal representative and to protect the inheritance he received from the late James Carroll.[8]

The Queen family remained illegally enslaved at White Marsh after James Carroll bequeathed the 2,000-acre plantation to the Mission Superior of the Maryland Jesuits. When Ashton took over management at White Marsh in 1774, he treated the lands and the enslaved families that his grand-uncle gifted to the Jesuits as if they were his own personal property.

The Auction

Priscilla Queen, born around 1762 at White Marsh, probably spent most of her adult years at the St Thomas Manor plantation in Charles County, before being forced to Georgetown College. The 1800 U.S. census reported

8 Will of James Carroll, Prerogative Court, Wills, 1728-1730, Lib. CC 2, pp. 700-730, S538-28, MSA; Mary Queen and her two children Nan (alias "Nanny Cooper"), and Ralph are listed on James Carroll's inventory dated July 1730. For reasons unknown Phillis Queen, born around 1721, was omitted from the list; see Inventory of James Carroll, Prerogative Court, Inventories, 1729-1730, Lib. 15, pp. 700-730, S534-15, MSA. In his deposition, Caleb Clarke declared that Mary Queen was "...sent across the Bay" to Anthony Carroll; see further *Edward Queen v. John Ashton*, Deposition of Caleb Clarke, 23 October 1793, General Court of the Western Shore, Judgments, S498-178, MSA; John Gilmary Shea, *Life and Times of the Most Rev. John Carroll, Bishop and First Archbishop of Baltimore: Embracing the History of the Catholic Church in the United States, 1763-1815, with portraits, views, fac-similes* (New York: J. G. Shea, 1888), 27-30; For a more in depth genealogy of the Carroll family, see Ronald Hoffman, Sally D. Mason, Eleanor S. Darcy, *Dear Papa, Dear Charley: The Peregrinations of a Revolutionary Aristocrat, as told by Charles Carroll of Carrollton and his father, Charles Carroll of Annapolis, with sundry observations on bastardy, child-rearing, romance, matrimony, commerce, tobacco, slavery, and the politics of revolutionary America* (Chapel Hill, NC: Published for the Omohundro Institute of Early American History and Culture, Williamsburg, Virginia, the Maryland Historical Society, Baltimore, and the Maryland State Archives, Annapolis, by the University of North Carolina Press, 2001); Thomas O'Brien Hanley, *Charles Carroll of Carrollton: The Making of a Revolutionary Gentleman* (Washington: Catholic University of America Press, 1970) 154.

that the Georgetown area had 1,449 slaves and 277 free African Americans out of a total population of 5,120. That same year, at least five members of the Queen family were listed as heads of household in Maryland. Priscilla's uncle, Simon Queen, was now a free man living with his enslaved children at the White Marsh plantation.[9] Priscilla Queen and her family were counted among the nearly 1,500 enslaved people living in Georgetown.

Alexis, Hester, and Mima Queen may have been the children of Priscilla Queen. Mima Queen had a daughter born Mary Louisa Queen—called Louisa—possibly Priscilla Queen's granddaughter. By 1809, they were enslaved on the property of Rebecca Nally in the District of Columbia near the Navy Yard. In her last will and testament, Mrs. Nally desired that the Queens "be sold for cash." She died on November 28, 1809.[10]

On December 11, 1809, Samuel N. Smallwood—Justice of the Peace and executor of the Nally's will—posted an advertisement in the *National Intelligencer* for the sale of Alexis, Hester, Mima and Louisa Queen. The auction, set for the following Monday at 11 o'clock, took place at Rebecca Nally's residence near the Navy Yard. John Davis of Abel purchased Alexis for $400.[11] It appears Richard Bennett Nally (son of the late Mrs. Nally) and his brother-in-law, James Nevitt, partnered up and bought Hester Queen, both had equal shares in her ownership. John Hepburn bought Mima and her daughter, Louisa.

Immediately after Nally's auction sale, the Queens devised a plan to delay any further separation. Word soon reached Priscilla Queen—possibly through her uncle Simon Queen—that her kinfolk was sold off from the estate of the late Rebecca Nally. Within days, they likely sought the aid of Phillip Barton Key, who had successfully represented their family members enslaved at the White Marsh plantation, now living at his Woodley estate

9 "Queen Family Network," in *OSCYS*, edited by William G. Thomas III, et al. University of Nebraska-Lincoln, https://earlywashingtondc.org/families/queen#priscilla-queen; U.S. Census, 1800.

10 Will of Rebecca Nally, 27 Nov 1809, District of Columbia Wills and Probate Records, Wills, Book 1, 1801-1815, pp. 289-290 (O.S. 373, Box 3), courtesy of Ali Rahmaan, Archivist, District of Columbia Office of Public Records (D.C. Archives), Washington, D.C.

11 Bill of Sale from Samuel N. Smallwood to John Davis of Abel, 22 December 1809, District of Columbia Land Records, 1792-1817, Lib. I9, p. 242, District of Columbia Office of Public Records, Washington, DC; in Wesley E. Pippenger, *Index to District of Columbia Land Records, 1792-1817* (Westminster, MD: Heritage Books, 2010), 305.

in Georgetown. Key referred the case to another Georgetown lawyer, his thirty-year-old nephew, Francis Scott Key.

The Trial

On the morning of 8 January 1810, Francis Scott Key handwrote three petitions for freedom and filed them at the U.S. Circuit Court for the District of Columbia. First for Priscilla Queen against the Reverend Francis Neale, the Jesuit priest and the incoming president of Georgetown College. Second, Mima Queen on behalf of herself and her minor child Louisa against John Hepburn. Third, Hester Queen against Richard Bennett Nally (son of the deceased Rebecca Nally) with his brother-in-law and co-owner James Nevitt. The following Wednesday, Key filed Alexis Queen's petition against John Davis of Georgetown, the son of Abel G. Davis—only seventeen days after he closed the deal with Samuel N. Smallwood.[12]

Both Priscilla and Mima Queen claimed to be the great-grandchildren of Mary Queen, "the mother of Nanny Cooper." If Mima Queen was indeed the great-granddaughter of the "Poppaw Queen," she was probably the sister or first cousin of Priscilla—as opposed to being her child. Key's strategy may have been to lead the trials with Priscilla Queen's case, as his uncle had done with her aunt Phillis Queen and the other litigants in 1794. However, Mima Queen's situation was dire. She feared "that she may be removed out" of the District of Columbia and prayed for immediate relief.

Gabriel Duvall and Philip Barton Key fought on opposite sides during the American Revolutionary War. Toward the end of the eighteenth century, they united to defend the "Revolutionary Generation" of enslaved people challenging the legality of their bondage in Maryland. Duvall and Key collected as many depositions as they could to support the Queen family's claim that they were descended from "a free woman." It would seem Francis Scott Key had an open and shut case, given the existing precedence in *Queen v. Ashton*. However, there was something more sinister at play.

---

12 *Priscilla Queen v. Francis Neale*, Petition for Freedom, 8 January 1810, OSCYS, https://earlywashingtondc.org/doc/oscys.case.0025.001; *Mima Queen v. John Hepburn*, Petition for Freedom, 8 January 1810, OSCYS, https://earlywashingtondc.org/doc/oscys.case.0011.001; *Hester Queen v. James Nevitt & Richard Nally*, Petition for Freedom, 8 January 1810, OSCYS, https://earlywashingtondc.org/doc/oscys.case.0026.001; *Alexis Queen v. John Davis*, Petition for Freedom, 10 January 1810, OSCYS, https://earlywashingtondc.org/doc/oscys.case.0012.001; Smallwood to Davis, 22 December 1809.

On June 16, 1794, several days after Nancy Queen filed her petition for freedom against the Reverend Charles Sewall—superior at St Thomas Manor—the Jesuits began tallying up their "lawsuit expenses against [the] freedom of negroes." In an underhanded scheme to thwart further freedom suits from their enslaved laborers, Sewall and his clergyman decisively acted "to . . . retain or stop the mouth of lawyer [Philip Barton] Key from speaking in favor of the Negroes who have sued for their freedom." On August 20, they borrowed £4 17s 6p (four pounds, seventeen schillings, and six pence) out of the general fund at St Thomas Manor and paid Philip Barton Key to stop taking on any new cases for Jesuit enslaved clients.[13]

After paying off Philip Barton Key, the Jesuits now had an advantage. Key knew the strategy of the plaintiffs and he himself set the game plan. Furthermore, it was probably Key that exposed the ambiguity in the deposition of Benjamin Duvall, which they later deployed as their ace-in-a-hole. As Nancy Queen's case proceeded, Sewall was so confident that in July 1796 he wrote to the Reverend Ambrose Maréchal at Bohemia telling him not to free Ralph—the only surviving son of Mary Queen. The next month, at the August 1796 term, the Charles County Court ruled in favor of Fr. Sewall and Nancy Queen remained enslaved.

Francis Scott Key accepted the cases of Priscilla, Mima, Louisa, Hester, and Alexis Queen in January 1810, however, this would not be his first time representing the Queen family. Five months prior, on 21 August 1809, the young Georgetown lawyer entered his name at the Charles County Court as one of the attorneys for Nancy Queen in her lawsuit against the Reverend Charles Neale, brother of Francis Neale and "agent for the Corporation of Roman Catholic Clergymen." Three other cases were filed in conjunction and consolidated under Nancy Queen's petition, including Stephen Queen, Mary Queen—on behalf of herself and her two children Charles and Elizabeth—against Neale, as well as Moses Queen, now enslaved by Henrietta (Wheeler) Sanders, the widow of Edward Sanders of Cain's Purchase. When Key and his team failed to secure freedom for the plaintiffs in August 1810, they immediately prayed for an appeal. However, at the

13 St Thomas Manor Account Book 1793-1821, Box 46, Folder 2, Maryland Province Archives, Society of Jesus, Georgetown University Manuscripts, via *OSCYS*, https://earlywashingtondc.org/stories/queen_v_hepburn.

December 1810 term, the High Court of Appeals upheld the lower court's decision and the Queens of Port Tobacco remained enslaved.[14]

Priscilla Queen's trial began on June 20, 1810, when the U.S. Circuit Court for the District of Columbia swore in the jury. One of the jurors was withdrawn after expressing "his detestation of slavery." The next day, Key introduced his first witness, Priscilla's uncle Simon Queen, who had been adjudicated a free man in Prince George's County. On June 15, 1810, most likely at the urging of Francis Scott Key, fifty-one-year-old Simon Queen hurried down to the courthouse in Upper Marlboro to get his freedom papers, which Key "produced in evidence a record [and] certificate of his freedom." Neale's attorney objected to the admission of Simon as a witness, but the Court overruled and allowed the testimony of Simon Queen, a free negro, even though the defendant was "a free Christian white person." Gabriel Duvall who represented Simon Queen from 1794 through 1796 was also called as a witness.[15]

The defendant's counsel then offered and read to the jury the entire deposition of Benjamin Duvall, which declared that Mary Queen "who is represented to be the mother of Nanny Cooper [and] living at James Carroll's" and who he referred to her as his "Poppaw Queen." Key then offered to read the eyewitness account of Fredus Ryland, who testified that Mary Queen told him that "she was born free and lived in [Guayaquil]" in South America. The court ruled that "The declarations of an ancestor, while held as a slave, cannot be given in evidence. Declarations of deceased persons, that the ancestor was free, may be given in evidence, to show that the ancestor was in fact free, that is, not held in slavery." As a result, the only eyewitness account, the only deposition containing the only words ever recorded from Mary Queen, was dismissed.[16]

---

14 Court of Appeals, Judgments, Western Shore, *Nancy Queen v. Charles Neale, Moses Queen v. Henrietta Sanders*, Dec. 1810: Nos. 106, 172, *Mary Queen and her children v. Charles Neale*, May 1815: No. 13, S382-132-1, MSA.

15 *Priscilla Queen v. Francis Neale*, Minute Book Entry, 20 June 1810, Minutes of the U.S. Circuit Court for the District of Columbia, 1801-1863, National Archives and Records Administration, Record Group 21, Microfilm 1021, Reel 1 in *OSCYS*, https://earlywashingtondc.org/doc/oscys.mb.0005.001.

16 William Cranch, *Reports of Cases Civil and Criminal in the United States Circuit Court of the District of Columbia, from 1801 to 1841, Volume II* (Boston: Little, Brown and Company, 1852), 3; Thomas, *Question of Freedom*, 173.

The court ruled in favor of the Reverend Francis Neale, the Jesuit priest and President of Georgetown College. Priscilla was sent back to Georgetown College in perpetual bondage.

At the trial of *Mima Queen v. John Hepburn*, Francis Scott Key, called Simon Queen back to the stand to testify on behalf of his grandnieces. Gabriel Duvall testified once again, but Key also called two other witnesses—two white women—including "Mrs. Nevitt," who may have been the daughter of the deceased Rebecca Nally, who had joint ownership of Hester Queen. John Hepburn's counsel called three witnesses, including Nicholas Young, son of Notley Young, and Daniel Carroll of Duddington, both men prominent members of Maryland's Catholic gentry and major contributors to the development of the nation's capital.[17]

All parties agreed that Mima and Louisa were descendants of Mary Queen, but the defendant's counsel argued that Mary Queen was not an indentured servant but held as a slave for life. Once again, the D.C. Court refused to enter critical evidence that declared Mary Queen's origin and status. On June 26, 1810, the jury affirmed the verdict in Priscilla Queen's case and Mima and her Louisa remained enslaved to John Hepburn.

Queen appealed the decision to the Supreme Court of the United States on a writ of error, arguing that the hearsay testimony should have been allowed in a petition for freedom case. Francis Scott Key's writ of error stated, "After a lapse of 100 years better evidence than this cannot be expected. The general reputation of the fact that the ancestor was free is sufficient to rebut the presumption arising from color, and throws the burden of proof on the other side."

While Priscilla and Mima Queen grew impatient for their second trial, Gabriel Duvall was nominated and seated on the Supreme Court of the United States, while his former partner Philip Barton Key was elected to the United States House of Representatives—both still slaveholders and now living in D.C. The young ambitious Francis Scott Key, now having several U.S. Supreme Court cases under his belt, began preparing for the trial.

After three years, the U.S. Supreme Court heard the case in February 1813. The majority opinion written by Chief Justice John Marshall denied

17 *Hester Queen v. James Nevitt and Richard Nally*, Petition of Freedom, in *OSCYS*.

the appeal and upheld the lower court, arguing that "hearsay evidence is incompetent to establish any specific fact, which fact is in its nature susceptible of being proved by witnesses who speak from their own knowledge."

Justice Duvall rendered the only dissenting opinion, in which he wrote that:

> *"To exclude hearsay in such cases, would leave the party interested without remedy. It was decided also that the issue could not be prejudiced by the neglect or omission of the ancestor. If the ancestor neglected to claim her right, the issue could not be bound by length of time, it being a natural inherent right. It appears to me that the reason for admitting hearsay evidence upon a question of freedom is much stronger than in cases of pedigree or in controversies relative to the boundaries of land. It will be universally admitted that the right to freedom is more important than the right of property."[18]*

Duvall further acknowledged that "people of color from their helpless condition under the uncontrolled authority of a master, are entitled to all reasonable protection."

As a result of *Queen v. Hepburn*, Priscilla's case was dismissed at the June 1813 term. Neale eventually returned to St Thomas Manor, where he served from 1819 until his death on December 20, 1837. Francis Scott Key, a slaveholder, later joined other anti-abolitionists in Georgetown and played a pivotal role in the development of the American Colonization Society—only a few years after arguing before the U.S. Supreme Court for the freedom of the Queens. Despite his efforts to secure their freedom, Key eventually advocated for their removal from American soil.

The fate of Priscilla Queen, Alexis Queen, Hester Queen, Mima and her daughter Louisa Queen after the 1813 verdict remains unknown.[19]

---

18 "The Timing of Queen v. Hepburn: An exploration of African American Networks in the Early Republic," in *OSCYS*, edited by William G. Thomas III, et al. University of Nebraska-Lincoln, https://earlywashingtondc.org/stories/queen_v_hepburn; *Mima Queen v. Hepburn*, 11 U.S. (7 Cranch) at 290-293 in "Not the Most Insignificant Justice: Reconsidering Justice Gabriel Duvall's Slavery Law Opinions Favoring Liberty," 2 March 2017, edited by Andrew T. Fede, *Journal of Supreme Court History, Vol. 42, Issue 1*, in *Wiley Online Library*, https://onlinelibrary.wiley.com/doi/10.1111/jsch.12132.

19 William G. Thomas III, "Priscilla Queen v. Francis Neale," in *OSCYS*, https://earlywashingtondc.org/cases/oscys.caseid.0025.

The Sale

The Reverend Francis Neale's worst fears were realized in 1838. The rural farms owned by the Jesuits were all in wretched condition and efforts to maintain Georgetown College led the Roman Catholic order into considerable debt. On October 10, 1837, the Reverend Thomas Mulledy became the second provincial superior of the Maryland Province of the Society of Jesus (formerly the "Maryland Mission"). Mulledy himself drove the Jesuits into debt with his ambitious ventures to expand facilities on the college campus. To settle the debt, Mulledy orchestrated the sale of over 272 enslaved people remaining on the Jesuit farms in Southern Maryland to two sugar planters in Louisiana: Henry Johnson and Jesse Batey.[20]

Before the 1838 sale, the Queen family was dispersed with clusters of free and enslaved groups throughout the Chesapeake and beyond. There were clusters of free Queens at Bohemia in Cecil County and at St Joseph's in Talbot County—some later migrated to Philadelphia. In 1820, Dennis Queen, a free man, was living near Georgetown College with four enslaved people in his household. They may have traveled with the Reverend Anthony Kohlmann in 1817 when he left White Marsh to assume his role as President of Georgetown College. In 1823, the Reverend Charles Van Quickenborne forced three families from White Marsh to labor at the new Novitiate in Florissant, Missouri near St Louis—including Susanna Queen and her husband Isaac Hawkins, Moses Queen and his wife Nancy, as well as Thomas Brown and his wife Molly (possibly a Queen). Then in 1829, Anna Hawkins and her children were forced from White Marsh and bound for Florissant. Her husband Proteus Queen—who we presume is the son of Phillis Queen, daughter of "Queen Mary"—forfeited his freedom to join his family. Jacks Queen—son of Nelly—and his wife Sally—daughter of Sally Harrison—were also uprooted from White Marsh and forced to labor for the Jesuits in Middle America. Their siblings remained in Maryland until 1838, when they were forced to Louisiana.[21]

20 "Major Superiors in the Northern United States," July 1962, Joseph H. Ramspacher, *Woodstock Letters*, vol. 91, no. 3, pp. 300-301.

21 Bohemia Parish Collection, 1789-1882, M11705, SC 3572-1-1, MSA; U.S. Census, 1820, Georgetown, Washington, District of Columbia, p. 57, NARA Roll: M33_5, Image: 64, RG 21, NARA via *Ancestry. com*; Robert Emmett Curran, *The Bicentennial History of Georgetown University: From Academy to University, 1789–1889, Vol. 1* (Washington, D.C.: Georgetown University Press, 1993), 84; "Beyond the 272

By the summer of 1838, Mulledy commissioned three vessels to transport the families from the port of Alexandria—then a part of the District of Columbia—to the port of New Orleans, bound for the estates of Jesse Batey and the former Governor of Louisiana the Honorable Henry Johnson. The first vessel the *Uncas* departed Alexandria in June 1838 with approximately 50 people. The *Katherine Jackson* shipped off 130 men, women, and children on 13 November and arrived on 6 December. Sixteen days later, the *Isaac Franklin* anchored in New Orleans on 22 December 1838, carrying 83 captive souls on board, several were not part of Mulledy's sale. Each vessel was associated with the notorious slave traffickers Isaac Franklin and John Armfield—the latter vessel obviously named after Franklin himself.[22]

"272 in all" was the number written on the list of people from the Jesuit plantations compiled in preparation for the sale in 1838. In actuality, the exact number was closer to 300 people—including the infant children. Originally, there were approximately 95 people accounted for at the White Marsh mission in Anne Arundel and Prince George's County—50 at St Thomas Manor in Charles County—49 at Newton and about 95 at St Inigoes in St Mary's County. The list recorded who had run away and who had been "married off." Rome gave the Jesuits strict orders not to separate immediate families. Yet, in all their efforts not to separate family units, Mulledy's sale did just that.[23]

"Old Isaac" Hawkins, his wife, and sixty-five-year-old Sally Harrison remained at White Marsh while their children and grandchildren were uprooted from their nuclear families.

Forty-three-year-old Rachel Queen would be leaving behind free and enslaved family members. Born about 1795, she was likely the daughter of

---

Sold in 1838, Plotting the National Diaspora of Jesuit-Owned Slaves," edited by Matthew Quallen, *Hoya Historian Columnist*, 29 April 2016; Bowie: Register of baptisms, marriages, etc., 1 January 1818 - 31 December 1895, Box 3, Folder 4, Whitemarsh Manor, Maryland Province Collection, Booth Family Center for Special Collections, Georgetown University, Washington, D.C.; See "Letter from the Novitiate Florissant," *Woodstock Letters*, Vol. 1, No. 1, 1 January 1872, for age of Proteus at time of death.

22 Slave Manifests of Coastwise Vessels Filed at New Orleans, Louisiana, 1807–1860, NARA microfilm M1895, Roll: 8, RG 36, NARA via *Ancestry.com*, in William G. Thomas III, *A Question of Freedom: The Families Who Challenged Slavery from the Nation's Founding to the Civil War* (New Haven: Yale University Press, 2020), 289-290.

23 Census of people to be sold in 1838, Maryland Province Archives, Oversize Box 4 (WO 112), Special Collections, Lauinger Library, Georgetown University in GSA, http://slaveryarchive.georgetown.edu/items/show/71.

Simon Queen—who recovered his freedom from Ashton in 1796. Simon had at least three other children that remained enslaved at White Marsh, namely, Simon Jr, Michael, and David Queen. In February 1806, Father Ashton demanded that the Corporation of Roman Catholic Clergymen give him "ye boy Davy … (Simon's son & now motherless)." Young David eventually secured his freedom and likely joined his father on the outskirts of Baltimore City near Marley Creek in Anne Arundel County. In the summer of 1806, Simon Jr and Michael Queen absconded from White Marsh; it's possible they never returned. By 1833, Rachel remained enslaved at White Marsh married to Ned Harrison—son of Old Sally—with five children. They named their firstborn son "Simon."[24]

"Old Isaac" knew the Queen family very well. In fact, the senior Simon Queen may have been his uncle. Historians and genealogists have drawn the conclusion that Isaac Hawkins was born at Port Tobacco on September 25, 1777, to Sam and Kate. There is a reasonable possibility that his mother Kate was the older sister of Priscilla Queen, who sued the Reverend Francis Neale for her freedom in 1810. If this is true, Isaac Hawkins would have had a legitimate claim to freedom. However, the U.S. Supreme Court decision in *Queen v. Hepburn* deterred any further petitions for freedom, as the very claim itself was ruled as inadmissible "hearsay."[25]

24 Ibid; Ashton to Rev. Mr. Germain Bitouzey, Proceedings of the Corporation of Roman Catholic Clergy, 3 February 1806, Maryland Province Archives, box 23, folder 13; See Certificate of Freedom for David Queen, 14 August 1817, Anne Arundel County Court, Certificates of Freedom, 1810-1831, p. 103, entry 1, C46-3, MSA, https://msa.maryland.gov/megafile/msa/coagser/c1/c46/000000/000003/pdf/mdsa_c46_3.pdf; U.S. Census, 1820, District 3, Anne Arundel, Maryland, p. 304, NARA Roll: M33_41, Image: 155, RG 29, NARA via *Ancestry.com*; *American and Commercial Daily Advertiser* (Baltimore), 3 June 1806 in Thomas, *Question of Freedom*, 137-138; List of slaves taxed at White Marsh in 1833, Prince George's County Levy Court, Assessment Record, 1830-1850, C1163-10, MSA in GSA, http://slaveryarchive.georgetown.edu/items/show/314; Baptism of Simon, 18 Jul 1820, Bowie: Register of baptisms, marriages, etc., 1 January 1818 - 31 December 1895, Box 3, Folder 4, p. 24, Whitemarsh Manor, Maryland Province Collection, Booth Family Center for Special Collections, Georgetown University, Washington, D.C.
25 Children born into slavery at Port Tobacco, 1750s-1770s, Box 3, Folder 8, Maryland Province Archives, Booth Family Center for Special Collections, Georgetown University, in GSA, http://slaveryarchive.georgetown.edu/items/show/45; Undated inventory of enslaved people and livestock at White Marsh and Fingal, ca. late 18th century, Inventory of Slaves Incapable to Work, Box 29, Folder 2, Maryland Province Archives, Booth Family Center for Special Collections, Georgetown University, in GSA, http://slaveryarchive.georgetown.edu/items/show/286; "Queen Family Network," in OSCYS, edited by William G. Thomas III, et al. University of Nebraska-Lincoln, https://earlywashingtondc.org/families/queen; Mima Queen v. Hepburn, 11 U.S. (7 Cranch) at 290-293 in "Not the Most Insignificant Justice: Reconsidering Justice Gabriel Duvall's Slavery Law Opinions Favoring Liberty," 2 March 2017, edited by Andrew T. Fede, *Journal of Supreme Court History, Vol. 42, Issue 1,* in *Wiley Online Library*, https://onlinelibrary.wiley.com/doi/10.1111/jsch.12132.

Len Queen and his family boarded the *Katherine Jackson* and were delivered to the West Oak plantation owned by Jesse Batey. Possibly the progeny of Nancy or her sister Priscilla Queen, he was one of those that remained enslaved at Port Tobacco after the freedom suits. Many of the "272" souls forced to Louisiana were descendants of the "Poppaw Queen." Several were sold to Henry Johnson, son-in-law of the late Maryland attorney Philip Barton Key. It is ironic that some of the families would end up harvesting sugarcane on the Acadia plantation for Philip Barton Key Jr—the son of the man that initially worked to secure their family's freedom.[26]

After the departure of the *Isaac Franklin* several families remained behind in Maryland. "Old" Isaac's daughter Nelly Hawkins was married to Peter Adams enslaved on the plantation of the late Notley Young in Prince George's County. His master Henry Young refused to purchase Nelly and her daughters. The Jesuits had a dilemma—either buy Peter or separate him from his wife and children. After weeks of negotiations, Governor Johnson agreed to purchase Peter Adams "from Henry Young," and prepared "a brig for carrying them [and] almost the rest at S[t]. Inigoes, W[hite] M[arsh], [and] S[t]. Thomas's servants."[27]

At White Marsh, Stephen Queen—a free man—must have watched in horror when Joshua T. Clarke began hauling off his aunts, uncles, cousins, and childhood friends on his wagon. Clarke the "Squire" of Clarke's Fancy—the northern tract adjoining White Marsh—was hired to transport the remaining slaves to the "brig" at Alexandria to be shipped to Louisiana. In a letter dated May 14, 1839, Clarke demanded that the Reverend Mulledy pay "thirty dollars" to him and his partners for "carr[y]ing off the servants

26 Slave Manifests of Coastwise Vessels Filed at New Orleans, Louisiana, 1807–1860, NARA microfilm M1895, Roll: 8, RG 36, NARA via *Ancestry.com*; Courtesy of Judy Riffel, *Georgetown Memory Project*, several White Marsh families were listed in the 1845 sale from Philip Barton Key's Acadia plantation, see Sale of an undivided one-half interest in a plantation in Ascension Parish from Philip B. Key to John Ryerss Thompson, 4 June 1845, Conveyance Book 19, p. 265, Ascension Parish Clerk of Court, Donaldsonville, La.

27 Grivel to Lancaster, February 8, 1839, Maryland Province Archives, Box 66, Folder 2, Booth Family Center for Special Collections, Georgetown University, in *Georgetown Slavery Archive*, https://slaveryarchive.georgetown.edu/items/show/229; "old Isaac remained": Fr. Grivel to Fr. Lancaster, May 4, 1839, Maryland Province Archives, Box 66, Folder 1, Booth Family Center for Special Collections, Georgetown University, in GSA, http://slaveryarchive.georgetown.edu/items/show/156; "Carring off the servants to Washington:" Joshua T. Clarke to Thomas Mulledy, May 14, 1839, Joshua T. Clarke to Thomas Mulledy, May 14, 1839 [Loose scrap of paper],Letter Book 1, Box 77, Addenda to the Maryland Province, Provincial Procurator Series, Maryland Province Archives, Booth Family Center for Special Collections, Georgetown University, in GSA, http://slaveryarchive.georgetown.edu/items/show/390.

to [W]ashington & one dollar thirty-seven cents for a pair of shoes which was bought for one of them." We can only imagine the distress in the young Stephen Queen when Joshua T. Clarke returned to White Marsh without his loved ones. Ironically, both men would eventually become the progenitors of one of the largest Queen families in Prince George's County, after Clarke's son William Henry fathered a "mulatto" child with Stephen's fifteen year-old daughter Lizzie Queen.[28]

To save Georgetown College, the Jesuits tore apart networks of free and enslaved family groups throughout Maryland. Twenty years after the horrific ordeal in 1838, Stephen Queen was still living on the White Marsh plantation with the remainder of his free and enslaved family members. All of his children and grandchildren were baptized there. He died in June 1883 and was buried in a shabby grave on the White Marsh estate. While many of his free Queen relatives moved away from the old plantation, Stephen Queen and his family remained hoping one day, perhaps, that his loved ones would return to their ancestral home.[29]

---

28 Referenced as "Squire Thomas Joshua Clarke" in Bowie: Baptismal Register, photocopy of., 6 July 1853 - 16 July 1872, Box 3, Folder 6, p. 101, Whitemarsh Manor, Maryland Province Collection, Booth Family Center for Special Collections, Georgetown University, Washington, D.C.; for Stephen Queen living free at White Marsh, see U.S. Census, 1850, Queen Anne, Prince George's, Maryland, Roll: 295, p. 86b, M432, RG 29, NARA via Ancestry.com (Joshua T. Clarke listed on the next page).

29 U.S. Census, 1850, Queen Anne, Prince George's, Maryland, Roll: 295, p. 86b, M432, RG 29, NARA via Ancestry.com; Burial Record for Stephen Queen, 5 June 1883, Bowie: Register of baptisms, marriages, etc., 1 January 1818 - 31 December 1895, Box 3, Folder 3, p. 122, Whitemarsh Manor, Maryland Province Collection, Booth Family Center for Special Collections, Georgetown University, Washington, D.C.

Bibliography

Archives and Archival Sources

1820 US Census Slave Schedules

1850 US Census Slave Schedules

1860 US Census for Free Inhabitants

1860 US Census Maryland Occupations

1860 US Census Slave Schedules

Archives of Maryland

Baltimore Jesuit Archives, Jesuit Residence of St. Claude La Colombière, Baltimore, MD.

British Jesuit Archives

Enoch Pratt Library
 MS6: Richard Malcolm Johnston Papers, 1841-1935

Georgetown University, Archives of the Maryland Province of the Society of Jesus

Georgetown Slavery Archive

Georgetown University Manuscripts, Booth Family Center for Special Collections Jesuit

GU272 Descendants Database, 1785-2020/GU272 Memory Project (online database: https://dbnews.americanancestors.org/2019/05/23/new-database-gu272-descendants-1785-2000/ https://gu272.americanancestors.org)

The Maryland Center for History and Culture

Maryland State Archives
 John J. Tierney Collection

Loyola Notre Dame Library (LNDL) Archives and Special Collections
 Loyola University Maryland Photograph Collection
 Nicholas Varga papers
 Oral History Archives

Dr. Lynn Nehemiah Personal Archive

Historical Newspapers and Periodicals

The American Catholic Historic Researches

Baltimore Afro-American

Baltimore Sun

Evening Sun

Evergreen Quarterly (Loyola University Maryland)

Evergreen Yearbook (Loyola University Maryland)

The Greyhound (Loyola University Maryland)

Loyola Annual

Loyola Magazine

The Loyola: A Semimonthly Published by the Literary Societies of Loyola College

Maryland Historical Magazine News-Post (Baltimore)

Woodstock Letters

Secondary Sources

Anderson, George M. "The Civil War Diary of John Abell Morgan, SJ.: A Jesuit Scholastic of the Maryland Province." *Records of the American Catholic Historical Society of Philadelphia* 101:3 (1990): 35-54.

Armitage, Ruth Ann, Leah Minc, David V. Hill, and Silas D. Hurry. "Characterization of Bricks and Tiles from the 17th-Century Brick Chapel, St. Mary's City, Maryland." *Journal of Archaeological Science* 33:5 (2006): 615–27.

Baker, Mitchell and Jean H. Baker, eds. *The Civil War in Maryland Reconsidered.* Baton Rouge: Louisiana State University Press, 2021

Barnvard, Joseph. *Pioneers of Maryland and the Old French War: With and Account of Various Interesting Contemporaneous Events Which Occurred in the Early Settlement of America.* Boston: Lothrop, 1875.

Baumann, Roland M. *Constructing Black Education at Oberlin College.* Athens: Ohio University Press, 2010.

Beitzell, Edwin Warfield. *The Jesuit Missions of St. Mary's County, Maryland.* Revised edition. Leonardtown, MD: St. Mary's County Historical Society, 1976.

Bell, Richard. "Border State, Border War: Fighting for Freedom and Slavery in Antebellum Maryland." In *The Civil War in Maryland Reconsidered,* edited by Charles W. Mitchell and Jean H. Baker, 16-45. Baton Rouge: Louisiana State University, 2021.

Berlin, Ira. *Generations of Captivity: A History of African-American Slaves.* Cambridge, MA:

Belknap Press of Harvard University Press, 2003.

Blight, David W. *Race and Reunion: The Civil War in American Memory*. Cambridge, MA: Belknap Press, 2001.

Brugger, Robert J. *Maryland: A Middle Temperment*, 1634-1980. Baltimore: Johns Hopkins University Press, 1988.

Campbell-Whatley, Gloria, Shaqwana Freeman-Green, Chris O'Brien, Kimm Reddig, and Ting Sun. "Non-Majority Student Perceptions of Diversity and Inclusion at a PWI and an HBCU." *Journal for Multicultural Education* 15:3 (2021): 253-269.

Carroll, John. "'The Present State of the Catholic Mission, Conducted by the Ex-Jesuits in North-America.' By Rev. Patrick Smyth: Unpublished Reply by Rev. John Carroll, 1788. Rev. John Carroll's Answer to Smyth." *The American Catholic Historical Researches* https:// www.jstor.org/journal/amercathhistrese 1:3 (1905): 193-206.

"Charles H. Dorsey, Jr., '57, Led Maryland's Legal Aid Bureau to National Prominence." Loyola Magazine https://www.loyola.edu/explore/magazine/stories/2016/ charles-dorsey-led-marylands-legal-aid-bureau

"Charles H. Dorsey, Jr. Historical Marker." *The Historical Marker Database*. Last modified April 17, 2020. https://www.hmdb.org/m.asp?m=6292.

"Charles H. Dorsey, Jr. Mentor Award." Baltimore City Bar Association. Accessed October 19, 2022. https://www.baltimorebar.org/awards/ charles-h-dorsey-jr-mentor-award

Connelly, Marc. *The Green Pastures*. New York: Farrar and Rinehart, 1929.

Cook, Bernard. "Maryland Jesuits and Slavery, Pt. I." *Cura Virtualis*, September 8, 2021, available at https://www.curavirtualis.org/post/maryland-jesuits-and-slavery-pt-i.

Cranch, William. *Reports of Cases Civil and Criminal in the United States Circuit Court of the District of Columbia, from 1801 to 1841*. Volume II. Boston: Little, Brown and Company, 1852.

Curran, Robert Emmet. *The Bicentennial History of Georgetown University: From Academy to University, 1789–1889*. Volume 1. Washington, D.C.: Georgetown University Press, 1993.

_____. *A History of Georgetown*. Volume 1. Washington, DC: Georgetown University Press, 2010.

Devitt, Edward. "History of the Maryland-New York Province, I. St. Inigoes, St. Mary's County, Maryland 1634-1915." *Woodstock Letters* 60: 2 (1931): 24-40.

Duhamel, Elizabeth. "Col. Henry Darnall and His Family." *Records of the Columbia Historical Society*, Washington, D.C., Vol. 26 (1924): 129-145.

Evans, Curtis J. "The Religious and Racial Meanings of The Green Pastures." *Religion and American Culture: A Journal of Interpretation* 18 (2009): 60-61.

Fede, Andrew T. Ed. "Not the Most Insignificant Justice: Reconsidering Justice Gabriel Duvall's Slavery Law Opinions Favoring Liberty." *Journal of Supreme Court History* 42, no. 1 (2017).

Fields, Barbara Jeanne. *Slavery and Freedom on the Middle Ground*. New Haven, CT: Yale University Press, 1985.

Flanagan, Charles M. "The Sweets of Independence: A Reading of the 'James Carroll Daybook, 1714-21." Ph.D. Dissertation, University of Maryland, College Park, 2005.

Flipper, Joseph J. "White Ecclesiology: The Identity of the Church in the Statements on Racism by United States Catholic Bishops." *Theological Studies* 82:3 (2021): 418–39. https://doi. org/10.1177/00405639211036477.

Fox, Craig. *Everyday Klansfolk: White Protestant Life and the KKK in 1920s Michigan*. East Lansing: Michigan State University Press, 2011.

Galke, Laura J. and Alyssa L. Loney, "Phase I Archaeological Investigations Aboard Webster Field Annex: NAS PAX, St. Mary's County, Maryland." Report presented to Natural Resources Branch Environmental and Natural Resources Division Department of Public Works Naval Air Station Patuxent River. St. Leonard, MD: Jefferson Patterson Park and Museum Maryland Historic Trust, 2000: 128–45.

Glotzer, Paige. *How the Suburbs Were Segregated: Developers and the Business of Exclusionary Housing, 1890-1960*. New York, NY: Columbia University Press, 2020.

Goldin, Claudia and Lawrence Katz. "Putting the CO in Education: Timing, Reasons, and Consequences of College Coeducation from 1835 to the Present." *Journal of Human Capital* 5.4 (2011): 379.

Griffith, Aisha N., Noelle M. Hurd, and Saida B. Hussain. "'I Didn't Come to School for This': A Qualitative Examination of Experiences with Race-Related Stressors and Coping Responses among Black Students Attending a Predominantly White Institution." *Journal of Adolescent Research* 34:2 (2019): 115-139.

Hanchin, Timothy. "Educating for/in Caritas: A Pedagogy of Friendship for Catholic Higher Education in Our Divided Time." *Horizons* 45:1 (2018): 74–104.

Harper, Shaun R. "Peer Support for African American Male College Achievement: Beyond Internalized Racism and the Burden of Acting White." *The Journal of Men's Studies* 14:3 (2007): 337–358.

Harris, Adam. *The State Must Provide: The Definitive History of Racial Inequality in Higher Education*. New York, NY: Harper Collins, 2022.

Harris, Jasmine L. "Inheriting Educational Capital : Black College Students, Nonbelonging, and Ignored Legacies at Predominantly White Institutions." *Women's Studies Quarterly* 48 (2020): 84-102.

Harris, Joel Chandler. *Uncle Remis: His Songs and His Sayings*. Gutenberg Project, 2020. Available at https://www.gutenberg.org/cache/epub/2306/pg2306-images. html#link2H_PREF.

Hartzler, Daniel D. *Marylanders in the Confederacy*. Silver Springs, MD: Family Line Publications, 1986.

Hawkins, Billy. "The White Supremacy Continuum of Images for Black Men." *Journal of*

African American Men 3: 3 (1998): 7-18.

Heppner, P. Paul, Peter Ji, Helen A. Neville, and Russell Thye. "The Relations among General and Race-Related Stressors and Psychoeducational Adjustment in Black Students Attending Predominantly White Institutions." *Journal of Black Studies* 34:4 (2004): 599-618.

Hoffman, Ronald, Sally D. Mason, and Eleanor S. Darcy. *Dear Papa, Dear Charley: The Peregrinations of a Revolutionary Aristocrat, as told by Charles Carroll of Carrollton and his father, Charles Carroll of Annapolis, with sundry observations on bastardy, child-rearing, romance, matrimony, commerce, tobacco, slavery, and the politics of revolutionary America.* Chapel Hill, NC: University of North Carolina Press, 2001.

Homan, Ken, Robin A. Proudie, Clarissa Ashton Stripling, and Greg Beaman, "What descendants felt during a dig at a Jesuit-owned plantation." *National Catholic Reporter*, August 19, 2021.

Hooper, J. Leon. "Report of the Working Group on Slavery, Memory, and Reconciliation to the President of Georgetown University. Washington, D.C. Summer 2016." *Jesuit Higher Education: A Journal* 6:1 (2017).

Hughes, Thomas. *History of the Society of Jesus in North America.* London: Longmans, Green, and Company, 1907.

Hughes, Thomas. *History of the Society of Jesus in North America: Colonial and Federal.* London: Forgotten Books, 2009.

Joerndt, Clarence V. *St. Ignatius, Hickory, and Its Missions.* Baltimore: Publication Press, 1972.

Johnson, Karen J. "Beyond Parish Boundaries: Black Catholics and the Quest for Racial Justice." *Religion and American Culture: A Journal of Interpretation* 25:2 (2015): 264–300.

Johnson, Richard Malcolm. *The Autobiography of Col. Richard Malcolm Johnston.* Washington: The Neale Company, 1900.

Kellerman, Christopher J. *All Oppression Shall Cease: A History of Slavery, Abolitionism, and the Catholic Church.* Maryknoll, NY: Orbis Books, 2022.

Key, Marcus, Leslie. Marcus Key, Leslie Milliman, Michael Smolek, and Silas Hurry. "Sourcing a Stone Paver from the Colonial St. Inigoes Manor, Maryland." *Northeast Historical Archaeology* 45:1 (2016): 132–55.

Kinniff, Jenny. "Aperio Research Report." Unpublished manuscript, 2023.

LaFarge, John. *The Manner is Ordinary.* New York: Harcourt, Brace and Company, 1954.

Le, Thomas P. "Racial Discrimination, gender role conflict, and depression in college men of color: A Longitudinal test of the racist-gender stress model." *Psychology of Men & Masculinities* 23 (2022): 4-12.

Mendoza, Elsa. "Catholic Slaveowners and the Development of Georgetown University's Slavey Hiring System, 1792-1862." *Journal of Jesuit Studies* 8 (2021): 56-80.

McPherson, James. *For Cause and Comrade: Why Men Fought in the Civil War.* New York, NY: Oxford Press, 1997.

Mitchell, Charles W., and Jean H. Baker, eds. *The Civil War in Maryland Reconsidered.* Baton Rouge: Louisiana State University Press, 2021.

Mitchell, Margaret. *Gone with the Wind.* New York: Macmillan Publishing, 1936.

Murphy, Thomas. *Jesuit Slaveholding in Maryland, 1717-1838.* New York, NY: Routledge, 2018.

O'Brien, Thomas Hanley. *Charles Carroll of Carrollton: The Making of a Revolutionary Gentleman.* Washington: Catholic University of America Press, 1970.

Ochs, Phils. "Changes." Recorded 1966. Elektra Records.

Odate, Karen. "Undergraduate Experience of a Black Haitian-American Female at a Competitive Predominantly White Institution." *International Journal of Social Sciences & Educational Studies* 9:1 (2022): 1-17.

Olson, Karen. "Old West Baltimore: Segregation, African-American Cultures, and the Struggle for Equality." *In The Baltimore Book: New Views of Local History.* Edited by Elizabeth Fee, Linda Shopes, and Linda Zeidman, 57-79. Philadelphia, PA: Temple University Press, 1991.

Osa, Justina O. "The pervasiveness of racial prejudice in higher education in the U.S: raising awareness and solution." *Forum on Public Policy Online* 3 (2007).

Pasquier, M. "Slavery, French Missionaries, and the Roman Catholic Priesthood in the American South, 1865." *Church History,* 77 (2008): 337-70.

Pettit, Emma, and Zipporah. "The 'Great College-Yearbook Reckoning': Why Scholars Say Blackface Images Aren't Outliers." *Chronicle of Higher Education,* February 7, 2019.

Phillips, Christopher. *Freedom's Port: The African American Community of Baltimore, 1790-1860.* Urbana, IL: University of Illinois Press, 1997.

Pike, Henrietta, Jeremy Alexander, Melissa Kemp, Negest Rucker, and Lynn Nehemiah. "Louisa Mahoney." *Still, We Speak.* January 26, 2023. https://stillwespeak.org/louisa-mahoney/.

Pippenger, Wesley E. *Index to District of Columbia Land Records, 1792-1817.* Westminster, MD: Heritage Books, 2010.

Quallen, Matthew, ed. "Beyond the 272 Sold in 1838, Plotting the National Diaspora of Jesuit-Owned Slaves." *Hoya Historian Columnist,* 29 April 2016.

Riordan, Timothy B. and Henry M. Miller, and Silas D. Hurry. "Birth of an American Freedom, Religion in Early Maryland: Archaeology of the St. Mary's City Chapel Field (18ST1-103)." Report submitted to National Endowment for the Humanities (NEH) Grants Office, Washington, D.C. 20506. Completion report for NEH grant RO-22102-90. St. Mary's City, MD: Historic St. Mary's City, 1994.

Rothman, Adam. "Archives and Historical Storytelling at Georgetown University." Paper delivered at Conference on Slavery and Johns Hopkins, Johns Hopkins University,

Baltimore, MD, 2021.

_____. "Georgetown University and the Business of Slavery." *Washington History* 29, no. 2 (2017): 18-22.

_____. "The Jesuits and Slavery." *Journal of Jesuit Studies* 8 (2021): 1-10.

Rothman, Adam, and Elsa Barraza Mendoza, eds. *Facing Georgetown's History: A Reader on Slavery, Memory, and Reconciliation.* Washington, DC: Georgetown University Press, 2021.

Ruffner, Malissa. "Ignatius "Nace" Butler Jr. (GMP-199)." Georgetown Memory Project. October 14, 2021. www.georgetownmemoryproject.org. Last accessed December 23, 2021.

Ryan, John J. Historical Sketch of Loyola College: 1825- 1902. *A Memorial of the Golden Jubilee of Fifty Years of Existence.* N.P., 1903?

Shakespeare, William. Othello. Edited by Barbara Mowat and Paul Werstine. Washington, DC: Folger Shakespeare Library, 2004.

Shea, John Gilmary. *Life and Times of the Most Rev. John Carroll, Bishop and First Archbishop of Baltimore: Embracing the History of the Catholic Church in the United States, 1763-1815, with portraits, views, fac-similes.* New York: J. G. Shea, 1888.

Stein, Sharon. *Unsettling the University: Confronting the Colonial Foundations of US Higher Education.* Baltimore: Johns Hopkins University Press, 2022.

Steiner, Bernard C. Ed. "The South Atlantic States in 1833, as Seen by a New Englander: Being a Narrative of a Tour Taken by Henry Barnard." *Maryland Historical Magazine* 13, no. 3 (1918).

Swarns, Rachel L. *The 272: The Families Who Were Enslaved and Sold to Build the American Catholic Church.* New York: Random House, 2023.

Thomas, William G. III. *A Question of Freedom: The Families Who Challenged Slavery from the Nation's Founding to the Civil War.* New Haven, CT: Yale University Press, 2020.

Thomas, William G. III et. al. "Priscilla Queen v. Francis Neale." OSCYS. University of Nebraska Lincoln. https://earlywashingtondc.org/cases/ oscys.caseid.0025.

Thomas, William G. III et. al. "Priscilla Queen v. Francis Neale." *Oh Say Can You See* (OSCYS), Early Washington DC Law and Family. https://earlywashingtondc.org/cases/ oscys.caseid.0025.

_____. "The Timing of Queen v. Hepburn: An Exploration of African American Networks in the Early Republic." *Oh Say Can You See* (OSCYS), Early Washington DC Law and Family. https://earlywashingtondc.org/stories/queen_v_hepburn.

U.S. Department of Education. *The Condition of Education* 2020. Bill Hussar, Jijun Zhang, Sarah Hein, Ke Wang, Ashley Roberts, Jiashan Cui, Mary Smith, Farrah Bullock Mann, Amy Barmer, and Rita Dilig. Washington, DC: National Center for Education Statistics, Institute for Education Studies, 2020. Last consulted October 25, 2023. https://nces.ed.gov/pubsearch/pubsinfo.asp?pubid=2020144.

Varga, Nicholas. *Baltimore's Loyola, Loyola's Baltimore*, 1851-1986. Baltimore, MD: Maryland Historical Society, 1990.

Wade, Lisa. "Racial Bias and Media Coverage of Violent Crime." *Sociological Images*, 2015.

Waite, Cally L. "The Segregation of Black Students at Oberlin College after Reconstruction." *History of Education Quarterly* 41:3 (2001): 344–364.

Weinberg, Carl R. "Does Lincoln Still Matter?" *OAH Magazine of History* 23:1 (2009) 64.

Welch, Emma. "Catholicism's Role in the Lives of African Americans: From Civil Rights to Today." *Journal of Theta Alpha Kappa* 45:1 (2021): 13–30.

Wilder, Craig Steven. *Ebony and Ivy: Race, Slavery, and the Troubled History of America's Universities*. New York, NY: Bloomsbury, 2013.

Williams, Frank. "Abraham Lincoln, Civil Liberties, and Maryland." *In The Civil War in Maryland Reconsidered*. Edited by Charles W. Mitchell and Jean H. Baker, 139-59. Baton Rouge, LA: Louisiana State University, 2021.

Wilmer, Allison, J.H. Jarrett, George W. F. Vernon. *History and Roster of Maryland Volunteers*. Baltimore: Guggenheimer, Weil & Company, 1898.

Zhuang, Juyan, and Wei Lu. "Deconstructing the Blackface Minstrel Show, (Re)constructing African American Identity: The Case of Olio by Tyehimba Jess." *Critical Sociology*, Vol. 48:4-5 (2021): 823-836.

Zwinge, Joseph. "The Jesuit Farms in Maryland. Facts and Anecdotes." *Woodstock Letters* *XXXIX*, no. 3 (1910): 374-82.

Index

1838 Georgetown sale 1-2, 3-4, 37-40, 48, 242, 251, 258, 264, 288, 296-297, 299, 311-313, 315
    Connection to Loyola 4, 37-38, 41, 43
    Georgetown public apology for, and actions for the descendants of sale 49, 300
    Ignatius Butler's escape from 252
    Impact on contemporary Loyola students 187
    J.R. Thompson request for payment extension 3-4; Jesuit letter in response 26-27
    Loyola's initial denial of connection, and avoidance of 38, 186-187, 216-217
    Lynn Locklear Nehemiah's reflections on, 299
    Mélisande Short-Colomb's learning of 276-278
    Payments from Henry Johnson and Jesse Batey 39; purchase of slaves by 296-297, 311-312, 314
    Queen family inclusion in 325
    Separation of families in 312, 314
    Silence around 268-270

African Student Association 225

ALANA organization 225, 232

Andrew White Student Center 9, 12, 138
    Decision not to rename, from administrative perspective 142

Anne Joice 255, 288, 272, 275, 288, 299
    Enslavement 291
    Insistence on indentured status and freedom 290-291
    Transport to Maryland 288-289

Ashton, Father John, manumission suits against 290, 291, 301

Ayd, Father Joseph 67, 115

Baltimore 4, 73, 245-246
    Black residents of 13n8, 73, 75, 245, 313
    Confederate sympathies in 42, 62, 65, 86
    Know-Nothing Party support in 57

Segregation in 7, 78, 14n22, 134

Lost Cause ideology in 5-6, 14n13, 62, 64; as a post-Civil War refuge for Confederate supporters 63

Loyola's relationship with city 73, 134, 245; hosting or sponsoring racist public events 65, 183

Opening of Loyola in 40-41, 132

Slaveowning in 4, 71

Battle of Bull Run; Jesuit ministry to wounded 61

Barnard, Henry 3, 243

Description of Father Thomas Mulledy 243

Bennet, Gabriel 298

Bennet, John 248, 252

Black Lives Matter 94

Blackface 6, 8, 49, 82, 85, 87, 163, 164-65, 167, 176, 182, 184,

Appearance in student yearbooks 88, 122, 181-190

Blackface minstrel shows: See "Minstrel shows"

Black laborers at Loyola 68; See also Alexander Briscoe, Thomas C. Burke, George C. Bush, Dominic Butler, Madison Fenwick, Matthew Fenwick, Ellen Mahoney, George Short, Thomas Short, Richard Thompson

Discriminatory treatment of 135, 208

Erasure of black labor xii, 74, 99, 136, 243, 245

Photographs of 108, 109

Unequal wages paid to black laborers 74-75, 135

Black students: See Charles Dorsey; Contemporary Experiences of Black Students; Paul Smith; Mary Frazier

Black Student Union 225

Bowman, Thea 94, 142

Renaming of Flannery O'Connor Hall to Thea Bowman Hall 94, 97; See also Flannery O'Connor, Hall

Meaning of building name change 103

Briscoe, Alexander 136, 245

Brown, Thomas 11, 311

Brown vs. Board of Education 7, 271

Burke, Thomas 136

Bush, George C. 136

Butler, Christopher 252, 253, 254, 258

Butler, Dominic 4, 136, 245

Butler, Ignatius 252, 258

Butler, Octavia 11

Campbell, Frank 284

Campus buildings 133, 134
   Andrew White 9, 12, 138; Decision not to rename, from administrative perspective 142
   Flannery O'Connor 139, 218; Renaming to Thea Bowman, 94, 97; Shallowness of gesture, 103; Resistance to and hesitation around 140; Dr. Rodney Parker's account of 141-142
   Jenkins Hall 12, 137

Campus culture
   As a reflection of the times 82, 85
   Avoidance of racist past 187-188
   Derogatory attitudes toward Native Americans 88, 138-139
   Economic ties to slavery in the student body 57
   Ineffectiveness of Community Standards 140
   Misogyny of, 89-91, 182
   Ongoing racism and impacts of 178-179, 185, 187-188
   Preconscious attitudes on campus 222
   Resistance to Civil Rights Movement, support for John Birch Society speaker 223-224
   White supremacy and silence around past 49

Carroll, Albert 58-59

Carroll, Charles 292, 293

Carroll, James 279, 292
   Endowment of Georgetown 279, 292, 304
   Enslavement of Queen Mary Papow 279
   Participation in slave trading 292

Carroll, R.G. 58-59

Co-education at Loyola 90-91, 211
   Celebration of in *The Greyhound* 214-215
   Current gender ratio 217
   Differences from integration, 219-220
   Parallels with integration 217
   Sexist attitudes toward 90-91, 215-216

Confederate flag, student display of 174, 179

Confederacy
   Enlistment in Confederate Army 4, 58-59, 85, 87
   Jesuits' support of 5
   Role of Catholicism in sympathies, 86
   Student ambivalence to the Union 57
   Sympathies on campus 35, 56, 62, 65, 76-77, 81, 85-86

Contemporary experiences of Black students 222
    Concerns about reinforcing stereotypes 229
    Experiences of racist language 228
    Feelings of judgment, concerns about white peers 227, 229
    Difficulty of inclusion for Black women compared to Black males 230-231
    Lack of awareness about resources 234
    Learning non-belonging 230
    "Multicultural House" establishment, and lack of institutional support for 224-225
    Racism from professors 229
    Reluctance to report racism 230

Cooper, Nanny 303, 308

Corporation of Roman Catholic Clergy 292, 298, 307

Curlett, John 90

Darnall, Colonel Henry 290-292
    Connection to Georgetown University 291

de Sousa, Mathias 288-289

Debate Club 53

Descendants of the 272 xiii, 2, 8, 9, 10, 12, 49, 246-247, 263, 276-277, 300

d'Invilliers, Dr. James 113

DiLorenzo, Thomas 66, 225
    Association with the League of the South 226
    Defense of Confederacy in class 226
    Impact on students 227

Diversity on campus 218

Dorsey, Charles 6, 133, 171-173, 186
    Education prior to Loyola 173-174
    Enrollment at Loyola 7, 174
    Exclusion from yearbooks 214
    Commitment to service 173
    Difficulties at Loyola 172
    Hostile campus climate during integration 171, 174
    Korean War service 176
    Legal career at Maryland Legal Aid Bureau 7, 177-178

Dorsey, Kathleen 180

Duvall, Gabriel 291, 301, 303, 306, 308, 309

Early, Father John 57, 83-84
    Attitudes toward enslaved people, 83, 84
    Petition on behalf of John Abell Morgan 60-61
    Photo of 19

Rental of servants 4, 68-69, 83

Emancipation Proclamation 77

Evergreen Campus, move to 6, 132-133, 199
    Photo of 23
    As an island 207-208

Fenwick, Madison 60, 74-75, 136, 245

Fenwick, Matthew 60, 136,

Fenwick, William Baugher 60

Flannery O'Connor, Hall 139; See also Bowman, Thea Hall
    Dr. Rodney Parker's account of 141-142
    Resistance to and hesitation around 140
    Shallowness of gesture, 103

Floyd, George 141

Frazier, Mary 8

Garrett, Isaiah 70

Garrett Family
    Family mansion as campus building 134-135
    Purchase of land from 78

Georgetown University 2-3

Green and grey school colors 199
    Choice of in 1922 199
    Grey as symbol of Confederacy at other institutions 202
    Memorialization of "Lost Cause" and connection to the Confederacy 200
    Official denial of origins in 1968 200

Harbard, Peter 290-291

Harbard, Sukey 292

Harris, Adam 10

Hawkins, Anna 311

Hawkins, Isaac 311, 313

Hawkins, Nelly 314

Ignatian Examen 54
    Examen for Racism 54

Integration at Loyola 49-50, 171
    Current student body composition 217-218, 232
    Exclusion of Black students from Junior prom 7
    Faculty event at club that did not allow Black members until 1995 14n22
    First Black Student: see Dorsey, Charles

Jesuit practices of white supremacy 50-52, 218-219
Hostile campus atmosphere 174
In yearbook circa 1971 213
"Policy on Admitting Negro Students" 130
White supremacy during, as documented in yearbooks 88

Jenkins, George Carrell 136
Support of Lost Cause 136

Jenkins Hall, and other buildings 12, 137

Jenkins Society 137

Jesuits slave owning xi-xii, 1, 3-4, 13n6, 13n11, 28, 46-47-49, 70-72, 154, 249-250, 292-293, 303-304
Acquisition of slaves 47, 293
Archeological erasure and prospects for new narratives 257-258
Archival silence around 72, 241-242
Connection to Loyola 3, 52, 71, 244-245, 293
Documented in 1860 Slave Schedule 4, 28, 242
Erasure of woman owned by Order of Jesuits in Baltimore 72, 242, 245
Experience of Nelly Mahoney and Louisa Mahoney Mason 255-257
Justification of 47, 218-219, 250, 281-282
Resistance to Queen family manumission suits 307
Sales to Louisiana, justifications for 72, 281-282
Silence around xii, 1-2, 46-47, 49, 268-270
Supposed "benevolent style" and resistance to 47, 72, 250

Jim Crow 1, 2, 272

Johns Hopkins University 14n13, 133-134, 212, 218

Johnston, Richard Malcolm 6, 21, 63-64
Photo of 21

Kane, George and Anna 41-42
Confederate sympathy and 1861 Baltimore Plot 42
Donation to Loyola 41, 43

Key, Francis Scott 280, 281, 291, 301, 306, 307, 308, 309, 310

Key, Philip Barton 306
Cooperation with Jesuits in manumission suits 307
Work with Gabriel Duvall to defend "Revolutionary Generation" of enslaved 306-307
Election to house of representatives 309

King Jr., Martin Luther 280

Know-Nothing party 57

Ku Klux Klan 6, 11, 34, 117, 124, 139
"klassy kut klothes" 117, 118

LaFarge, Reverend John 114

Lancaster, Charles C. 244

Lawless Smith, Geneva Ruby Taylor 272, 275

League of the South 225-226

Lee, Robert E. 5, 42, 77

Lincoln, Abraham 42, 64, 66, 77, 86, 225, 283

Lord Baltimore 289-292

Lost Cause ideology 2, 5-6, 62, 65-66
    Connection to choice of grey for school colors 200
    Espoused in Col. Charles Marshall lecture 243-244
    George Jenkins support of 136
    In Father John J. Ryan's Historical Sketch of Loyola College, Baltimore 243-244
    In Leo A. Codd's "Clansmen" 6; Photo of "Clansmen" 34
    In student publications 65, 121, 123
    Lingering presence today 10, 66

Loyola College 4, 132
    Photo of 24
    Map of 111

Loyola land deed, race-exclusive covenants 6, 78, 132-133, 186
    Current status of 132
    Inclusion in sale of Guilford property 134
    Loyola's acceptance of 133
    Photo of 29

Loyola Night School 14n19, 126
    Emotional impact of 154-155

Loyola and Slavery 69-71, 73, 245
    Documented in 1860 Slave Schedule 4, 28
    Lingering impacts of 5, 232
    Loyola's resistance to change around slavery 79, 82

Mahoney, Charles, Daniel, and Patrick 290
    Manumission suits 290-291

Mahoney, Ellen 136

Mahoney Family 264-65, 281

Mahoney, Harry and Anna 255, 294

Mahoney, Harry 294-295
    Role in hiding money during British raid 295
    Decision to protect his Jesuit enslavers 296
    Sold by Jesuits despite promises 297-298

Mahoney Mason, Louisa 254, 258, 288, 298-299
    Archaeology of former home 255
    Escape from 1838 sale 298

Mahoney Mason, Nelly 256-257, 258, 265
    Difficulty of reconstructing her story 257

Magevney, Father Hugh 64

Manning, Mrs. Henry S. 70
    Father John Early's rental of servants from 4, 69, 83, 245, 259
    Slaveholder 4, 70, 84

Mason-Dixon Line 56, 87

Mason, Robert 254

Matthew, slave at St. Inigoes 253-254

McElroy, Father John 40

McSherry, Father William 40

Miller, Reverend Peter
    Ministry to Black Baltimoreans 5, 62

Minstrel shows 164-165
    In Baltimore Sun 31-32
    In yearbooks 182
    Lingering impact of 182-185
    Performance for charity 183
    Production by Edward P. Duffy, S.J. 169, 182
    Program for 33

Morgan, Father John Abell 5, 76, 84, 244
    Anger over emancipation proclamation 77
    Attitudes as a southerner 84-85, 87
    Avoidance of Union Civil War draft 60
    Bigotry 84
    Confederate sympathies 5, 76-77, 84-85
    Family's slaveowning 76, 84, 258
    Friendship with Richard Malcolm Johnston 63

Morrison, Toni 11

Mount Saint Agnes College 212
    Connections to slavery 212-213
    Discussion of co-education in The Greyhound 214-215
    Erasure of Mount Saint Agnes through merger 211-212
    Lack of diversity at time of merger with Loyola 213
    Merger with Loyola 89, 211, 214

Mulledy, Reverend Thomas F. 3, 39, 243, 325

Role in 1838 sale 39-41, 311-312, 315

Nally, Rebecca 305
    Auction of slaves from Queen family after death 305

Nativism 57

Nehemiah, Lynn Locklear xiii, 8, 9, 10, 12n1, 263, 288

Noonan, James 4-5

Oberlin College 211, 212

O'Callaghan, Father Joseph 61-62

Ochs, Phil 215

O'Connor, Flannery 94, 139
    Racism of, 139

O'Donnell, Angela Alaimo 140, 142

Old Chapel Field 249, 251 253
    Slaves Ben, Jenny, Betty, Matthew 253

Peroutka, Michael 66

Plessy vs. Ferguson 272

Port Tobacco 245, 303, 308, 313, 314

Porter, Kevin 10, 263, 301

Predominantly White Institution (PWI), experience of 96, 179, 228, 233

Prom, Junior 7

Proudie, Robin 258-259

Queen family 265, 275, 283, 301-3, 305-9, 311-15
    Illegal enslavement of at White Marsh Plantation 304
    Manumission suits 306-310

Queen, Edward 280, 301

Queen, Guilford 258

Queen, Mary 301-303, 307, 308, 309
    Breach of indenture by James Carroll 304

Queen, Mary Ellen 264, 265, 275, 281, 283

Queen, Mary Louisa 305

Queen Mary Papow 279-280, 302-303

Queen, Priscilla 280, 303, 305, 306, 307, 308, 311, 313, 314
    Defeat in manumission suit 309-310

Racism 2, 3, 5-12, 54, 65, 178-79, 183, 185, 187-88, 229, 230

Republican Party 56

Roland Park Company (RPC) 6, 78, 133
  Segregation and use of exclusionary covenants 6, 78, 133

Roothaan, Superior General Jan 40, 282

Ryan, Father Abram Joseph 6, 64
  Photo of 20
  Ryan Poetry medal 6, 64

Ryan, Father John J. 243

Segregation, Jesuit complicity with 50

Sellinger, Father Joseph A. 89
  Resistance to merger with Mt. Saint Agnes 89

Short, George, 74-75, 245

Short, Thomas 245

Short-Colomb, Mélisande xiii, 8, 10, 15n29, 188, 263, 264, 271, 300

Sisters of Mercy 212-213
  Relationship with slavery 213

Smith, Paul 7, 8, 14n20

Society of Jesus: See "Jesuits"

Summerville, Donald 135

St. Mary's City 251

St. Mary's Church 267

St. Inigoes plantation 248
  British raids on 295
  Expansion and slavery in 18th century 253
  Experience of Harry Mahoney at, 294-296
  Experience of enslaved person "Matthew" 253-254
  History of Louisa Mahoney Mason 254-256

Susan, laborer at Loyola in 1850s 74

Theater department 163
  Erasure of blackness in Othello 164, 166
  Institutionalized racism 168
  Teaching of white supremacy 164, 167
  The Green Pastures 167-168; Appeal to white audience 168; Use of blackface in 168;
  Popularity of 1956 performance 168
  Progress toward inclusion 170
  The Emperor's Doll 169; Use of yellowface in 6, 169; Victory in 1955 Provincial One
  Act Play Contest 169

Thomas, Robert 256

Thompson, Richard 136

Trossbach, Lynn 252

Union
    Enlistment in army of 4-5, 59
    Maryland's relationship with 56, 87

Vashon, George B. 212

Webster Field Annex 248

White, Andrew 8, 137-138
    Missionary work 9, 138

White Marsh plantation 267, 290, 292-293, 304
    Connection to Georgetown University 292-293
    Sale of enslaved people from 315

White Power 2, 5, 9, 10, 11

White supremacist pedagogy 9-10, 52-53, 115, 119
    Curriculum diversity requirement, shallowness of 233
    In Social Science Club programs 119-120

Wilson, Angela 248-249, 251

Apprentice House Press

Loyola University Maryland

Apprentice House is the country's only campus-based, student-staffed book publishing company. Directed by professors and industry professionals, it is a nonprofit activity of the Communication Department at Loyola University Maryland.

Using state-of-the-art technology and an experiential learning model of education, Apprentice House publishes books in untraditional ways. This dual responsibility as publishers and educators creates an unprecedented collaborative environment among faculty and students, while teaching tomorrow's editors, designers, and marketers.

Eclectic and provocative, Apprentice House titles intend to entertain as well as spark dialogue on a variety of topics. Financial contributions to sustain the press's work are welcomed. Contributions are tax deductible to the fullest extent allowed by the IRS.

To learn more about Apprentice House books or to obtain submission guidelines, please visit www.apprenticehouse.com.

Apprentice House Press
Communication Department
Loyola University Maryland
4501 N. Charles Street
Baltimore, MD 21210
Ph: 410-617-5265
info@apprenticehouse.com • www.apprenticehouse.com